earner
rvices

Dyslexia and Vision

Dedication

To Ben, Josie, and Dorothy
Thank you

Dyslexia and Vision

BRUCE JW EVANS

PhD, FCOptom, DipCLP, FAAO

Director of Research, Institute of Optometry, London
Visiting Professor, City University, London
Independent optometrist, Brentwood, Essex

Consultant in Dyslexia

Professor Margaret Snowling

University of York

W
WHURR PUBLISHERS
LONDON AND PHILADELPHIA

© 2001 Bruce JW Evans
First published 2001 by
Whurr Publishers Ltd
19b Compton Terrace, London N1 2UN, England and
325 Chestnut Street, Philadelphia PA 19106, USA

Reprinted 2002 and 2003

British Library Cataloguing in Publication Data
A catalogue record for this book is available from the
British Library.

ISBN 978-1-86156-242-5

Contents

Preface

Teachers, psychologists, parents, and others who are involved in the care of dyslexic people often ask whether visual factors play a role in dyslexia. The goal of *Dyslexia and Vision* is to answer this question. More specifically, the visual factors which have been claimed to be associated with dyslexia are explained, and the evidence relating to their association with dyslexia is reviewed.

The chapters of this book are intended primarily for educational psychologists, teachers, paediatricians, and members of the public (e.g. parents or adults with an interest in dyslexia), and no specialist knowledge about the eyes or vision is required. Terms are introduced and explained when they are first used so that, as long as the book is read in sequence, the reader's knowledge should be built up as they progress through the book. Lay language is used wherever possible, but the technical terms are also quoted. This is to assist readers in interpreting the terminology used in reports by eyecare practitioners.

The general format, after the introductory chapter, is to cover different visual problems in each chapter of the book. Typically, a section with a heading such as 'What is long-sightedness?' will be followed by a section headed 'Long-sightedness and dyslexia'.

Real-life examples can help to relate technical details to everyday life. To this end, there are several case studies quoted in *Dyslexia and Vision*. These are examples selected from patients whom the author has seen in his optometric practice. These cases have been selected because they clearly illustrate the condition under discussion.

Most of these cases are children and there is a greater emphasis throughout the book on dyslexia in children than in adults. Dyslexia is most often investigated in childhood and visual factors ought to be detected at as young an age as possible. Unfortunately, this is often not the case and the visual investigations and treatments discussed in this book can apply to adults just as readily as to children.

A great many theories have been suggested relating to dyslexia and vision and it can be difficult to 'sort the wheat from the chaff'. The healthcare disciplines are increasingly tending to cope with controversial topics by adopting an 'evidence-based approach'. In this approach high-quality scientific research is used to investigate old and new techniques alike. Investigative approaches and treatments that have been validated in this way are taken most seriously, and ones that have less rigorous support should be openly acknowledged as unproven.

An attempt has been made in *Dyslexia and Vision* to rank different methods, especially treatments, according to an evidence-based approach. Appendices are given at the end of the book which provide brief summaries of the scientific literature that supports the statements made in the main body of the book. The appendices are numbered from 1 to 8, one for each chapter, and fairly closely follow the format of the relevant chapters. Whereas the chapters are written for those who are not familiar with vision science, the appendices are specifically aimed at eyecare practitioners and vision scientists who may require references for further reading.

I am grateful to Dr Dorothy Thompson, Professor Arnold Wilkins and Dr Ian Richards for their helpful comments on sections of the manuscript. I would also like to thank all the children, parents, and teachers who have freely given their time to help with various research studies over the years. Finally, I would like to thank my young patients, who teach, amuse, correct and enlighten me whenever I remember to listen to what they say.

Ethical statement

I do not have a financial interest in any of the investigative tools or diagnostic instruments described in this book. I developed a booklet of eye exercises for people with certain problems of binocular co-ordination, which are sometimes prescribed for people with dyslexia. I receive a small remuneration based on sales of these, but the exercises can only be purchased by eyecare professionals. I do not have a financial interest in any of the coloured filter treatments described in this book.

CHAPTER 1

Introduction

Overview of learning difficulties

The skills that we learn at school are important for success in later life and difficulties with learning at school, or *learning difficulties*, can in some cases continue to impact on a person's life long after they leave school. Apart from this direct effect, there is also an indirect effect of learning difficulties in that they can lead to a sense of failure and of low self-esteem. The prevention of this is crucial and this is one reason why the two most important influences on young people with learning difficulties are their parents and their teachers.

This book concentrates on visual factors and for a more detailed description of the nature and classification of learning difficulties the reader is referred to the references in Appendix 1.

Learning difficulties can be broadly classified into non-specific and specific. The non-specific category can be further sub-divided into mild and profound.

Non-specific learning difficulties

People with *non-specific learning difficulties* have general learning difficulties across a wide range of activities and the person's intelligence quotient (IQ) would also be significantly below average.

A mild non-specific learning difficulty is not a disease or a reason for excessive concern. Not everyone is average: some people perform better than average and some people worse than average. Some individuals will be 'not as bright' as others, and this may just be the way that they are.

1

This is not to say that they cannot be helped: an individualized and structured educational approach that takes account of the child's strengths and weaknesses will doubtless aid their progress.

The term profound learning difficulties, or *learning disabilities*, is usually reserved for people who have a severe intellectual impairment. In the past, people with profound learning difficulties might have been described as mentally retarded. In some cases, there can be a constitutional cause for the learning disability, such as a genetic (chromosomal) defect in Down's syndrome, fragile X syndrome, or problems around the time of birth in cerebral palsy (although many people with cerebral palsy have normal intellectual functions). There are visual anomalies that are particularly likely to affect people with profound learning difficulties. But this subject is beyond the scope of this book (see Appendices 1 and 8 for further reading). The term 'learning disabilities' is sometimes used differently in North America to refer to specific learning difficulties (e.g. dyslexia), which are described below.

Specific learning difficulties

As the name suggests, people with *specific learning difficulties* (SpLD) have specific difficulties with certain aspects of learning. The diagnosis of SpLD is best made by a specially qualified teacher or by an educational or child psychologist.

One approach to diagnosis is to ensure that the person has had adequate opportunity to learn and then to measure the intelligence quotient (IQ). From the IQ, a psychologist can calculate the expected performance on a range of tasks. For example, children with an unusually high IQ would be expected to read and spell better than most children of their age. As well as calculating the *expected* performance at a range of skills, the psychologist would also measure the *actual* performance at, for example, reading, spelling and mathematics. They could then calculate the *discrepancy* between the expected and the actual performance (i.e. the degree of 'under-achievement').

If there is a large discrepancy between expected and actual performance at a given task, then this suggests that the person has a specific learning difficulty in this area. For example, people whose actual reading ability falls far below the level expected from their intelligence and age are described as having specific reading difficulties. Some definitions state that a person has to be at least 18 months behind expectation to be diagnosed as having a specific learning difficulty. In research, a fixed criterion like this is important. But in practice, it is best not to attach too much significance to a strict cut-off.

People with SpLD do not always have a high IQ. An advantage of the method of diagnosis described above is that people with average or below average IQ can still be diagnosed as having a specific learning difficulty, as long as their performance at some academic task(s) is significantly below that expected from their age and intelligence.

So far, we have discussed the psychometric diagnosis of SpLD by educationalists. Often, SpLD are first identified by parents who recognize that their child's abilities at certain tasks are far worse than they would expect from the child's capabilities in other areas. Typically, the performance at written tasks is much worse than at spoken tasks.

Dyslexia

Dyslexia is the most common of the SpLD and is a specific learning difficulty with literacy (reading and spelling). It affects about 5% of the population and persists throughout life. Dyslexia often runs in families and many people believe it to be more common in males than females, although this has been disputed.

Some definitions of dyslexia refer solely to a difficulty with reading, but dyslexia is almost invariably associated with specific spelling difficulty. Indeed, some adults with dyslexia have learnt ways to minimize the apparent reading difficulty so that the spelling difficulty is the most obvious feature of their dyslexia.

Although no single definition of dyslexia is universally accepted, the following working definition will be used in this book: *A specific learning difficulty where reading and/or spelling is markedly below that expected on the basis of age and intelligence.*

Dyslexia, or alexia (a total inability to read), can be acquired following some damage to the brain, for example after a stroke. This is rare and this book concentrates on the more common type of 'developmental' dyslexia.

Dyslexia is, by definition, a description of a disability. But many dyslexic people have exceptional abilities. For example, Leonardo da Vinci, Shakespeare and Einstein are all believed to have been dyslexic. Perhaps a day will come when computers completely remove the need for humans to be able to read and spell. Then we may view dyslexia in a more positive light, for the outstanding contribution that many people with dyslexia can make to society.

Dyscalculia

Dyscalculia is a specific learning difficulty affecting numerical skills, such as mathematics. It is sometimes associated with dyslexia. Compared with dyslexia, dyscalculia receives relatively little attention and it is much less frequently diagnosed.

Dyspraxia

Dyspraxia is a disorder of voluntary movement. People with dyspraxia have an inability to perform, command or imitate a familiar action, even though they understand the action that they have been asked to do. Dyspraxia cannot be accounted for by severe incoordination or paralysis of the parts concerned.

Attention deficit disorder (ADD)

ADD is characterized by inattention, impulsivity, poor vigilance, motor impersistence, and sometimes hyperactivity. ADD is correlated with dyslexia: the two conditions sometimes, but not always, go hand in hand.

Causes of dyslexia

There can be many different reasons why a person reads below expectation and one or all of these reasons may account for the reading difficulty in a given individual.

Phonological processing deficits

Phonology refers to the study of sounds in a language. Reading requires considerable skills of phonological processing to convert a written image into the sounds of spoken language. There is a substantial amount of research suggesting that most people with dyslexia have difficulties with their phonological processing and that these difficulties are usually the major cause of their reading and spelling difficulty.

Phonological deficits are such a common finding in dyslexia that this has led some people actually to define dyslexia as the presence of a phonological decoding deficit. But, as explained below, dyslexia is a complex condition that can have many contributory factors. The condition is not fully understood and, when defining the condition, it may be better at this time to avoid making assumptions about an exclusive cause.

Other possible contributory factors

Most people with dyslexia do not have overt difficulties with spoken language, yet do have marked difficulties with written language. The obvious difference between written and spoken language is that written language is seen and spoken language is heard. This may be why, since the earliest days of the quest for the causes of dyslexia, vision has been high on the list of suspects. This is discussed more in the next section.

Many other factors have been associated with dyslexia, such as hearing problems including 'glue ear' early in life.

Several researchers have looked at brain structure and function in dyslexia, using post mortem studies or studies of the electrical activity in the brain. Some studies have found slight abnormalities in dyslexia. It should be stressed that these abnormalities are extremely subtle and it should not be inferred that people with dyslexia have some sort of brain damage. Indeed, one of the findings is that the brain is actually larger than average in dyslexia.

The role of visual problems and therapies in dyslexia

For many years dyslexia researchers tended to fall in one of two camps. The majority researched phonological factors in dyslexia and argued that, because they found phonological deficits, there must be 'no visual deficit' in dyslexia. Others researched visual factors and, on finding visual deficits in dyslexia, argued that these must be the cause of dyslexia. The 'third way' is to acknowledge that there is evidence supporting both of these arguments so they must both be correct and need not be mutually exclusive.

Dyslexia: not one cause but many

Some conditions, for example malaria, have one cause (in the case of malaria, a tiny parasite). Other conditions, like headaches, have a variety of different factors that can cause or contribute to the condition. Dyslexia is this type of complex condition and there are probably a range of factors that can cause or contribute to dyslexia. This is not surprising since many different skills are involved in the reading process.

This may explain the countless theories that have been proposed for different factors causing dyslexia. If one of these is correct it does not necessarily mean that all the others are wrong.

Dyslexia: not one condition but many

Many people have attempted to classify dyslexia. These classifications usually result in three groups based on the types of reading and/or spelling errors that tend to be made. Typically, the largest group contains people whose reading/spelling errors are those that one might expect from difficulty with phonological processing ('dysphonetic'). People with this type of dyslexia generally read quickly but inaccurately and rely on the visual appearance of words. People in the second group tend to read slowly, relying on phonetic analysis rather than on their limited sight vocabulary ('dyseidectic'). The third group make a combination of both types of errors and usually have the severest problems.

Classifications like this seem to make sense but are probably an oversimplification. Indeed, some studies have concluded that dyslexia is so varied that it defies classification.

Both roads to reading start with vision

The classifications of dyslexia described in the previous section are based on a model of the reading process in which reading is believed to occur through two pathways (Figure 1.1).

Early readers tend to build up and use a sight vocabulary comprising familiar words which are recognized by their shape. To read more complex words, developing readers employ phonetic analysis skills to

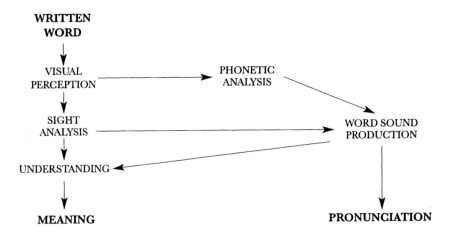

Figure 1.1. Diagram representing a simplified model of reading in which reading occurs via two different pathways, one using the 'sight vocabulary' and the other 'phonetic analysis'. Both pathways start with visual perception: the written word must be seen before it can be analysed.

break down unfamiliar words into their sound units. Usually, mature readers use both pathways together when they are reading.

The dysphonetic dyslexia described in the preceding section is characterized by a difficulty with the phonetic analysis pathway. Dyseidectic dyslexia is characterized by a difficulty with the sight analysis pathway.

It might be thought that a deficit of the sight analysis pathway suggests that the person may have a visual problem. But this is not necessarily the case. As can be seen in Figure 1.1, both pathways start with a visual perception of the written word. So, it is not possible to predict how likely a person is to suffer from the visual problems described in this book from a superficial analysis of the type of reading and spelling errors that they make.

As an aside, there is one exception to the statement that all roads to reading start with vision. This is people who are blind or have a severe visual disability and read by Braille. Unfortunately, there has been relatively little research on dyslexia in Braille readers.

Correlates versus causes

A common source of confusion is the difference between a correlate and a cause. If two things are correlated then it means that they are associated. They may be two things that often go together (blond hair is correlated with blue eyes) or variables where as one increases the other tends to increase or decrease (e.g. height is correlated with weight: people who are taller tend to weigh more than people who are shorter). A great deal of research is about identifying correlates, but there are two important limitations of correlates.

First, correlates are not necessarily causes. For example, blond hair does not cause blue eyes, nor vice versa. Second, even if one correlate does cause another, it is very unlikely that the relationship between the two factors is so strong that it is predictive. For example, although it is known that smoking can cause heart disease one cannot predict that a person will die of heart disease just because they smoke.

Researchers, like everyone else, want their work to be important. So there is a temptation for them to assume, when they identify a correlate of a disorder, that they have found a cause of the condition. But this is not necessarily the case. For example, certain visual factors (including poor focusing) are correlated with the profound learning disability of Down's syndrome. But no-one suggests that poor focusing causes Down's syndrome. Of course, the poor focusing may give the person an added burden, so it might need treatment.

Similar logic applies to many of the visual correlates of dyslexia. They may not be major causes of the dyslexia, but they might contribute to the overall difficulty that a person experiences. In this case treatment of the visual problems may help, although it should not be expected to be a cure for the dyslexia.

As will be seen in the following chapters, visual problems can contribute to dyslexia in two ways. They can impair visual perception and thus *directly* contribute to the learning difficulty. Alternatively (or additionally), some visual problems can cause eyestrain or headaches when reading. This might make a person reluctant to read and hence *indirectly* contribute to a reading problem.

The placebo effect

A *placebo* is a remedy without any direct action on the disease or condition that is being treated. In essence, the patient gets better just because they believe that the treatment is making them better. The *placebo effect* should not be underestimated: placebos work, and they work for just about everyone. Up to one-third of all drugs prescribed in the USA may effectively be placebos. To healthcare workers, the placebo effect can be a good thing: it helps their patients to get better.

It is in research that the placebo effect can cause problems. Research is used to discover the truth about whether a treatment helps a condition, and the placebo effect obscures this truth. Parents of dyslexic children often say 'I tried *such-and-such* treatment, and it helped my son's reading; so, the treatment must work.' The key question for the researcher is why the treatment worked. Was it just because of a placebo effect, or did it work because of a genuine *treatment effect* in addition to any placebo?

Genuinely effective treatments are likely to help people for two reasons. First, from the genuine treatment effect and second, from the placebo effect. So, if time and resources are spent giving a genuine treatment then the person will be receiving a treatment effect plus a placebo effect, compared with just a placebo effect if they receive a placebo treatment.

One of the goals of dyslexia research is to discover new ways of helping dyslexic people. If people are encouraged to invest time and resources in treatments that are just placebos then this will slow down the development of new treatments and will in the long term impede the battle to overcome the difficulties associated with dyslexia.

The evidence-based approach

The problems described above apply to all branches of the healthcare sciences and have led to *evidence-based medicine*. The evidence-based approach uses scientific tools to objectively evaluate products and treatments.

The usual type of research study to investigate the correlates of a condition is a *matched group controlled study*. In dyslexia, this usually means that a group of people with dyslexia are compared with a control group. Ideally, the control group should be matched to the dyslexic group so that both groups have the same age, intelligence, opportunity to learn, socio-economic background, and proportion of males and females.

When assessing the effect of treatments (interventions), the appropriate type of research is a *double-masked randomized placebo-controlled trial* (RCT). A group of people with dyslexia would be allocated, at random, to one of two groups. The *treatment group*, would be given the treatment that is under investigation and the *control group*, would be given a sham (placebo) treatment. The placebo treatment should lack the component that is thought to be helpful, but should otherwise be as similar as possible to the real treatment: both treatments should give the subjects the same degree of time and attention, should involve the same degree of high tech equipment, and should generally be equally convincing for the subject. Neither the subjects (or their parents), nor the researchers should know the identity of the treatments until the research is completed. In this way, people's expectations cannot influence the outcome.

Sometimes, it may be unethical to withhold a treatment from subjects in a research study. In these cases, the placebo treatment may be replaced by the currently available 'gold standard' treatment.

Scientists generally wish to have their work published in the highest quality journal that will accept the paper. So, the reputation of a journal is a useful guide to the quality of research. Over 9.2 million records from 1966 to the present from 3,800 leading international biomedical journals are indexed by *Medline*, which is a free (on the Internet) resource facilitating searches for published work in a given field. The publications that are included in Medline are typically inter-disciplinary peer-reviewed journals. *Peer-reviewed* means that papers are only accepted for a journal if they meet basic criteria of scientific rigour. *Inter-disciplinary* ensures that research is not just accepted by 'believers' within a certain profession. Much of the background reading for this book started with Medline.

The opinions stated in the chapters of this book are supported by statements made in the appendices at the end of the book. These appendices include references to the original scientific research behind the statements. I have tried to give greatest weighting to views supported by rigorous research (see Appendix 1).

Professionals who help people with dyslexia

Since there are usually many facets to a person's dyslexic difficulties, it follows that there are many facets to the help that they need to receive. The most crucial people in providing this help are parents. They often have to co-ordinate the activities of other professionals, and to encourage, teach, counsel, and generally support their dyslexic child.

Several other professionals are involved in helping people with dyslexia and some of these are outlined below.

Teachers

Clearly, teachers play a central role in helping the dyslexic child. The special needs support team will be aware of the special needs of people with dyslexia, although they may not always be fully aware of recent research on vision and dyslexia. Ideally, all teachers should have an awareness of dyslexia and of how best to help children with SpLD.

Psychologists

Educational and child psychologists are usually involved in the diagnosis of dyslexia and other learning difficulties. A detailed psychological assessment is crucial for people with severe degrees of dyslexia. Ideally, such an assessment should be available from an educational psychologist provided by the Local Education Authority, but resources can be short. An alternative route is to seek a private psychological assessment through a child or educational psychologist who may work at a local branch of the Dyslexia Institute (see page 157). A complementary organization, the British Dyslexia Association, provides support for people with dyslexia and can provide advice on how to pursue an educational assessment through the state system (see page 157).

Eyecare professionals

The largest eyecare profession in the UK is optometry. There are approximately 8,500 optometrists who are trained to diagnose diseases, diagnose and treat refractive and orthoptic (binocular vision) anomalies, and to dispense spectacles and contact lenses. There are about 1,500 ophthalmologists who are medical specialists trained in eye examination, and medical and surgical treatment of eye diseases. There are about 1,000 orthoptists, most of whom work with ophthalmologists. Orthoptists are principally concerned with detecting and treating binocular vision anomalies. About 4,500 registered dispensing opticians supply and fit glasses and sometimes, with additional qualifications, contact lenses.

The vast majority of optometrists work in city centre locations and patients do not need a referral from a GP to see an optometrist. Most ophthalmologists work in hospitals and their patients are referred by GPs or optometrists. Most orthoptists work in hospital practice and receive the majority of their patients via an ophthalmologist.

Optometrists receive a fixed fee from the NHS for a child's eye examination. This fee has reduced in real terms since its introduction and only a basic eye examination is usually covered. Because of the various visual anomalies that need to be looked for in people with (suspected) dyslexia, these eye examinations usually take about twice as long as a normal eye examination. Therefore, optometrists who have specialized in investigating people with reading difficulties almost always charge a private fee for these additional tests.

Unfortunately, there are no specific qualifications that eyecare practitioners can take to indicate specialist expertise in the assessment of people with dyslexia. The College of Optometrists has shown an interest in developing a specialist diploma in this subject and we are currently trying to instigate a *code of conduct* for eyecare practitioners. In the meantime, the best method of finding eyecare practitioners who have specialized in this field is by personal recommendation.

Others

Some general medical practitioners (GPs) have an interest in dyslexia and are able to provide support and advice. Paediatricians, who are medical specialists in children's health problems, also sometimes have specialist knowledge in this area. Their expertise can be very important in managing the hyperactivity that is sometimes associated with Attention Deficit Disorder, which often can be alleviated with medication (e.g. Ritalin).

Paediatric occupational therapists also play a role in the care of some dyslexic children, as do speech and language therapists.

Some experts recommend that people with SpLD should have an assessment of their auditory function (hearing). GPs can inspect the outer ear and check for conditions like glue ear. More expert assessment can be obtained from ear, nose and throat (ENT) surgeons and audiologists.

Structure of the eye and basic visual functions

Structure of the eye

The eye is illustrated in Figure 1.2. In optical terms, the eye can be compared with a camera. There are two lenses at the front of the eye (like the lenses at the front of a camera) which form an image onto a screen (*retina*) at the back of the eye (like the film at the back of a camera). The front lens of the eye is the *cornea*, and the second lens, inside the eye but near the front, is the *crystalline lens*. Each eye is surrounded by six muscles (*extra-ocular muscles*) which move the eyes in various directions of gaze.

Basic visual functions and terminology

Just like a camera, if the lenses of the eye do not focus correctly then the vision will be blurred. If the lenses of the eye are too weak then objects close to will be more blurred than objects in the distance and the eye is said to be *long-sighted*. If the lenses of the eye are too strong then objects far away will be more blurred than objects close to and the eye is said to be

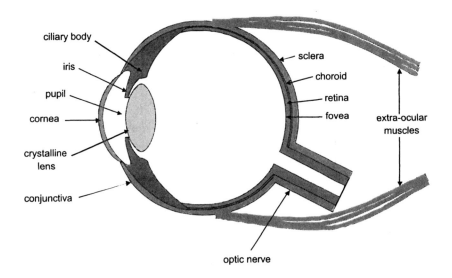

Figure 1.2. Diagram of the human eye.

short-sighted. Refraction refers to the focusing of the eye, and long- and short-sightedness are *refractive errors*.

In an ideal world, the eyeball should be exactly spherical (round, like a football). In the real world, it is often not precisely spherical, but is shaped a little more like a rugby ball. This causes another type of refractive error, *astigmatism*. Refractive errors are discussed further in Chapter 2.

To take clear photographs a camera has to be properly focused for the distance between the camera and the object that is being photographed. The eye automatically adjusts its focus to maintain a clear image. This focusing takes place at the lens inside the eye and is called *accommodation* (see Chapter 3).

There are about a million fibres running from each eye through the *optic nerve* to the brain. An enormous amount of processing occurs in the eye and the brain to analyse and make sense of the image. This is called *visual processing* and is a part of visual perception. The extent of space in which objects are visible to an eye is called the *visual field*. Visual processing and visual fields are discussed in Chapter 6.

For the eyes to work well they must be precisely pointing at what we want to see. The extra-ocular muscles hold the eyes steady whilst they *fix* a stationary object. If the object moves slowly the eyes make *pursuit eye movements* to follow the object. If the object moves fast then the eyes can no longer follow it smoothly and they make a series of flick eye movements to keep up with the object: these are *saccadic eye movements*.

When we read, the eyes pause on a group of 5–10 letters while the brain processes the information from these. After about a quarter of a second the eyes make a saccadic eye movement to the next group of letters. The information from these is processed, the eyes move again, and so on. Most of the eye movements (for people reading European languages) are from left to right, but opposite (right to left) eye movements occur at the end of a line and when the eyes make *regressions* to a previous section, usually to aid understanding.

Ideally, the two eyes should work together as a team demonstrating *co-ordinated binocular vision*. When we look at an object that is approaching us our eyes should both keep lined up on the object so that they have to turn inwards, or *converge*. If the object is moving away then the eyes have to turn outwards, or *diverge*. Binocular co-ordination and eye movements are discussed in Chapter 3.

Low level versus high level visual sensory functions

The brain is such a complex organ that in order to understand it better we need to, so far as is practicable, break down its activities into their component parts. Different parts of the brain concentrate on different functions. The first very broad distinction that can be drawn is between *sensory* and *motor* function. Sensory function describes how the brain processes and analyses information that flows into it from our senses, particularly vision. Motor visual function describes how the brain controls the muscles that focus and move the eyes.

Sensory visual function can further be divided into *low level* and *high level*. Although the distinction between these two is not always clear, low level refers more to the early stages of visual processing where the visual image is processed and enhanced. High level refers to the later stages of visual processing where the visual image is analysed and interpreted.

In reports by educational psychologists about dyslexic people there is often a section describing visual or visuo-spatial abilities. This refers to high level sensory visual function (and frequently to tasks requiring memory and reasoning), which is very different from the low level sensory visual function or motor visual factors that are discussed in this book. The problem is that the word *vision* is rather vague.

Components of the eye examination

Table 1.1 lists the basic components of the eye examination. Most of these elements will be described in more detail later in the book. Many tests can be carried out without any response from the child: children do not need to be able to read before they can consult an optometrist (Figure 1.3).

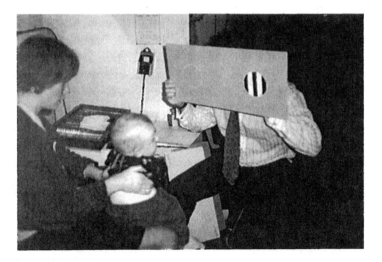

Figure 1.3. The assessment of visual acuity in a pre-school child. Children do not need to be able to read before they can have an eye examination.

Table 1.1. Components of the eye examination. Synonyms are in square brackets. The most common tests are in normal print, more specialist tests are in italics. With children, a subjective refraction is sometimes inappropriate. The terms are explained in more detail in subsequent chapters

Component	Test	Explanation
Ocular health	Ophthalmoscopy	Using an instrument to view the eye, especially the inside of the eye
	Pupil reactions	Ensuring that the pupils function normally; a test of neurological function as well as eye health
	Visual fields	*Determining the peripheral vision*
	Tonometry	Measuring the pressure inside the eye which is one of the glaucoma tests that is recommended for people over 40
	Slit lamp biomicroscopy	*Using a binocular microscope to examine the front of the eye under magnification. Essential in contact lens practice and used, for example, to diagnose hay fever*
	Colour vision	*To determine the presence of any colour vision defects*
Vision	Charts and text	Measures the resolving power of the eye; often checked with and without glasses
Refraction	Retinoscopy [objective refraction]	Objective method of determining the refractive error by using reflected light
	Subjective refraction	Testing the patient's response to different lenses to determine the precise prescription. Always includes a large element of re-checking
Binocular co-ordination [orthoptic status] [ocular motor function]	Ocular motility	Observing the eye movements in extreme positions of gaze to look for weak eye muscles and unstable (jerky) eye movements
	Cover test	Checking the ocular alignment to determine the presence and size of any strabismus or heterophoria
	Dissociation test	*Measuring the absolute size of any strabismus or heterophoria. Less useful than the cover test or aligning prism*
	Aligning prism [associated phoria] [fixation disparity]	Assessing the precise degree of alignment of the two eyes. A good indicator of how well a person can compensate for a heterophoria
	Fusional reserves	*Measurement of the maximum amount by which a person can converge or diverge the eyes. An indicator of how much 'power' a person has in reserve to overcome a heterophoria*

(contd)

Table 1.1. (contd)

Component	Test	Explanation
	Near point of convergence	Measurement of the closest point to which a person can converge the eyes
	Stereo-acuity	Measurement of the ability to use the images from the two eyes to assess depth
	Foveal suppression	*Assesses whether the brain is using the images from both eyes*
	Near point of accommodation	Measurement of the closest point to which a person can focus
	Accommodative facility	*Assessment of the rate at which a person can change their accommodation*
	Accommodative lag	*The accuracy of accommodation*

Many of the tests of visual function can be carried out at *distance* and *near*. Distance vision tests assess the function of the eyes for seeing objects a long way away, such as signs when driving, or writing on a board in class. Distance tests are usually carried out at 6 metres which, optically speaking, is close to infinity. Near vision tests assess functioning for near tasks, such as reading.

When eyecare practitioners talk about their patient's right eye they mean the eye on the patient's right hand side. When talking to dyslexic patients, it is often best for practitioners to avoid using descriptions of right or left.

Visual symptoms

Some research studies have found that children with dyslexia report more visual symptoms than good readers. However, children might not report their symptoms: they assume that everyone has the same experience. It is not uncommon for a child to fail to describe any symptoms for a visual condition that would, in an adult, cause acute complaints of blurring, eyestrain, or headaches. Yet, once the condition has been corrected the child then describes the initial symptom that has now been alleviated.

Even when children do report visual symptoms, their reports are often difficult to interpret. While many adults can clearly differentiate between blurring, doubling, and words moving, many children cannot. And even if they can, these symptoms are non-specific. In other words, different visual problems can cause similar symptoms.

Some research studies have tried to discover questions that parents or teachers can ask children to try and identify those with visual problems. But such studies have been largely unsuccessful. Hence, although it is sensible for parents or teachers to question dyslexic children carefully about any symptoms that they may have, it is not safe to conclude that people who do not report symptoms do not need an eye examination.

Summary

- In dyslexia, reading and/or spelling are markedly below the level expected on the basis of age and intelligence.
- A major cause of dyslexia is a deficit of phonological processing.
- It has also been suggested that visual factors may contribute to dyslexia.
- Correlates and treatments of dyslexia should be investigated with objective, evidence-based, research.
- The largest eyecare profession in the UK is optometry.
- Children do not need to be able to read to have an eye examination.

CHAPTER 2

Ocular health and refractive errors

Ocular health

Thankfully, eye diseases are rare in childhood and are not especially common in people with dyslexia. Children who are partially sighted as a result of eye diseases may have impaired reading, but they often seem to adjust their reading speed to minimize errors. However, there has been very little research on the type of reading errors made by people with visual impairment from eye diseases. Some references to the effect of eye diseases and brain diseases (e.g. loss of half the visual field) can be found in Appendix 2.

Refractive errors, vision, and visual acuity

Eyecare professionals use the term *vision* to describe how well an eye sees (usually tested by reading down a letter chart). Uncorrected vision is measured without glasses, corrected vision (or *visual acuity*) is measured with appropriate glasses. The *refractive error* refers to the optical error of an eye (e.g. short-sightedness). Sometimes, an eye with a high refractive error actually achieves good visual acuity with glasses, yet an eye without any significant refractive error might, for a variety of reasons, be quite poor at reading a letter chart.

To determine refractive errors, optometrists use both objective (requiring no response from the patient) and subjective (requiring responses) methods. A complete, albeit basic, eye examination can be carried out objectively and this is how infants' eyes can be examined (Figure 1.3). If a child is being inconsistent or uncooperative then the optometrist will base their results on objective tests.

Vision and visual acuity do not appear to be strong correlates of dyslexia (see Appendix 2). However, there are a few studies which have found dyslexia to be associated with poor near visual acuity. This could be explained by poor naming skills, reduced accommodation (see Chapter 3), or uncorrected hypermetropia (see below). Whatever the explanation, these few studies have only found a small degree of reduced visual acuity in dyslexia which is unlikely to interfere with reading in the vast majority of cases.

Short-sightedness (myopia)

What is short-sightedness?

The main types of refractive errors that affect children and young adults were described at the end of Chapter 1. Short-sightedness is when the lenses of the eye are too strong and the person's vision is most blurred for distant objects. This is one of the few visual problems that would be detected in a standard letter chart test, as long as each eye was tested and the untested eye was covered properly. About 10% of schoolchildren are short-sighted.

If a significant degree of short-sightedness is present (see later), then it should be corrected with glasses. The glasses will need to be worn when viewing the board in class or, if there is high degree of short-sightedness, they may need to be worn all the time. Glasses or contact lenses are the only effective method of correcting short-sightedness in children. Wearing glasses to correct short-sightedness should not be expected to make the short-sightedness get any better or worse. Short-sightedness usually increases for a few years, and it will do this whether glasses are worn or not.

Occasionally, claims have been made that short-sightedness can be corrected or prevented by eye exercises or by prescribing reading glasses or bifocals for children. Research shows that eye exercises will not prevent or control short-sightedness. Similarly, bifocals or reading glasses (sometimes called 'learning lenses' or 'low plus lenses') will not have a significant effect on the development of short-sightedness for the vast majority of children. There is one small group of children (those who have esophoria at near, see Chapter 3) for whom the progression of short-sightedness might be slowed down with bifocals. Even in this group, the average effect of bifocals on the development of short-sightedness is very small.

Short-sightedness and dyslexia

The research literature is very clear on the relationship between short-sightedness and dyslexia: there isn't one! Dyslexic people are no more likely to be short-sighted than are good readers.

Any child can become short-sighted, and this is especially likely if short-sightedness is present in the family. If a child reports difficulty seeing writing on the board then it is a sensible precaution to take them to an optometrist. The detection of short-sightedness is a part of the basic NHS eye examination, which is usually free of charge in the UK.

Long-sightedness (hypermetropia or hyperopia)

What is long-sightedness?

Long-sightedness is when the lenses of the eye are too weak and the vision will usually be more blurred for near objects than for distant objects. About 5% of school-children have a potentially significant degree of long-sightedness.

The eye has two lenses, the cornea at the front of the eye which is a powerful fixed lens and the crystalline lens inside the eye (see p. 12 and Figure 1.2). The crystalline lens is flexible and focuses the eye through a process called *ocular accommodation* (see Chapter 3). When people with perfect eyesight look in the distance this lens is set at its lowest power. If an object is approaching a person then the lens will gradually increase its power, to keep the object in focus (see Figure 3.1). The lens is very power-ful in children and this is why most young children can focus on objects that are very close to their noses.

When a person views an approaching object something else happens in addition to this accommodation. We have two eyes and for the binocu-lar vision (binocular co-ordination) to be effective the two eyes must keep pointing at the object of regard. Thus, the eyes react to an approaching object not only by accommodating but also by turning inwards, or *converg-ing* (Figure 3.5).

Since accommodation and convergence naturally go hand in hand, the brain automatically links the two functions so that a given amount of accommodation triggers a given amount of convergence, and vice versa.

If a person who is long-sighted tries to focus on a distant object then the object ought to be blurred because the lenses of the eye are too weak. But young people can try to compensate for the long-sightedness by 'over-focusing' the lens inside the eye. In other words, they can exert accommodation so that, for distance vision, the lens inside the eye is not relaxed as it should be but is focused to compensate for the long-sightedness. For near vision the lens will have to make a considerable effort to focus, because a near object requires accommodation in addition to that which has to occur to overcome the long-sightedness.

Not everyone who is long-sighted is able to over-accommodate in this way. If a person cannot do this then their long-sightedness may cause blurred vision. Even if a person can use ocular accommodation to over-come long-sightedness then this can cause two problems. First, the constant effort to maintain a higher than usual degree of accommodation can cause eyestrain and headaches.

The second problem results from the link described above between accommodation and convergence. When accommodation is exerted this is associated with a tendency to converge, or turn the eyes inwards. Therefore, when people over-accommodate to compensate for long-sightedness this can cause a tendency for the eyes to turn inwards. This may result in a convergent strabismus (see Chapter 3). The only correct treatment for this type of strabismus is to take away the cause of the problem: to correct the long-sightedness with glasses. For this particular type of convergent strabismus, an operation is not an appropriate treatment.

In some cases, long-sightedness causes the eyes to try to turn inwards but the person manages to overcome this by constantly straining to stop the eyes from turning. This straining can cause symptoms of eyestrain and headaches (see Chapter 3).

Many programmes for screening vision in pre-school and in school-age children are poor at detecting long-sightedness. Indeed, long-sightedness occasionally can even be missed in a thorough eye examination by an eyecare professional. This is because of the potential for ocular accommodation compensating for, or masking, long-sightedness. Optometrists or ophthalmologists use an instrument called a retinoscope to determine objectively (without asking any questions) the refractive error. In older children, they may also use subjective questions and trial lenses to refine their estimate of the refractive error. Retinoscopy is quite good at detecting long-sightedness, but can sometimes miss the condition, particularly in younger children. If the symptoms or other test results suggest that significant long-sightedness may be present, then the practitioner may use drops (cycloplegic) to relax the focusing muscle in the eye and to reveal the full refractive error.

Eye exercises are not likely to have a significant effect on long-sightedness. Similarly, if school-aged children or adults wear glasses this will not make long-sightedness get appreciably better or worse. Unlike short-sightedness, long-sightedness does not usually get worse: the degree of long-sightedness that a child has when they enter school is often not too dissimilar from the degree that they have when they leave school. What will happen is that, as they become older and do more tasks that require concentrated vision, they may become progressively less able to compensate for the long-sightedness. Hence, the strength of glasses that long-sighted children need does often change over time.

Long-sightedness and dyslexia

Some research studies suggest that dyslexia is especially likely to be associated with long-sightedness. However, other research studies suggest that long-sightedness is no more common in dyslexia than it is in good readers. The only safe conclusion to draw is that long-sightedness is not strongly correlated with dyslexia: people who are dyslexic are not very highly likely to be long-sighted. But they are at least as likely to be long-sighted as other children.

As described above, long-sightedness can cause blurring, eyestrain, and headaches. These problems can discourage children from reading and could, in severe cases, directly impede their reading progress. Hence, although long-sightedness is not a cause of dyslexia, it may contribute to a dyslexic person's difficulties. Occasionally, a person with a significant degree of uncorrected long-sightedness is misdiagnosed as having dyslexia. The boy in Case study 2.1 had suspected dyslexia and correction of the long-sightedness greatly improved his symptoms and reading.

Case study 2.1: Ref. G0596

BACKGROUND: Boy, aged 6, referred to the author because of reading difficulties for which the child was receiving extra teaching. Psychologist diagnosed attention deficit disorder (ADD) with speech/language problems.

SYMPTOMS: Text blurs, changes size; skips and re-reads words or lines; eyes become sore and tired after reading for even a short time. Headache in right side of head, on average once a fortnight, associated with much schoolwork.

CLINICAL FINDINGS: Visual acuities normal. Ocular health normal. Refractive error (objective) without cycloplegic: R = L = +1.50DS; with cycloplegic: R = L = +2.75DS (the notation for refractive errors is explained near the end of this chapter). Normal amplitude of accommodation and no significant heterophoria or heterotropia.

MANAGEMENT: Glasses were prescribed (R = L = +1.50DS).

FOLLOW-UP 4 MONTHS LATER: Voluntarily wears glasses for all schoolwork. 'Much better at school'. No symptoms. No more headaches since received glasses. Reading has improved from 1 year behind to now at average level for patient's age. Clinical findings essentially as above.

COMMENT: It is likely that this child is still not achieving to his full potential, since the glasses would have little effect on his attentional and speech and language problems. Nonetheless, it seems likely that there was a visual component to his difficulties and that the glasses have corrected this.

Astigmatism

What is astigmatism?

In Chapter 1 astigmatism was described as the condition when the eyeball is not exactly spherical but is shaped more like a rugby ball than a football. In fact, most people have a low degree of astigmatism, simply because it is difficult for nature to make a perfect sphere.

The effect of astigmatism is to make the vision blurred at all distances. The higher the degree of astigmatism, the worse the blur. As with all types of blur, the effect is most noticeable when the person is trying to resolve fine detail. About 5% of schoolchildren have a potentially significant degree of astigmatism.

People with astigmatism perceive lines at certain angles as being clearer than others. For example, people with a certain type of astigmatism (with the rule astigmatism) will find vertical lines to be clearer than horizontal lines. So, they might find the letter 'l' to be easier to make out than the letter 'e'.

Astigmatism cannot be helped by eye exercises; although the term *astigmatism* is occasionally confused with the term *strabismus* which describes a very different condition (see Chapter 3) that can sometimes be treated with eye exercises. Occasionally, astigmatism can be progressive and increase throughout life (e.g. in a condition called *keratoconus*), but usually this is not the case. However, astigmatism does often fluctuate over the years, requiring fairly frequent changes of glasses during childhood.

Astigmatism and dyslexia

Most research studies have not found astigmatism to be especially prevalent in dyslexia. Astigmatism can occur in anyone, and therefore can occur in dyslexia. Astigmatism is routinely detected in optometric eye examinations and, if significant, can be corrected with glasses. There is no reason to believe that a low degree of astigmatism, which would not ordinarily require correction, should be corrected just because a person has dyslexia. Since astigmatism is not a cause of dyslexia, its treatment should not be expected to cure dyslexia. But anyone who has a significant degree of astigmatism will find concentrated visual tasks, like reading, easier with glasses.

Occasionally, optometrists encounter cases where there is fairly high degree of uncorrected astigmatism in a child with reading problems. It sometimes turns out that the uncorrected astigmatism is the only problem and correction of this with glasses will, with time, allow the child to catch up in class. These cases should not have been diagnosed as dyslexic.

Anisometropia

In most people, the refractive error of the two eyes is fairly similar. The term *anisometropia* describes the situation when the two eyes have markedly different refractive errors. About 10% of the population have a potentially significant degree of anisometropia.

In one type of anisometropia, when both eyes are long-sighted but one is more so than the other, there is a risk of the worse eye becoming 'lazy' or *amblyopic*. This occurs because the brain attempts to overcome the long-sightedness by over-focusing (accommodating, as described above). Both eyes tend to accommodate by about the same amount and the degree of accommodation is usually set to match that required to correct the long-sightedness of the better eye. In other words, the accommodation does not fully compensate for the higher degree of long-sightedness in the worse eye. This eye therefore perceives a constantly blurred image and the nerves running from the eye to the brain fail to develop fully. Since they never perceive a clear image, they never develop with the potential for analysing a clear image. Hence, even when the full degree of long-sightedness in each eye is corrected with glasses, the worse eye will still not see clearly. This is why it is said to be 'lazy', although it should be stressed to children that it is not them who are lazy.

Often, when the anisometropia is corrected and the person gets used to the glasses then the vision of the lazy eye improves. In other cases it does not and, for children, a patch may need to be worn over the better eye to train the lazy eye.

Anisometropia is not especially prevalent in dyslexia. Children with anisometropia often do not have symptoms since young people adapt to the condition and tend to automatically use their better eye, ignoring the blurred vision in the other eye.

Presbyopia

Chapter 1 explained how the lens inside the eye focuses the eye to maintain clear vision on near objects. When we are young, this lens is very powerful and can focus on objects that are very close. As we age, this lens becomes less flexible and less able to focus until, for most people at about the age of 45, we become unable to focus at a normal reading distance. At this stage, reading glasses are required and the person is said to have *pres-byopia*.

Presbyopia is a condition affecting people in their middle age and does not affect children. There is no evidence to suggest that it affects adults with dyslexia any earlier than usual.

Understanding an optical prescription

Optical prescriptions are recorded in *dioptres*, which is a unit of focusing power and can be best understood by thinking of the magnifying lenses that children might use to focus the sun into a spot of light. The distance of the spot of light (point focus) from the lens is the focal length of the lens (Figure 2.1). The reciprocal of the focal length (in metres) gives the power of the lens (in dioptres). For example, a weak lens of 1 dioptre (1.00D) will bring the sun's rays to focus at a distance of 1 metre (1m) from the lens. A strong lens, of say 20.00D, will focus the sun at 5cm from the lens (1/20 = 0.05 and 0.05m is 5cm).

A typical optical prescription is shown below:

Example A: R +0.50/–0.50 x 180 = 6/6   L +1.50DS = 6/12

The abbreviation 'R' refers to the right eye (sometimes abbreviated 'OD') and the 'L' relates to the left eye (sometimes abbreviated 'OS'). The prescription for the right eye is +0.50/–0.50 x 180 and the level of visual acuity that this gives is 6/6. The first part of the prescription (+0.50) is the spherical component which usually determines whether a person is long- or short-sighted. If it is '+', as in Example A, then the person is long-sighted. As a very general rule, in school age children long-sightedness up to about +0.75 would not usually need glasses. Long-sightedness between

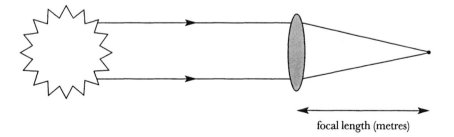

focal length (metres)

Figure 2.1. Schematic illustration of a lens bringing rays of light from a very distant object (e.g. the sun) to focus at the focal length of the lens.

+0.75 and +2.00 might need glasses. Long-sightedness over +2.00 would usually need to be corrected with glasses.

The second part of the prescription (–0.50 x 180) gives the astigmatism, which is usually recorded, by convention, as a negative value. Astigmatism below 0.75 would not normally need correction, between 0.75 and 1.25 might, and over 1.25 probably would require correction. The last part of the prescription (x 180) refers to the axis of the astigmatism. In Example A the left eye does not have any astigmatism, which is confirmed by the letters 'DS'.

To understand the visual acuity it is best to consider the 6/6 and 6/12 as fractions and to divide them out. When 6 is divided by 6 it gives 1.0, or 100%. Thus the right eye has normal visual acuity: at a given distance it can resolve detail about as well as an average eye. In fact, most children's eyes have better than average visual acuity and can resolve 6/5 or even 6/4. Literally speaking, children's visual acuity is often, therefore, 120% or 150%!

When 6 is divided by 12 it gives 0.5, or 50% so that the left eye sees about half as well as an average eye. In other words, an object that an average eye could just resolve would have to be twice as large for it to be resolved by this person's left eye.

A comparison of the spherical part of the prescription (+0.50 in the right eye and +1.50 in the left eye) shows that there is some anisometropia (the two eyes are different). A difference of about half a dioptre is common and of little significance. But a difference of 1.00 dioptres is unusual and represents a significant degree of anisometropia. Indeed, in this example the anisometropia is probably the reason why the left eye sees less well than the right (anisometropic amblyopia).

Example B: R –2.00/–0.25 x 90 = 6/5   L -2.25/-0.50 x 95 = 6/5   Add +1.50

Example B is a typical prescription for a middle-aged person who is moderately short-sighted. A low degree of short-sightedness, of –0.25 to –0.75, might not need correction with glasses. Short-sightedness of about –0.75 upwards would probably necessitate glasses in order to see the board in class or for driving. The prescription in Example B, showing about –2.00 dioptres of short-sightedness, would need glasses for many tasks, but not for near vision (i.e. not necessarily for reading).

The astigmatism in Example B is low and the visual acuities are very good. So, although without glasses the person has poor sight for looking at objects in the distance, with glasses or contact lenses they would have no problem in seeing as well as anyone else.

The final part of the prescription in Example B is the 'Add', which is an abbreviation for the *near addition*. This is the additional prescription that has to be added to the glasses to help with near vision (for presbyopia). Because the person is short-sighted, the add almost cancels out the short-sightedness (for the right eye −2.00 + 1.50 = −0.50). This is why people with a low or moderate degree of short-sightedness can read comfortably by removing their glasses, when other people of a similar age might start to need reading glasses.

Summary

The key points of this chapter are summarized in the box. Although this book is about the specific learning difficulty of dyslexia, it should be noted in passing that high refractive errors are common in profound learning disabilities, such as Down's syndrome. People with profound learning disabilities should have regular eye examinations from very young ages.

Summary

- Refractive errors are not strong correlates of dyslexia.
- Refractive errors can, for dyslexic and non-dyslexic children, impede performance in the classroom.
- Refractive errors are not always detected by visual screening tests.
- Wearing glasses to correct refractive errors will not cause the refractive error to become worse.
- Refractive errors cannot be helped by eye exercises.

CHAPTER 3

Ocular motor factors

Introduction

In Chapter 1 a distinction was drawn between *sensory* and *motor* visual function. Motor visual function describes how the brain controls the muscles that focus and move the eyes. Ocular refers to the eye, so motor visual function is also known as ocular motor function. Confusingly, the term *oculomotor* function is sometimes used in North America to refer to studies of eye movements, particularly saccadic eye movements (discussed on p. 47–52). In fact, the term *oculomotor* literally refers to one of the twelve nerves through which the brain controls our actions (third cranial nerve). This controls some, but not all, of the eye muscles. Hence, the term *oculomotor* is potentially misleading and is avoided in this book.

Different test methods tend to obtain different results, even when they purport to assess the same function. There has been a trend in optometry over the last 20 years or so to develop tests of ocular motor function which are as natural as possible and which do not interfere significantly with normal viewing conditions (e.g. aligning prism and foveal suppression tests in Table 3.4). Results obtained with naturalistic tests are more likely to give an accurate reflection of the real situation in everyday life than are more artificial tests.

Accommodative function (focusing)

What is accommodation?

The crystalline lens, situated inside but near the front of the eye (see Figure 1.2), is responsible for adjusting the focus of the eye. Unlike a camera lens, which focuses by moving backwards and forwards, the crystalline lens does not appreciably change its position but instead changes its shape to focus the eye (Figure 3.1). It is assisted in this by a ring of muscle that surrounds the lens, called the *ciliary muscle*.

When we look in the distance this lens is relaxed and has a thin shape, like a weakly powered magnifying glass. When a child focuses to look at a near object the lens becomes fatter which increases its power, like a high powered magnifying glass (Figure 3.1).

The *amplitude of accommodation* is the maximum amount of accommodation that an eye can exert. It is usually measured by bringing small text in towards the eye and measuring the distance at which it becomes blurred. The reciprocal of this distance (in metres) gives the amplitude of accommodation (in dioptres). The maximum amplitude of accommodation that a person can exert decreases with age, as shown in Table 3.1. In Chapter 2 *presbyopia* was described as the condition which usually affects people between age 40 and 50 years when the crystalline lens becomes less able to focus close to, so that reading glasses are required. This is just a part of the normal ageing process.

Types of accommodative anomalies

Accommodative insufficiency occurs when the amplitude of accommodation is significantly below average for a person's age. The most severe form of accommodative insufficiency is *accommodative paralysis* when the ciliary muscle is paralysed. This can result from injury, illness, or for no apparent reason.

The accommodative amplitude does not necessarily predict how accurately a person is accommodating at a normal reading distance. This accommodative accuracy can be assessed by using an objective tech-

crystalline lens
in relaxed
state as in
distance vision

crystalline lens
in accommodated
state as in
near vision

Figure 3.1. Schematic diagram of relaxed and focused crystalline lens.

nique, called dynamic retinoscopy, to measure the *accommodative lag*. Usually, a small positive accommodative lag is present, of about 0.5D. This means that, when a person is focusing on a book, their accommodation is lagging slightly behind the target, usually focused about 2cm behind the target. This small error of accommodation does not cause a significant blur. If the accommodative lag is much greater than this then it might cause blur and is likely to be associated with symptoms.

Since accommodative lag is measured objectively, the optometrist does not rely on a response from the patient. This test can therefore be used to check children's claims about whether they are seeing clearly.

Occasionally, a person may over-accommodate on a target, exhibiting *accommodative spasm*. There may be a number of reasons for this, including poor control over the high accommodative amplitude that children possess.

A child should be able to change their accommodation rapidly, for example when changing their focus from the classroom board to a book. An inability to rapidly change accommodation is called *accommodative infacility*. Unfortunately, the standard clinical method of testing accommodative facility is prone to errors.

Table 3.1. The second column shows typical values of the amplitude of accommodation (dioptres) for the ages (years) in the first column. The amplitude of accommodation (in dioptres) is the reciprocal of the closest distance at which an eye can focus and these distances are given in centimetres in the last column

Age	Normal (D)	Normal (cm)
4	17	6
6	17	6
8	16	6
10	16	6
12	15	7
14	14	7
20	13	8
30	10	10
40	7	14
50	4	25

Table 3.2 summarizes the causes and treatments of accommodative anomalies. It can be seen that a common cause of these problems is long-sightedness. As was explained in Chapter 2, children may attempt to compensate for long-sightedness by over-accommodating. This can cause symptoms and can also cause accommodative anomalies. In these cases

the appropriate treatment is to correct the cause; that is to wear glasses to correct long-sightedness.

Other cases of accommodative anomalies are often treated with eye exercises (sometimes called orthoptic exercises or vision therapy).

Table 3.2. Table summarizing causes and treatments of accommodative anomalies. Bifocals and varifocals are spectacles with lenses that have more than one focal length

Condition	Causes	Treatment
Accommodative paralysis	Trauma	Reading glasses
	Some illnesses	Bifocals or varifocals
	Sometimes no known cause	Exercises (often unsuccessful)
Accommodative insufficiency	Long-sightedness	If long-sightedness, glasses
	Sometimes no known cause	Eye exercises
Accommodative lag	Long-sightedness	If long-sightedness, glasses
	Sometimes no known cause	Eye exercises
Accommodative spasm	Long-sightedness	If long-sightedness, glasses
	Sometimes no known cause	Eye exercises
Accommodative infacility	Long-sightedness	If long- or short-sightedness,
	Short-sightedness	glasses
	Sometimes no known cause	Eye exercises

Accommodation and dyslexia

Some research studies suggest that a low amplitude of accommodation is a correlate of dyslexia. Typically, a research study might compare the amplitude of accommodation of a group of people with dyslexia to that of a group of good readers (see Appendix 3). Research of this type has tended to find a significantly lower *average* amplitude of accommodation in dyslexia than in good readers. But, as was discussed in Chapter 1, a correlate is very different from a cause and a difference between the average performance of two groups does not mean that many *individual* cases of dyslexia will require treatment for poor accommodation. The amplitude of accommodation of most individuals with dyslexia is more than adequate to allow comfortable focusing at the distances at which children would usually hold a book to read.

Nonetheless, any child can have accommodative insufficiency and, since the accommodative amplitude is on average lower in dyslexia, it seems likely that a higher than usual proportion of dyslexic children will have accommodative insufficiency. Case study 3.1 on page 32 describes a case who reported difficulties at school and was found to have an accommodative anomaly.

Case study 3.1: F0352

BACKGROUND: Girl, aged 11, routine eye check but mentioned difficulties at school and near vision blur.

SYMPTOMS: About twice a day at school the near vision blurs. No other symptoms.

CLINICAL FINDINGS: Visual acuities: normal. Ocular health: normal. Refractive error (objective) without cycloplegic: low degree of long-sightedness in both eyes. Slightly low amplitude of accommodation (R = L = 8D). Accommodative facility normal, but high accommodative lag (R +1.50, L +1.00). Binocular vision test normal.

MANAGEMENT: Given eye exercises to improve accommodative control (focus on a detailed target and then bring this towards her until it blurs, repeat for 5 minutes twice a day) until symptoms better (or return).

FOLLOW-UP APPOINTMENT: Near blur is much rarer, now just occurs about once a week. No other symptoms. Accommodative function now much better (lag R = L = +0.75). Other results similar to before.

COMMENT: The patient's symptoms were helped by simple eye exercises, which could be done at home.

Relatively few research studies have assessed accommodative lag in dyslexia, and these suggest that accommodative lag is not a strong correlate of dyslexia. This is important because, compared with accommodative amplitude, accommodative lag is a more meaningful measure of how well a person accommodates during the actual reading process.

Similarly, the research on accommodative infacility and dyslexia is equivocal. Some studies have suggested that accommodative infacility is particularly common in dyslexia, but other studies have not supported this conclusion. One possible reason for this confusion may be that many tests of accommodative facility require the person to read out words or letters. Word recognition and possibly letter recognition may be impaired in dyslexia. Hence, dyslexic people could do poorly in accommodative facility tests not because of poor accommodation but because of their reading problem.

Accommodative facility testing is helpful in cases where a child reports difficulty changing focus from the board to a book, or vice versa. It may occasionally provide useful information in other cases, particularly if the child does poorly on other tests of accommodative function.

Binocular co-ordination (eye teaming)

What is binocular co-ordination?

Each eyeball is surrounded by six *extra-ocular muscles* which move the eyes into various positions of gaze. The muscles are controlled by nerves which run from specific areas in the brain which control eye movements. Ideally, each eye should point precisely at the object of regard and similar images will be formed at the back of each eye. These images are transmitted along each optic nerve to the brain where the images from each eye eventually come together to form a single perception.

Binocular incoordination means that the co-ordination between the two eyes is not as good as it ought to be. If the two eyes are misaligned, so that one is not pointing precisely at the object of regard, then the person may have double vision (*diplopia*). If the two eyes become very misaligned then the two doubled image will be situated a long way apart and the person will have recognizable double vision (Figure 3.2, top row). If the misalignment between the two eyes is slight then the person's perception may not be one of double vision (Figure 3.2, bottom row). If the misalignment of the visual axes is variable then, depending on the degree of misalignment, letters or words may appear to blur, move, wobble, or even flicker and shimmer. Hence, binocular incoordination does not just result in diplopia, but can also result in visual perceptual distortions.

The reason why we have evolved to have good binocular co-ordination is not just to avoid double vision and visual perceptual distortions. When the brain combines the images from each eye together to gain a single view of world, it is able to extract information about the depth of objects. Anyone who has ever closed one eye during a 3D movie will know that the remarkable depth perception immediately disappears.

Problems with binocular co-ordination are sometimes described as *binocular vision anomalies* or *orthoptic anomalies*. About 5% of the population have a significant degree of binocular incoordination.

What is strabismus?

We have all encountered people who have a *strabismus*, which is when there is a manifest (obvious) misalignment of the eyes. When in conversa-

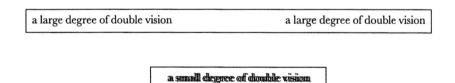

Figure 3.2. Illustration of double vision. The top row represents the patient's perception if the two eyes are misaligned by a large amount, such as in a 12° strabismus. The bottom row represents a much more subtle degree of misalignment, when the visual axes are misaligned by about half of one degree. The figure is a simplification: the images may move, flicker, or fade.

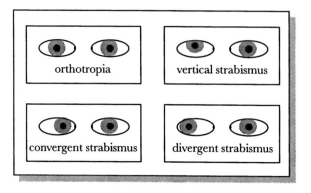

Figure 3.3. Strabismus. The top left diagram shows good ocular alignment, when there is no strabismus, termed *orthotropia*. The top right diagram shows a vertical strabismus, a right *hypertropia*. The bottom left diagram demonstrates a convergent strabismus, a right *esotropia*. The bottom right diagram shows a divergent strabismus, a right *exotropia*.

tion with a person who has a large angle strabismus it can be quite unnerving trying to decide which of their eyes is looking at you. A strabismus is also known as a *cast*, *lazy eye*, or *wandering eye*, but the most accurate scientific term is heterotropia. Unfortunately, some authorities continue to call it a *squint*, which to lay people often means something quite different: when a person screws the eyes partially shut. Sometimes, 'a strabismus' is confused with 'astigmatism', although this is quite different (see Chapter 2). The main types of strabismus are illustrated in Figure 3.3.

Not every case of strabismus will be as obvious as those illustrated in Figure 3.3. The strabismus may be so slight that it cannot be detected by an untrained observer. The misalignment reflects a problem in the *motor* control of the eyes: either a problem with the extra-ocular muscles or with the outgoing nerve signal from the brain.

Surprisingly, most people with strabismus do not have double vision, despite the fact that the eyes are pointing at different objects. Strabismus usually occurs at a young age when the brain can develop adaptations to avoid perceiving double vision. There are two types of these *sensory adaptations* and the first is *suppression*, when the brain simply 'switches off' the image from the strabismic eye. The suppression will only occur when the person is using both eyes: if one is covered then there is no risk of double vision so the suppression will cease.

Although suppression will prevent double vision, it is wasteful to discard the image from one eye. The second type of adaptation is much less wasteful and goes by the unwieldy name of *harmonious anomalous retinal correspondence (HARC)*. HARC is a fascinating but complicated phenomenon and is described in more detail in another book by the author (see Appendix 3). HARC may be thought of as a sort of 're-wiring' (although this phrase is probably an over-simplification). HARC means that, even although the two eyes are not pointing at the same object, the brain can still use the images from both eyes at the same time and see singly.

One of the commonest causes of *convergent strabismus* is long-sightedness. It was noted earlier in this chapter that the visual system usually attempts to compensate for long-sightedness by accommodating, or 'over-focusing' the eyes. But the natural purpose of accommodation is to keep objects clear as they approach the observer. A second function that occurs during near vision is convergence to keep the object single. Accommodation and convergence naturally occur together and the two are *cross-linked*: a given degree of accommodation induces a corresponding amount of convergence, and vice versa.

It is this link between convergence and accommodation that causes problems in long-sightedness. A person may over-accommodate to compensate for the long-sightedness and this over-accommodation induces a corresponding over-convergence. The over-convergence can cause a convergent strabismus (esotropia). The proper treatment for this type of strabismus is to correct the underlying problem: the long-sightedness. This can be done with glasses, which sometimes need to be bifocals or varifocals (glasses that have more than one focal length; for example to allow different corrections for distance and near).

Generally speaking, mild degrees of strabismus that occur in school-aged children can often be treated with glasses or exercises. If parents suspect strabismus in a child then they should see an optometrist as soon as possible. Very rarely, a strabismus can be caused by an eye disease or other health problem in which case the optometrist will refer for a medical opinion. Large angle strabismus usually needs an operation and the optometrist will refer for the opinion of an eye surgeon. Most surgeons work with orthoptists who would assess the characteristics of the strabismus before and after surgery.

Strabismus and dyslexia

Most relevant research studies agree that strabismus is not a strong correlate of dyslexia. Strabismus does occasionally occur in dyslexic people, but it is no more likely to be present in dyslexic people than in good readers.

As an interesting aside, a tribe of Aztec Indians, the Maya, deliberately made their offspring esotropic, possibly for religious reasons. This did not prevent them from establishing an advanced civilization for several centuries, with a form of writing and expertise in astronomy and mathematics.

The reason why strabismus does not impair reading is probably because of sensory adaptations. People with long-standing strabismus usually have a stable sensory adaptation which prevents the strabismus from interfering with their visual perception. Occasionally, eyecare practitioners encounter patients whose sensory adaptation to strabismus is unstable and these people may benefit from treatment, sometimes in the form of eye exercises.

What is heterophoria?

For people who do not have a strabismus then, as long as the two eyes are free to view the object of regard, they will be aligned. The brain will see two matching images and will combine them together in the process of *sensory fusion*. But if one eye is covered then the two eyes no longer have matching images for the brain to fuse. In this situation, the eyes are said to be *dissociated* and the covered eye can turn to take up any position. The covered eye usually turns in or out to take up its *position of rest*. This means that the person has a tendency for the eyes to misalign which, under normal conditions, the person is automatically overcoming. This tendency to misalign, which is revealed when the eyes are dissociated, is called a *heterophoria*. When the cover is taken away, the eye that was covered will move from its position of rest to take up fixation. This movement is a measure of the heterophoria. Nearly always, the heterophoria is the same whichever eye is covered.

Eyecare practitioners use this *cover test* to detect, classify, and measure the heterophoria. The main types of heterophoria are illustrated in Figure 3.4.

The types of heterophoria in Figure 3.4 closely correspond with the main types of strabismus, or heterotropia, described in Figure 3.3. Indeed, a heterophoria can 'break down' to a strabismus and a heterophoria used to be called a *latent strabismus*.

If a person is placed in a completely darkened room then there will be no objects for the eyes to fix upon. Typically, the eyes would then adopt a resting posture of being lined up on an imaginary object about a metre away. One way of thinking about binocular co-ordination is to think of distance vision as an active divergence (eyes turning outwards) from this resting position, and of near vision as an active convergence (eyes turning inwards) from the resting position (Figure 3.5). For many people, their heterophoria can be explained as a slight underaction of the required

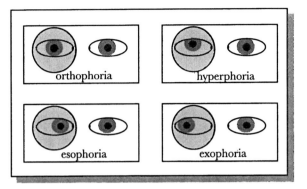

Figure 3.4. Heterophoria: an ocular deviation that occurs when an eye is covered. The diagrams show the position of the left (uncovered) eye and the right eye which, for the purposes of the diagram, is 'seen through' a cover (shaded circle). The top left diagram shows the situation where the eye behind the cover is straight and there is no heterophoria, termed *orthophoria*. In the top right diagram the eye behind the cover has moved up: a *hyperphoria*. In the bottom left diagram the eye behind the cover has moved in: an *esophoria*. In the bottom right diagram the eye behind the cover has moved out: an *exophoria*.

convergence or divergence. Hence, the average heterophoria to have at distance is a low degree of esophoria, as if the eyes are not quite diverging enough when one eye is covered. Similarly, the average heterophoria to have at near is an exophoria, as if the eyes are not quite converging enough when one eye is covered.

Nearly everyone has a heterophoria and there are usually no signs or adverse effects of the heterophoria under normal viewing conditions. This is because when the brain receives similar images from each eye it initiates the appropriate convergence or divergence movement to overcome the heterophoria and to keep the eyes straight. In these cases the heterophoria is said to be *compensated*.

Occasionally, a heterophoria is too great or the available convergence or divergence is inadequate and the heterophoria becomes *decompensated*. A decompensated heterophoria may cause problems for two reasons: it can break down to a strabismus and/or it may cause the symptoms in Table 3.3.

Symptoms are important, but many of the symptoms in Table 3.3 can have other causes. Hence, eyecare practitioners use a battery of tests to assess whether a heterophoria is compensated and the key tests are listed in Table 3.4.

When tested for near vision (e.g. reading), most people have an exophoria (Figure 3.4). If it is decompensated then the exophoria is usually treated with eye exercises or glasses. Eye exercises (also called

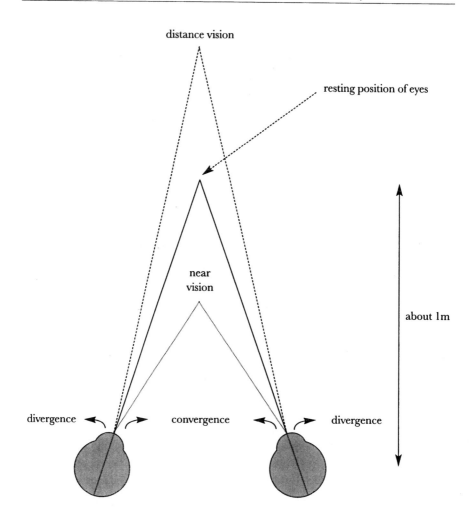

Figure 3.5. Diagram (not to scale) illustrating vergence eye movements away from the resting position that the eyes typically take up in a completely dark room. In this situation, when nothing is seen to permit fusion, the eyes usually align on an imaginary object about 1 metre away. During normal viewing, distance vision may be thought of as a turning out of the eyes (divergence) and near vision as a turning in of the eyes (convergence) away from this resting position.

vision therapy or *orthoptic exercises*) are the preferred treatment in most cases (see Case study 3.2 and Figure 3.7). Although exercises are often effective, they require hard work and co-operation from both the child and the parent.

In cases where the child is not likely to co-operate, or when exercises have not worked, then the exophoria can be treated with glasses. Glasses

Table 3.3. Symptoms of a decompensated heterophoria. Those numbered 1–3 are sometimes described as asthenopia, 2–3 as visual discomfort, and 4–6 as visual perceptual distortions

Symptoms of decompensated heterophoria

1. headaches
2. aching eyes
3. sore eyes
4. blurred vision
5. double vision
6. letters or words moving
7. losing place when reading
8. difficulty with depth perception
9. tendency to close or cover one eye
10. general irritation

Table 3.4. Tests that are sometimes used to determine whether a heterophoria is compensated. The tests can be carried out at any distance at which the person usually works, typically at 6 metres and at reading distance. The tests are listed in order of usefulness, with the most useful tests at the top

Test	Explanation
Cover test	Checks the ocular alignment to determine the presence and size of any strabismus or heterophoria. The speed and smoothness of the movements of the eyes during the test indicate whether the heterophoria is compensated
Aligning prism	Measures the precise degree of alignment of the two eyes under natural conditions. A good indicator of how well a person can compensate for a heterophoria. This test is also known as an associated heterophoria or fixation disparity (OXO) test (Figure 3.6)
Fusional reserves	Measurement of the maximum amount by which a person can converge or diverge the eyes. An indicator of the 'power in reserve' to overcome a heterophoria (Figure 3.8)
Foveal suppression	Assesses whether the brain is using the images from both eyes. In some cases of decompensated heterophoria, a person may suppress the fovea of one eye. This may help to avoid symptoms, but can be a sign that the heterophoria may be breaking down into a strabismus and requires treatment
Stereo-acuity	Measures the ability to use the images from the two eyes to assess depth
Dissociation test	Measures the absolute size of any strabismus or heterophoria. This is a poor predictor of whether a heterophoria is compensated

with negative lenses are often used to make the patient accommodate, which induces convergence to help overcome the exophoria. These are sometimes called *exercise glasses* since the goal is to reduce the strength of the glasses over a period of months as the child becomes more able to overcome the exophoria themselves. In most cases, the strength of the glasses is eventually reduced to a point where they are no longer required.

Figure 3.6. Mallett fixation disparity test. This test detects the aligning prism and is a good indicator of whether a heterophoria is compensated. When it is appropriate to correct the heterophoria with lenses or prisms, the test can also be used to determine the required correction.

Figure 3.7. Institute Free-space Stereograms, a type of eye exercises developed by the author. The booklet of exercises is given to the patient to do at home, often helped by a parent. The child looks at various targets and the parent reads out instructions. Eyecare professionals use these, and other, exercises to treat convergence insufficiency, decompensated exophoria, exotropia, and binocular instability.

Case study 3.2: F7086

BACKGROUND: Referred to the author by a teacher because of spelling difficulties. Teacher tested with a coloured overlay and patient has been using an overlay for 5 weeks, which 'makes reading easier'.

SYMPTOMS: Small text 'blurs and jumps around'; skips or omits words or lines. 'Five headaches in the last five months'.

CLINICAL FINDINGS: Decompensated exophoria at near.

MANAGEMENT: Given Institute Free-space Stereogram eye exercises (Figure 3.7) to improve ability to converge and overcome decompensated exophoria.

FOLLOW-UP 1 & 5 MONTHS LATER: No more symptoms (no blurring, no movement of text, no headaches). Exophoria now compensated. No longer receives any benefit from a coloured overlay. Reading and spelling slightly better, but still specific spelling difficulty.

COMMENT: The decompensated exophoria responded well to treatment with exercises and his visual symptoms were cured; but he still has a specific learning difficulty. Some people who report eyestrain, headaches, and perceptual distortions require coloured filters, but in this case the symptoms resulted from the exophoria.

The most common cause of decompensated esophoria (Figure 3.4) is long-sightedness. A person might try to compensate for uncorrected long-sightedness by over-accommodating. The over-accommodation would trigger over-convergence which could cause an esophoria. If the esophoria is too great for the person to overcome then it may break down into a convergent strabismus, which was described above. The correct treatment in these cases is to correct the underlying problem: the long-sightedness (see Case study 3.3). Some other cases of esophoria, even when there is no significant long-sightedness, can also be corrected with glasses, including bifocals or varifocals. Although esophoria can be treated with exercises, esophoria is harder to treat this way than exophoria.

Hyperphorias (Figure 3.4) are very rare and when they do occur they are likely to cause symptoms. They can be corrected with a type of spectacle lens called a prism, which allows the eyes to turn towards their resting position. Prisms are a 'crutch': they do not usually make the problem better or worse because they are a correction rather than a treatment.

Prisms can also be used to treat cases of exophoria and esophoria (Figure 3.6). But prisms are usually a last resort, in cases that do not respond to other types of treatment. Prisms are also sometimes used as a temporary measure, for example to correct a decompensated exophoria during exams, with the understanding that the patient will start eye exercises when they have more time.

Heterophoria and dyslexia

No clear consensus emerges from the research literature concerning any relationship between heterophoria and dyslexia. Several studies have found no relationship: others have found increased levels of heterophoria of various types, most commonly exophoria at near. With conflicting results in the literature, the best that one can say is that heterophoria is not a strong correlate of dyslexia. From the description of heterophoria in the last section it is clear that the most relevant question is whether there is a greater prevalence of decompensated heterophoria in dyslexia and this is discussed below.

Several studies have found that the fusional reserves (the ability to exert convergence or divergence; Table 3.4 and Figure 3.8) are, on average, a little lower than usual in dyslexia. But, as was discussed in Chapter 1, an *average* difference does not mean than many *individual* cases will require treatment. Since fusional reserves are used to overcome a heterophoria, one might expect decompensated heterophoria to be particularly common in dyslexia. But the research evidence suggests that decompensated heterophoria is not a strong correlate of dyslexia.

Decompensated heterophoria is fairly common and a conservative summary is that it is at least as common in dyslexia as it is in the general population. Some of the symptoms of decompensated heterophoria (visual perceptual distortions; numbers 4–6 in Table 3.3) can directly contribute to reading difficulties and others (asthenopia, numbers 1–3; and 10 in Table 3.3) may indirectly contribute to reading problems through making the person less willing to read.

Figure 3.8. The measurement of fusional reserves in a child. Several methods can be used, and in the illustration the fusional reserves are being measured with a prism bar.

Many eyecare practitioners have encountered rare cases in which the symptoms of a decompensated heterophoria have been so severe as to make reading very difficult for the patient. Once the visual problem has been resolved, the reading performance of these cases can rapidly improve to 'normal' levels, although the child may need extra teaching to help them make up for lost ground. A few of these cases have been misdiagnosed as dyslexic (see Case study 3.3) and this highlights the need for professional eyecare from a young age in suspected cases of dyslexia.

Case study 3.3: F9033

BACKGROUND: Referred by educational psychologist who had found borderline dyslexic and dyspraxic difficulties.

SYMPTOMS: Text sometimes appears to change size, faint colours appear to be present around words, eyes become tired after reading for a long time, tendency to skip or omit words or lines, rubs eyes.

CLINICAL FINDINGS: Moderate degree of long-sightedness (+1.50) in each eye and decompensated esophoria at distance and near.

MANAGEMENT: Prescribed glasses for all schoolwork and reading.

FOLLOW-UP 4 MONTHS LATER: 'Reading much better since glasses, almost up to average'. All the initial symptoms have resolved. The esophoria was corrected while the glasses were worn.

COMMENT: This was a simple case of long-sightedness causing esophoria and symptoms. Correcting the underlying problem, the long-sightedness, alleviated the visual symptoms.

What is binocular instability?

The fusional reserves (Table 3.4) represent the motor fusion (convergence and divergence) that a person has 'in reserve' to overcome their heterophoria. From this statement it might seem safe to assume that if a person does not have any heterophoria (they are *orthophoric*; Figure 3.4) then they will not require any fusional reserves. But this is not the case and the reason relates to the fact that all the tests in Table 3.4 assess the eyes while they are relatively stationary.

During everyday tasks, such as reading, the eyes are not stationary but constantly move. The eyes are fairly soft 'balls' moving in a bed of soft tissue and even in people with normal visual function there are bound to be small errors in the alignment of the eyes that occur as they move. In fact, as the eyes move along a line of text errors of alignment of up to 2–3° may occur, even in a person with good binocular co-ordination. Hence, even a person with orthophoria will need to have some fusional reserves available just to maintain alignment as the eyes move.

People with binocular instability have low fusional reserves and an unstable heterophoria. The symptoms of binocular instability are the same as the symptoms of decompensated heterophoria (Table 3.3). The treatment of the condition is usually by eye exercises (e.g. Figure 3.7), although sometimes glasses are required.

Binocular instability and dyslexia

Most research studies which have looked for binocular instability in dyslexia have found that people with dyslexia are more likely to have binocular instability than good readers. Although people with dyslexia tend to have a fairly normal heterophoria (tendency for the eyes to maintain alignment), they often have lower than average fusional reserves, which suggests that they may have to work harder than usual to maintain alignment. This means that they are more likely than usual to have binocular instability, and are therefore more likely to have the symptoms in Table 3.3.

Like decompensated heterophoria, the symptoms of binocular instability can contribute to a reading difficulty either directly or indirectly. Of course, treatment of binocular instability will not affect the phonological problems that are usually present in dyslexia. But if binocular instability is contributing to the dyslexic difficulties then treatment will be of some help.

What is convergence insufficiency?

If a person looks at the tip of a pencil as it approaches their nose then, when it gets very close, they will appear to be 'cross-eyed': they will be exerting a considerable degree of convergence. Some people can converge until the pencil touches their nose; others can only converge to a lesser extent. The distance from the tip of the pencil to the eye at this point of maximum convergence is called the *near point of convergence*. For most children, this is 5cm or less, when it is about 10cm or greater it is described as *convergence insufficiency*. Convergence insufficiency is one of the most common binocular vision anomalies, affecting about 8% of the population.

There is an important difference between the convergent fusional reserve and the near point of convergence. During fusional reserve testing the object of regard is kept at a constant distance from the patient, whereas the object approaches the patient when the near point of convergence is tested. An awareness of the closeness of the object causes the brain to induce extra convergence.

Nonetheless, convergence insufficiency is often associated with a decompensated heterophoria at a normal reading distance, and can cause the symptoms in Table 3.3. Convergence insufficiency can nearly always be treated successfully using simple eye exercises (e.g. Figure 3.7). Sometimes, convergence insufficiency is associated with accommodative insufficiency and some of these cases respond to exercises while others require glasses.

Convergence insufficiency and dyslexia

The research literature is divided on whether convergence insufficiency is a correlate of dyslexia (see Appendix 3). In any event, convergence insufficiency is so common that it is bound to affect many people with dyslexia. If the convergence sufficiency is severe enough to produce symptoms then treatment may help reading performance, for the same reasons as given above for decompensated heterophoria.

What is amblyopia?

Amblyopia is reduced vision in an eye which has become disused during childhood. An amblyopic eye would not be able to read very far down a letter chart, even if any refractive error was corrected. The most common causes of amblyopia are a strabismus or an uncorrected refractive error. Amblyopia can be treated, if detected before the age of about 8 years, by wearing a patch over the good eye to encourage use of the amblyopic eye.

Amblyopia and dyslexia

The research literature suggests that amblyopia is no more common in people with dyslexia than it is in the rest of the population. When amblyopia is present, it nearly always only affects one eye. During everyday tasks, when both eyes are in use, the brain simply chooses to use the better eye. So, amblyopia usually has no significant effect on reading.

Stereopsis, foveal suppression, and aniseikonia

It was noted earlier in this chapter that one of the reasons why we have two eyes is to allow the brain to combine the images together to see objects in depth. *Stereopsis* and *stereo-acuity* refer to our ability to do this. To some extent, stereo-acuity is a barometer of binocular co-ordination: people with good binocular co-ordination tend to have good stereo-acuity. But there are exceptions to this rule because other factors in addition to binocular co-ordination also influence stereo-acuity. Most

well-controlled research studies suggest that stereo-acuity is not correlated with dyslexia (Appendix 3).

Foveal suppression (Table 3.4) can exist as a compensatory mechanism
to avoid the symptoms from decompensated heterophoria. Its presence
may indicate that a heterophoria is progressing to a strabismus and
requires treatment. Foveal suppression does not appear to be strongly
correlated with dyslexia, although few research studies have investigated
this.

Aniseikonia occurs when the images that the brain receives from each
eye are different sizes, causing problems in fusing these images together.
The most common cause of aniseikonia is unequal refractive errors
(anisometropia; see Chapter 2) and correction with contact lenses may be
necessary to minimize aniseikonia. About 50 years ago, there was a fairly
common view in the eyecare professions that aniseikonia frequently
occurred in the absence of anisometropia and was a common bar to
stable and comfortable visual perception. These days this view is very
rarely held. It seems unlikely that aniseikonia is a major factor by itself,
and most attention is given to detecting and correcting the underlying
problem of anisometropia. As contact lenses have become safer they are
being fitted more commonly to children and this helps to reduce the
effects of anisometropia. I do not know of any researchers who have
argued in recent times that aniseikonia is a significant factor in dyslexia.

A note on eye exercises

Many of the most common types of binocular vision anomalies can be
treated with eye exercises. Specifically, decompensated exophoria,
convergence insufficiency, and binocular instability can all be treated
with exercises to train the fusional reserves (e.g. Figure 3.7). Eye exercises
to treat fusional reserves are not controversial and have been used for
many decades and validated by controlled research studies.

These eye exercises are not a treatment for dyslexia, but rather treat
people with dyslexia (and without) who have one of the above types of
binocular incoordination. These exercises will not cure dyslexia, but
may correct a visual problem which might be causing symptoms when
reading.

Eyecare practitioners will only be likely to prescribe these exercises to
a small proportion of the patients they see with dyslexia (about 1 in 5,
according to one research study). There are other types of exercises which
are more controversial and are prescribed, by a few practitioners, to the

vast majority of children they see with dyslexia. There is relatively little evidence to support the use of these exercises, which are discussed in Chapter 5.

Eye movements (eye tracking)

The need for eye movements

The retina contains about 136 million receptor cells. One way of using these to gain information about the visual world might be for a nerve fibre to run from each of these cells to the visual part of the brain. But this is just not practical. There are twelve main nerves that feed into the brain and the optic nerve contains more nerve fibres than the other eleven, but even so the optic nerve only contains about 1.2 million nerve fibres. So, there is no way that every receptor cell on the retina can have its own nerve fibre running to the visual area of the brain.

Nature has evolved a clever way round this problem. The central area of the retina (the fovea or macula) has a very dense concentration of receptor cells and does have nerve fibres running from virtually each receptor to the brain. It is this central region that is capable of resolving very fine detail.

The rest of the retina does not have individual nerve fibres running from the receptors to the brain so cannot resolve fine detail. Instead, the retinal periphery recognizes general shapes and outlines and is very good at localizing objects and at detecting movement and flicker. It is this region that draws our attention to objects that may be interesting. An eye movement then takes place so that the object of interest becomes imaged on the fovea and can then be analysed in detail. So, the retinal periphery tells us most about where to look and the fovea specializes in telling us what we are looking at. The main purpose of eye movements is to keep objects of maximum interest imaged on to the fovea.

Overview of eye movements

The first function that we should consider in this section is fixation, which is not really an eye movement at all. If we are steadily looking at a stationary object then the fixation reflex will keep the object imaged on the fovea. Fixation should be stable, since fixation instability would make it harder to analyse the object.

The three main types of eye movements are vergence, pursuit and saccades. Vergence eye movements help to keep track of objects at different distances and convergence and divergence have already been discussed. Pursuit eye movements are used to track a slowly moving object, such as an aeroplane flying across the sky. They are fairly slow eye movements and are not usually used during reading.

Saccadic eye movements are rapid, 'flick', eye movements. They can have a speed of up to 800 degrees per second. Saccadic eye movements are used when observing objects that are moving too fast for pursuit eye movements to keep up with them. Saccades are also used to follow a sequence of stimuli, like the eye movement that occurs to change fixation from a red traffic light to a green one.

Saccadic eye movements are also used to search visual scenes. For example, if someone is looking for a friend in a crowd then their eyes will be searching through the crowd with a series of saccadic eye movements. What is really happening is that the eyes pause to fix (fixation pause) on a group of people so that this image can be resolved by the fovea and analysed by the brain. The eyes then make a saccade to the next group of people and once the brain has processed the image of this group the eyes make another saccade to the next group, and so on. This pattern of eye movements is used to analyse any detailed visual scene; for example, when we enter an unfamiliar room, look at a picture, or walk down a street. Each of us makes about 150,000 saccades a day.

When we read a page of text we are analysing a detailed visual scene so we use this pattern of saccadic eye movements. Three things about reading make it a slightly unusual saccadic task. First, for people reading Western languages the required sequence of saccades is unusually regular, requiring most successive saccades to be in a horizontal line and from left to right. Second, the visual scene is, in terms of its general appearance, composed of very similar objects. The visual task of reading has been likened to standing back from a brick wall and trying to count the bricks. Third, the visual task of reading occurs predominantly in two dimensions (i.e. the page is flat).

The pattern of eye movements during reading can be recorded using special equipment and this usually results in a trace rather like that illustrated in Figure 3.9. The eyes proceed along a line in a series of step-like saccades, which are separated by fixation pauses. During the fixation pauses, information is acquired from the relevant section of text; the width of this section, normally measured in the number of letters, is termed the *perceptual span*. Most saccades are in a left-to-right direction, but occasionally one is made in the opposite direction. These *regressions* are to return to previously read text, normally to aid understanding. At the end of a line the eyes make a large right to left saccade, or *return sweep*. Reading of more complicated text is usually associated with an increase in the number of regressions and fixations and a decrease in the perceptual span and speed of reading.

To some extent the pattern of saccadic eye movements during reading is automatic. It has been shown that while the fovea is analysing the small group of centrally fixed letters the 'peripheral retina' is processing the general shape of letters and words ahead to determine where the eyes will move to in the next fixation. This is *bottom-up* processing: automatic low level processing that is distinct from the higher level parts of the brain that interpret the meaning of the words. But *top-down* processing also occurs. The higher level areas of the brain whose role is to extract meaning from the page can influence the pattern of saccadic eye movements during reading. This is how the pattern of saccadic eye movements changes for more complicated text, as described above.

What is tracking?

The term *tracking* is sometimes used to refer to eye movements, but the term is used in many different ways. To assess tracking, some people see how smoothly a subject's eyes can follow a slowly moving target, which is assessing pursuit eye movements. Others hold two targets, for example pencils, about 20cm apart and have the person look alternately at one and then the other. The observer sees whether the subject can alternate their fixation with just one accurate saccade, or whether they have to make additional small corrective saccades. Other testers assess the person's ability to 'track' a slowly moving target as it approaches their nose, which is assessing convergence.

Each of these tasks is attempting to assess fundamentally different types of eye movements, so the term tracking is so vague as to be virtually

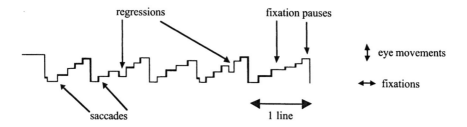

Figure 3.9. Schematic illustration of eye movements during reading. Vertical lines represent eye movements, horizontal lines fixation pauses.

meaningless. In any event, watching a person's eyes while they attempt to follow a target is probably too coarse to provide much useful clinical information. A third problem is the confounding issue of attention. If a person's attention wanders during any 'tracking' task then this may be mistakenly recorded as an abnormal eye movement. This is discussed further below.

Eye movements and dyslexia

Vergence eye movements were discussed earlier in this chapter and are returned to in Chapter 8.

A few research studies have investigated pursuit eye movements in dyslexia and most of these have found irregularities of smooth pursuit to be a fairly common feature of dyslexia. Yet, pursuit eye movements do not usually occur during reading. So this correlate of dyslexia could not be a cause or even a contributory factor to the reading difficulty. One possible explanation might relate to attentional difficulties. It was noted in Chapter 1 that attention deficit disorder (ADD) commonly co-exists with dyslexia. One of the features of ADD is motor impersistence, which is a difficulty in sustaining motor control. This could easily account for saccadation of pursuit eye movements and is discussed further in Chapter 8.

There have been many research studies in 'quality' scientific journals relating to the role of saccadic eye movements in dyslexia, yet this remains a controversial topic. It is widely agreed that dyslexic people tend to make an increased number of fixations, particularly regressions, when they read. But the crucial question is whether this is a cause or an effect of their problem. Some people have argued that dyslexics have a fundamental eye movement problem which is a cause of their reading difficulty.

A second hypothesis is that the increased fixations, especially regressions, that occur in dyslexia are not the cause but are the result of the dyslexic difficulties. Because the person has trouble understanding the text then they have to make more fixations to 'search' for meaning. According to this hypothesis, the fundamental eye movement skills in dyslexia are normal. The third hypothesis is that abnormal patterns of eye movements are neither the cause nor the effect of the dyslexia, but are a non-causal correlate.

Several research approaches have been used to try to decide which of these hypotheses is correct and these are outlined in Appendix 3. It seems that the majority of rigorous studies have found that there is no fundamental deficit of saccadic eye movements in dyslexia. This is not surprising since nearly *everything* that we do requires saccadic eye movements and yet dyslexia is a *specific* difficulty with a certain area of academic performance (see p. 2–3).

One possible explanation for the disparate findings of different research studies on saccades and dyslexia may be the effect of attention. If a person has an attentional deficit then this might be expected to result in fewer regular saccades, more fixations, and especially more regressions. Although 'lapses of attention' might cause lapses of eye movement control, this does not necessarily mean that the poor eye movement control will impair performance during reading. It seems more likely that the lapses of attention will directly interfere with reading. Very little work on eye movements and dyslexia has investigated the role of attentional deficits and this is a priority for future work.

The research evidence summarized above relates to studies that have used one of several devices to objectively measure eye movements (Figure 3.9). There are two clinical tests available which, it is claimed, can assess saccadic eye movement function without having to use sophisticated equipment. These two tests are the King-Devick Saccade test and the Developmental Eye Movement Test (DEM). The King-Devick Test has randomly spaced numbers in horizontal rows and the speed with which a person can read these is assumed to be a test of saccadic function. While saccadic dysfunction would impair performance at this task, so would many other factors. For example, performance at the test might be influenced by virtually all of the visual factors described in this book, as well as other skills including character recognition, phonological decoding, attention, and intelligence. Hence, the test does not specifically assess saccadic eye movement skills.

The DEM test also has numbers in horizontal rows but additionally has a control condition where there are just two vertical columns of numbers to be read. The assumption seems to be that if a person has saccadic dysfunction then they will make abnormal horizontal saccades but normal vertical saccades. The horizontal digits are randomly spaced, but this might simply make the horizontal task harder than the vertical rather than necessarily measuring any aspect of eye movement skills. No-one has yet carried out a research study that objectively records eye movements in patients who have been tested with the DEM test.

In summary, it is unclear whether the King-Devick and DEM tests are reliable measures of saccadic eye movement skills. In any event, saccadic eye movement dysfunction does not seem to be a robust correlate of dyslexia so it is probably not a valuable use of clinical time to investigate saccadic eye movements. A few practitioners recommend eye exercises to treat saccadic eye movements in dyslexia, but this is highly controversial and requires more research to establish whether it is anything more than a placebo (see Chapter 5).

Summary

The key points of this chapter are summarized in the box. Although this book is about the specific learning difficulty of dyslexia, it is worth mentioning that the profound learning disabilities, such as Down's syndrome, are often associated with accommodative problems and binocular incoordination, especially strabismus.

Summary

- A reduced amplitude of accommodation is a correlate of dyslexia and can produce blurred vision.
- Strabismus and amblyopia are not correlates of dyslexia.
- Decompensated heterophoria and convergence insufficiency are common, but are probably not especially common in dyslexia.
- Binocular instability is a correlate of dyslexia.
- The above anomalies can make reading harder and can be treated with eye exercises or glasses.
- Saccadic eye movement skills are probably normal in dyslexia

CHAPTER 4

Ocular dominance

What is ocular dominance?

The dominant (or controlling) eye is the eye whose visual function predominates over the other eye. Most people would say that the dominant eye is simply the eye that they would use, for example, to sight a gun.

Unfortunately, the situation is far more complicated than one might expect. Part of the reason for this complexity is the phrase *visual function* in the definition above. So far, this book has described many different types of visual function including visual acuity, ocular alignment (binocular co-ordination), suppression, stereopsis, and saccadic eye movements. Each of these types of visual function can be assessed in a variety of ways and, for a given person, the right eye may be dominant for some tasks and the left eye dominant for other tasks.

So it seems that the notion that a person has *a* dominant eye is, for most people, inaccurate. Rather, there are different types of ocular dominance with the eye that is dominant depending on the test conditions.

Classification of ocular dominance

One approach to the classification of ocular dominance is given in Figure 4.1. Tests of ocular dominance can be broadly classified into those that assess sensory function, motor function, and sighting dominance. It was noted at the beginning of Chapter 3 that different ocular motor tests (eye focusing, alignment, and movement) produce different results and, for dyslexia research, tests that reflect the *natural* situation during reading may produce more relevant results than tests that use *artificial* conditions.

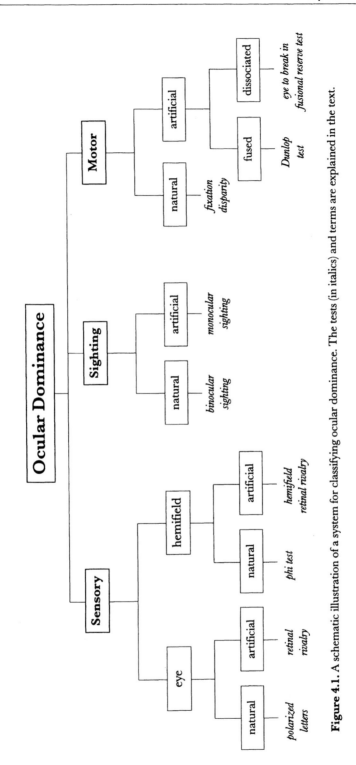

Figure 4.1. A schematic illustration of a system for classifying ocular dominance. The tests (in italics) and terms are explained in the text.

Sensory ocular dominance

Tests of *sensory ocular dominance* assess which image is selected as predominant by the visual cortex in the brain (Figure 4.1). To explain the distinction between eye and hemifield let us imagine that a person is viewing a point straight ahead with the left eye covered. Everything the person sees to the left of this point is in the *left visual hemifield*, and the rest the *right visual hemifield*. The nerve fibres that carry the visual image from the eye to the brain are arranged such that objects in the right visual field (right hemifield), of both eyes, are initially processed in the left visual cortex, and vice versa. *Hemispheric dominance* refers to dominance of one half of the brain over the other and this may impact on the dominant visual field.

The foveal suppression test was described in Table 3.4 and this is a way of determining, under natural conditions, which eye is most likely to be suppressed. The eye that is less likely to be suppressed is the dominant eye for this task. A problem with this test is that there is often no foveal suppression, although it can sometimes be induced by dimming the illumination. Another way of assessing the sensory dominant eye is to determine the eye that has better visual acuity.

Retinal rivalry occurs when each eye is presented with a dissimilar image so that the brain has to choose which eye's image it prefers. For the phi test the person rapidly alternates fixation between a distant and a near light and describes the perception of movement.

Motor ocular dominance

Tests of *motor ocular dominance* assess the eye with most accurate fixation or which is least likely to lose fixation (Figure 4.1). The fixation disparity (aligning prism; Table 3.4) test detects a minute tendency for the eyes to misalign. It is usually the eye that becomes misaligned that is the non-dominant eye under these test conditions.

A problem with this method is that, if a fixation disparity test is used that has been carefully designed to be natural, then most people do not have a fixation disparity. The *Dunlop test* attempts to get round this problem by forcing the eyes to diverge beyond the parallel position, which usually induces a fixation disparity. But it is not natural for the eyes to diverge beyond parallel (Figure 3.5) and the instrument that is used for this test (synoptophore) creates unusual viewing conditions so that the test creates a highly artificial environment. The test has been claimed to be important for assessing people with dyslexia (see below).

The Dunlop test assesses the dominance as the eyes are starting to 'break down', or stop working together. If a little more divergence is induced then the eyes would no longer be able to fuse and a strabismus would have been temporarily induced. Usually, when this happens one of the eyes maintains fixation and the other gives up and deviates. Under the dissociated conditions of this test, the eye that maintains fixation is the dominant eye. In essence, this example gives the dominant eye in a divergent fusional reserve test (Table 3.4). It is usually, but not always, the same as the eye in which the fixation disparity occurs.

Both these methods of measuring the motor ocular dominance (fused or dissociated) could be attempted either with the eyes diverging or converging.

Sighting dominance

When most people talk of a dominant eye they mean the *sighting dominant eye*. It is the 'eye that is used to line something up' and has also been called directional dominance. In fact, there are many different ways of assessing sighting dominance which tend to produce different results (Figure 4.1). The simplest method is for the practitioner to stand across the room from the subject and to hold up a finger at the end of an outstretched arm. The practitioner asks the subject to point to this finger and the watches to see which one of the subject's eyes is lined up with the finger.

There are several problems with this method. Right handed subjects will tend to point with their right hand, which will be nearer their right eye: this error can be minimized by asking the subject to hole both hands together and point with these. Alternatively, a piece of card with a hold in the centre can be used. Some subjects may close one eye (*monocular sighting*) and it is better to ask them to keep the eyes open (*binocular sighting*). Many authors have argued that a single test of sighting dominance is inadequate, and instead a battery of tests should be used.

What underlies sighting dominance?

Surprisingly, all the time our eyes are open we have a form of double vision. If the reader holds up a finger about halfway between the page of this book and their nose and keeps looking at a word in the book then they should see that the finger is doubled. This is called *physiological diplopia* and occurs when we contemplate an object at a different distance to the object that we are viewing.

One of the most interesting things about physiological diplopia is that we are not normally aware of it. This is because the human mind ignores irrelevant objects in the visual field. The subconscious mind, rather than allowing us to experience physiological diplopia, will choose which one of the doubled images to ignore and which one to attend to. The sighting dominant eye is the eye whose image is not ignored. To put it another way, the sighting dominant eye is the eye to whose image the brain allocates most attention. This might suggest that sighting dominance is a form of sensory ocular dominance. Yet, the initial description in this section of the sighting dominant eye as the eye that a person uses to line up with a target suggests that it is a form of motor ocular dominance. It seems that this is one occasion where the distinction between sensory and motor breaks down. It could almost be said that sighting dominance is where sensory visual function meets motor visual function.

Sensitive tests of sighting dominance sometimes reveal an even more complicated situation. The sighting dominant eye is often described as a *cyclopean eye*, a sort of imaginary third eye which lies somewhere between the two eyes. So, for example, rather than being 100% right eye sighting dominant a person might be 60% right eye sighting dominant.

Stability of dominance

We have seen that ocular dominance is not a single entity, but rather a manifestation of the conditions created by the method of testing. But, for some forms of ocular dominance, even if the same test is carried out in exactly the same way on the same person then the dominant eye may change from moment to moment. This raises the concept of the *stability* of ocular dominance and has formed the basis for a great deal of research on dyslexia with the Dunlop test, as described below.

Ocular dominance and dyslexia

Sighting dominance and crossed dominance

Crossed dominance occurs when the sighting eye is on the opposite side of the body to the dominant hand. In the 1960s there was a fairly commonly held view that people with dyslexia were particularly likely to have crossed dominance. Some researchers argued that crossed dominance or unstable sighting dominance (ambi-ocular) were causes of dyslexia. A teacher at my primary school found that I was left handed and right eyed and, in line with the views of the day, taught me to write with my right hand to avoid being crossed dominant.

It has also been suggested that it is undesirable for the sighting dominant eye to be the eye with worse visual acuity. It has even been argued that 'over-dominance', when one eye is too strongly dominant, could cause reading difficulties.

These views are not generally supported by rigorous research. Although some studies have found a slight tendency for people with dyslexic difficulties to have crossed dominance, other studies do not support this finding. There is no convincing evidence to suggest that crossed dominance plays a causal role in dyslexia, or reversals (see Appendix 4). Attempts to treat or train children to 'correct' crossed dominance would appear to be unfounded. Indeed, it is very doubtful whether there are any practical advantages to determining the sighting dominant eye in dyslexia.

Sensory ocular dominance

From the available research, which is fairly sparse, it is not possible to reach a consensus on the role of sensory ocular dominance in dyslexia. Sensory ocular dominance is not routinely tested and there is no evidence at present to suggest that it should be.

Motor ocular dominance and the Dunlop test

The Dunlop test, which is described in the box, assesses the motor ocular dominance under artificial conditions of divergence. The test was originally researched by Dunlop and Dunlop, a husband and wife team, in the 1970s. They found that dyslexic people were particularly likely to exhibit crossed handedness and eyedness with this test and they believed that this caused letter reversals.

A large amount of research by another team, including Stein and Fowler, used the Dunlop test in a different way. To avoid confusion with sighting dominance, they called the dominant eye with the Dunlop test the *reference eye*. Stein and Fowler argued that it did not matter which was the reference eye, nor how this related to the dominant hand. Rather, they attached great importance to the *stability* of the reference eye. They repeated the Dunlop test 10 times and if either eye was the reference eye 8 or more times out of 10 then the person was said to have a stable reference eye. Otherwise, there was an unstable reference eye, allegedly signifying that the brain was confused about co-ordinating each eye's images with an awareness of where the eyes were pointing. Stein and Fowler described this as *visual dyslexia*. They treated an unstable reference eye by patching (covering with a patch) the left eye, during reading, for a few months and found that this helped to establish a stable reference eye and was associated with improved reading performance.

The Dunlop test

The original version of the Dunlop test was carried out with an instrument called a synoptophore. The patient looks through tubes at two pictures, one for each eye. The pictures are very similar, with most of the detail identical in both images so that it is easy for the patient to 'fuse' them into one image. But there is a piece of detail that is unique to each eye's image; these are the *monocular markers*.

The tubes of the synoptophore are set parallel, to simulate the situation when the patient is looking into the distance. Once the patient has fused the images the tubes are slowly diverged, so that the eyes have to turn out beyond parallel to maintain a single, fused, perception.

Eventually, the patient will not be able to diverge any further and may experience double vision. Before this happens, one of the monocular markers may appear to move. This means that one eye has become very slightly misaligned, although not enough for the patient to have double vision. The eye which sees the monocular marker that does *not* move is the dominant, or 'reference' eye.

Stein and Fowler's research caused quite a stir in the UK. Although in the early twentieth century visual factors were thought to be major causes of dyslexia, since then the tide had steadily turned away from this viewpoint so that the vast majority of researchers believed that visual factors were not causes of dyslexia. Then Stein and Fowler came along claiming that 50% of people with dyslexia had 'visual dyslexia' which could be treated by patching.

Unfortunately, when other researchers investigated Stein and Fowler's findings they generally failed to obtain the same result. Throughout the 1980s there was a heated debate between a small group of people who believed in the Dunlop test and those who did not. Each side repeated the other side's research, sometimes even using different techniques to re-analyse the results of studies with which they did not agree. By the end of the 1980s a general picture was emerging, that the Dunlop test was an exceptionally unreliable test. Most research studies did not find that dyslexic people were especially likely to have an unstable reference eye, but the results with the test were very variable. The Dunlop test creates the artificial condition of diverging the eyes beyond parallel and it is quite difficult for children to correctly describe what they are seeing. Patching, as a treatment for dyslexia, was also heavily criticized.

Some of the later research with the Dunlop test linked its result with other visual correlates of dyslexia, including binocular instability. Of most interest, are painstaking studies comparing the types of reading and spelling errors that are made by people who fail the Dunlop test with the errors made by those who pass the test. These data do suggest that 'Dunlop test failures' make more of the reading and spelling errors that would be expected to result from visual confusions than do subjects who pass the Dunlop test.

It is impossible to deny that several good studies have effectively discredited the Dunlop test. But one is still left feeling that, despite all the test's failings, perhaps there was in some cases a genuine visual problem that the test was inadequately assessing.

Stein and Fowler's theories about what the Dunlop test was measuring developed over time. At one point, they claimed that the test detected *binocular instability*, and they did find that an unstable reference eye was associated with low fusional reserves (ability to converge and diverge the eyes) and reduced stereo-acuity (see Chapter 3). It is possible that the Dunlop test might be another way of detecting binocular instability (p. 43–44), although it is not a very reliable method.

If a person has binocular instability, as diagnosed by conventional methods, then during reading their eyes may not be precisely aligned on the word that they are viewing. In this situation it may be important for the brain to consistently choose which of the two eyes' images it is going to use. Hence, it may be that a stable motor dominant eye is only important when a person's binocular co-ordination is imperfect.

In such cases, it would seem that the most appropriate treatment is to correct the binocular incoordination. Patching is a temporary cure for any binocular vision anomaly since, for as long as the patch is worn, the person is no longer binocular. But a more permanent solution would be to improve the binocular co-ordination, for example with eye exercises (p. 37–40).

Summary

The idea that ocular dominance may be important in dyslexia has risen and fallen in popularity over the last 60 years. It has become clear that the concept of *a* dominant eye is an over-simplification, since there are many different types of ocular dominance. Not only does the dominant eye, for a given person, vary depending on the task but it may also vary, even for the same task, from one moment to another.

The overall conclusion seems to be that ocular dominance is not commonly atypical in dyslexia. The key findings of this chapter are summarized in the box.

Summary

- The dominant eye is the eye whose function predominates over the other eye.
- For most people, the eye that is dominant changes depending on the test conditions.
- Crossed dominance (sighting eye on different side to dominant hand) is not much more common in dyslexia than in good readers and is unlikely to be relevant.
- The Dunlop test assesses the motor ocular dominance (reference eye) under artificial test conditions.
- The Dunlop test is unreliable.
- The Dunlop test may indicate binocular instability, but it is probably an inadequate method of identifying binocular instability.
- Occlusion (patching) is unlikely to be the best method of treating binocular instability.

CHAPTER 5

Behavioural optometry and other controversial visual approaches

Behavioural optometry and developmental vision therapy

What is behavioural optometry?

Behavioural optometry (BO) is a sub-discipline of optometry which is fairly popular in the United States and has a few followers in the UK. The 'father' of behavioural optometry was an American optometrist, A.M. Skeffington, who founded the *Optometric Extension Program* in 1928. Behavioural optometry is controversial, with its supporters arguing that many thousands of patients have been helped by this new extension of the optometrist's role. Its critics have argued that BO reflects an attempt by optometrists to expand their role into areas that they either don't fully understand and/or that are poorly validated.

Behavioural optometrists (BOs) are perhaps most active in the management of people with difficulties at school, including dyslexia. Some BOs treat virtually all the dyslexic children they see. The treatment is often highly intensive, so their fees can be high. This has further fuelled the controversy.

Behavioural optometry is a broad discipline and exists on many different levels. At its simplest level, BOs argue that patients should not just be treated as a pair of eyes, but should be viewed as a complex interaction of many factors, including the home and school environment. This holistic approach is, of course, sound advice for any healthcare practitioner. If a patient sees their family doctor with a headache then a good doctor will enquire about the home, work, or school life, amongst many other things.

On another level, many BOs take a very keen interest in assessing the ocular motor factors described in Chapter 3. In particular, many carry out a detailed assessment of binocular co-ordination (how well the eyes work together as a team) and accommodative function (focusing) and treat when appropriate, as outlined in Chapter 3. Many of these treatments have been validated with the type of rigorous research described on p. 9 (randomized controlled trials; RCTs) and are not controversial.

A distinction between conventional optometry/orthoptics and BO starts to become apparent when one considers the extent of ocular motor (eye movement and focusing) factors that BOs treat. BOs are likely to treat patients with very subtle ocular motor abnormalities, whose function is perhaps not abnormal but is really at the lower end of the normal range. A basic tenet of BO is that *vision is learned and therefore it can be trained*. So, some BOs argue that vision therapy may even help patients who have normal visual function.

An example of this is eye movements. Some BOs treat saccadic and/or pursuit eye movements (called, confusingly, oculomotor dysfunction; see p. 28) in dyslexic children. Yet, as is discussed in Chapter 3 and Appendix 3, pursuit eye movements are not usually involved in reading and there is very little scientific evidence to suggest that saccadic eye movement dysfunction is a cause of dyslexia.

BOs are much more optimistic about the management of short-sightedness (myopia; see p. 19) than conventional optometrists and ophthalmologists. BOs sometimes treat myopia with vision therapy, although this is not supported by RCTs. The philosophy behind BO argues that myopia is the result of *near point stress* and that reading glasses or bifocals relieve near point stress and reduce the progression of myopia. Most of the objective scientific evidence does not support this assertion (see Appendix 5), except for a small subgroup of people who are esophoric at near (see p. 37). Even for this small subgroup, the effect of bifocals at reducing the progression of myopia is marginal.

Although myopia control does not specifically relate to dyslexia, some BOs prescribe low powered plus lenses (in the form of reading glasses, bifocals, or varifocals) to many dyslexic children to relieve near point stress. These low powered glasses are sometimes called 'learning lenses'. It is argued that, quite apart from any effect on myopia, the glasses may help reading. Again, there is very little objective evidence to support these claims (see Appendix 5).

Some BOs are involved in psychometric and educational testing. For example, they might attempt to diagnose or classify a person's dyslexia.

This type of work would conventionally be the province of psychologists or teachers and one has to ask whether the optometrist is the best trained person to carry out this sort of work. Also, the tests that are sometimes used by optometrists for these sorts of investigations have not all been standardized with the rigorous research that is typical for tests developed by psychologists.

BOs also often give treatments aimed to improve higher level *visual perceptual skills* or *visual perceptual motor skills*. This might involve training hand–eye co-ordination, laterality, directionality, form perception, visual memory and visualization, and visual motor integration. Many of these areas have more conventionally been the province of other professionals, such as occupational therapists.

Behavioural optometry: effective treatment or placebo?

Commonly, one seems to encounter a rather unquestioning acceptance by BOs of the theories to which they subscribe. There is frequently an absence of an 'evidence-based' approach (p. 9) and, in their desire to help patients, BOs adopt treatments that have not yet been validated (see Appendix 5). It was noted on p. 8 that the placebo effect can be very large. It is likely to be a major factor in treatments where a child is given an expensive and intensive therapy by a healthcare professional, such as in BO. Hence, it is especially important for BO to be validated by RCTs. Yet, a recent review of BO 'found no randomized controlled trials' (see Appendix 5). So, one is often unable to determine whether the treatments used in BO are anything more than a placebo. In the absence of RCTs, one can only conclude that BO is unproven, and that the benefits that are sometimes attributed to BO might not result from genuine treatment effects.

It is sometimes argued that it does not matter if a treatment is a placebo or not, as long as it helps the child. But children and their families only have a finite amount of time and resources. A proven treatment for dyslexia, such as individually structured extra teaching, will also be associated with a placebo effect as well as a genuine treatment effect. Clearly, this is likely to be more helpful to the child than a treatment which is only a placebo. So, it is better to spend resources on validated treatments than on ones that have not been validated.

Another argument that has been used by BOs is 'I know that my treatment works, if you want proof then do the research yourself'. This approach does not stand up to close scrutiny. When it comes to treatments, humans are extremely inventive and there are thousands of unproven treatments, for conditions ranging from headaches to acne, and from hangovers to the common cold. It usually takes relatively little time to invent a treatment and far longer to research it. The primary responsibility for proving that a treatment works must lie with those who wish to provide the treatment.

Behavioural optometry and dyslexia

One can think of dyslexia as a disturbance in the smooth flow of information from the images of text on the retina through to the spoken (read) word. Treatment of a visual problem can only help in two ways. First, if it helps to alleviate a bottleneck in this pathway and second, if it removes symptoms (e.g. eyestrain) and so makes the child more willing to try to read.

The evidence reviewed in Chapter 3 and Appendix 3 suggests that saccadic eye movement dysfunction is probably not a cause of poor reading or symptoms in dyslexic children. So, it seems unlikely that treating saccadic eye movements in dyslexia will be much help.

Likewise, there is little evidence to suggest that 'learning lenses' (low powered plus lenses) are beneficial in dyslexia. In the absence of significant refractive errors, accommodative anomalies, or binocular misalignment, refractive glasses are not likely to help. The term 'learning lenses' implies that they help learning, but this claim does not appear to have been supported by RCTs.

Similarly, most of the research on higher level cognitive functions and dyslexia (see Appendix 1) shows that although poor phonological skills do cause dyslexia, other factors such as directionality, form perception, and visual–motor integration are not major causes of dyslexia.

Apart from the placebo effect, there is another reason why any sort of intensive exercise regimen might appear to be helpful for children with dyslexia. So much that children do at school involves reading and this can mean that people with dyslexia may develop a sense of failure and of poor self worth. To achieve success in a different field is bound to help such children, just through improving their self-confidence. Success at a course of vision therapy will help, as would success in a new sport or another recreational activity. Clearly, the importance of an improvement in a child's self-confidence should not be under-estimated. But if this is the primary reason for a benefit from BO vision therapy then perhaps a more enjoyable extra-curricula activity should be recommended!

Children with dyslexia are particularly likely to have attention deficit disorder (ADD; p. 4), with its characteristic features of inattention, impulsivity, and sometimes hyperactivity. It seems likely that these children might benefit from some sort of activity that involves them in a novel task which encourages them to concentrate on some aspect of their motor control. This might explain the benefit that some parents and children report from BO vision therapy. But one again wonders if the child might find coaching in a new sport, or even judo, karate or tai chi, to be a more interesting diversion than BO vision therapy.

Conclusions

Many of the theories and methods in BO are not supported by evidence-based research (see Appendix 5). Until the advocates of BO can provide objective support for their methods, BO will remain one of the many unproven approaches for people with dyslexia. There is nothing to stop the public from trying BO, but there is also very little objective evidence to commend them to do so.

Neuro-developmental and neuro-physiological retraining (patterning)

Another controversial assertion is that many people with dyslexia have *neuro-developmental delay* and benefit from *neuro-physiological retraining* or *patterning*. The hypothesis seems to be that many of the primitive reflexes that normally develop in young children fail to develop in some people with dyslexia. The patterning training attempts, through a range of exercises, to re-establish the appropriate reflexes, following the correct developmental sequence of events. Some of these exercise regimens involve eye exercises.

There is a lack of rigorous research in this area (see Appendix 5) and it is impossible to make informed comments about the validity of this approach. Like behavioural optometry, children may benefit through a placebo effect and through the effect of success in an extra-curricula activity on the child's self-confidence.

Cerebello-vestibular dysfunction

The visual image is processed in a part of the brain called the cerebral cortex (see Chapter 6). The cerebellum is a separate part of the brain, which is mainly concerned with the reflex adjustment of voluntary movements, with muscle tone, and with balance. The vestibular apparatus is the part of the inner ear concerned with balance. Hence, cerebello-vestibular dysfunction implies a problem with balance and posture.

There have been a few claims in the research literature, mostly originating from one research group, suggesting that cerebello-vestibular dysfunction is present in 97% of cases of dyslexia (see Appendix 5). It is claimed that this results in a mild eye movement instability and an unstable perception of text. Treatments that have been recommended include eye exercises, modifying the reading technique, and drugs (medication for motion sickness). The original research in this field was very weak, with the only well controlled study suggesting that cerebello-vestibular dysfunction is not a correlate of dyslexia.

Recently, more thorough research has provided evidence to support the notion of a cerebellar deficit in dyslexia. The role of this, if any, in causing reading difficulties has still to be established, as has the effect of any treatments.

Ocular lock and chiropractic treatment

A chiropractic theory suggests that reading disability is caused by 'ocular lock' resulting from damage to two cranial bones. This theory holds that cranial massage (massaging the head), or cranial osteopathy, can help in dyslexia. There also appears to be a lack of objective research on this subject (see Appendix 5), so it is unclear whether this represents anything more than a placebo.

Summary

- Behavioural optometry is a controversial field and has many unproven treatments, including:
  - low plus and bifocal glasses for near point stress;
  - exercises to train saccadic eye movements;
  - gross motor exercises;
  - visual perceptual training.
- Neuro-developmental and neuro-physiological retraining are also controversial.
- Cerebello-vestibular dysfunction seems unlikely to be a significant cause of dyslexia.
- Ocular lock and chiropractic treatment also lack objective evidence.

CHAPTER 6
Visual processing

Low level versus high level visual function

On p. 14 a distinction was drawn between *low level* and *high level* sensory visual function. Although the distinction between these two is not always clear, low level refers more to the early stages of visual processing where the visual image is processed and enhanced. High level refers to the later stages of visual processing where the visual image is analysed and interpreted.

In psychological reports about dyslexic people there is often a section describing visual or visuo-spatial abilities. This refers to high level sensory visual function, which is very different from the low level sensory visual function or motor visual function that are discussed in this book. The available evidence suggests that people with weak higher level, visuo-spatial function are not especially likely to have the low level visual deficits described in this book. It is encouraging that although some IQ tests divide performance into *visual* and *verbal* IQs, one test avoids confusion over the word *visual* by breaking IQ down in *verbal* and *performance* IQ.

The magnocellular pathway deficit and dyslexia

Magnocellular (M) and parvocellular (P) visual function

During normal daylight vision our visual systems analyse the world around us in two main ways. One visual sub-system tells about *what* an object is and the other concentrates on *where* an object is. This distinction is part of an overall division in the visual system between two parallel pathways, the magnocellular (M) and parvocellular (P) pathways. The M system (*where*) is a rapid 'early warning' system to draw our attention to new or changing objects in our visual field. The P system (*what*) is a slower system for analysing in fine detail the precise characteristics of the object of interest. The M system tends to make a rapid, *transient*, response; whereas the P system makes a slower, more *sustained*, response. The characteristics of these systems are summarized in Table 6.1.

It is an over-simplification to think of these systems as two distinct and separate pathways. In fact, their functions overlap and there are numerous inter-connections between the two pathways.

Evidence for an M system deficit in dyslexia

There is very convincing research evidence to suggest that about two-thirds of dyslexic people have a deficit of the M visual system. This

Table 6.1. Table differentiating between magnocellular (M) and parvocellular (P) visual systems

Characteristic	Magnocellular (M, transient)	Parvocellular (P, sustained)
Type of cell in the optic nerve	Magno or M-cells	Parvo or P-cells
Ultimate destination in the brain	Parietal lobe (this part of the brain covers about the same area as a cardinal's skullcap)	Temporal lobe (the part of the brain adjacent to the temple and ear)
Sensitivity to movement and flicker	Very sensitive	Insensitive
Ability to resolve detail	Good at resolving coarse detail	Good at resolving fine detail
Ability to detect contrasts	Sensitive to low contrast objects	Sensitive to high contrast objects
Effect of blur	Relatively insensitive to blur	Greatly affected by blur
Area of visual field where most sensitive	Peripheral vision	Central vision
Persistence of response to a stimulus	Nerve cells respond briefly at the onset and offset of a stimulus (transient)	The response of the nerve cells persists throughout the stimulus (sustained)
Ability to discriminate colours	Unable to discriminate colours	Good at discriminating colours

evidence comes from four types of research study where the *average* performance of dyslexic people has been compared with that of good readers. These studies are summarized in more detail in Appendix 6, but in general terms they have found that:

- there is a reduced ability to detect flicker in dyslexia;
- there is a reduced ability to detect coarse detail, but a normal ability to detect fine detail;
- there tends to be a prolonged persistence of the visual image in dyslexia; and
- dyslexia is associated with a decreased ability to detect fine motion.

It should be noted that the M system deficit in dyslexia is subtle and can only be detected with carefully designed experiments and, usually, special stimuli. This is an exciting research finding but, as we shall see, it does not necessarily mean that this correlate of dyslexia impairs anyone's performance in everyday life.

Role of the magnocellular (M) visual deficit in dyslexia

It was noted in Chapter 1 that it is much easier to detect a correlate of dyslexia than it is to determine whether this correlate is a cause of the reading difficulty. There have been several models for how an M visual deficit *might* contribute to a reading difficulty, but as yet relatively little research on whether such a deficit really does contribute to the reading problem.

One early theory relates to the interaction between the M and P systems during reading. It was noted on pp. 48–49 that during reading the eyes pause (*a fixation pause*) while the information is absorbed from a section of text and then make a rapid 'flick' eye movement (*saccade*) so the eyes can fix upon the next section of text, and so on. It was suggested that the P system is responsible for analysing the image of the letters or word during a fixation pause. The theory supposed that the P image is then 'wiped clean' by *saccadic suppression* from the M system during the following saccade. An M deficit might mean that the image is not effectively 'wiped clean' so that one sustained image persists into the next fixation. This image persistence could cause confusion during reading. This hypothesis was such a neat idea that many people took it to be fact, despite a lack of direct research evidence. Now, recent research papers have shown that this hypothesis is unlikely to be correct, since the M system does not seem to be responsible for saccadic suppression (see Appendix 6).

Other research has linked the M deficit in dyslexia with the presence of binocular instability and with an unstable reference eye on the Dunlop test (Appendix 6). The M pathway is very likely to play a key role in the feedback in the brain that is used to control eye alignment (the P system is also likely to play a lesser role). If the M pathway deficit causes binocular instability (unstable eye alignment; see p. 43) then it could be indirectly responsible for the perceptual distortions and eyestrain that can occur in binocular instability (see Chapter 8). However, this hypothesis has not been evaluated. While it is known that dyslexic people with the M deficit tend to be those with binocular instability, it remains to be proven whether one of these deficits is the cause of the other.

Does the M deficit cause dyslexia?

One study has demonstrated that children with signs of an M deficit are more likely to make reading errors that are suggestive of visual confusion than are other children (see Appendix 6). But this study did not look specifically at dyslexia. Another study, also not specifically of dyslexia, suggests that there is a link between an M deficit and awareness of the precise position of letters in a word. It remains to be seen whether the M visual deficit directly causes these visual confusions or whether the M deficit causes binocular instability resulting in the confusions (see Chapter 8).

One might assume from this that dyslexic people with signs of the M deficit tend to be those with the dyseidectic form of dyslexia (see pp. 6–7), which is characterized by the types of reading errors that one would expect to result from visual confusions. Surprisingly, two different research groups have actually supported the opposite conclusion: that it is the dyslexic people who tend to have a phonological weakness who have the M deficit (see Appendix 6).

It has been suggested that this might be explained by the presence of fast, transient (magnocellular), processing channels in other senses as well as vision. If some people with dyslexia have a *general* magnocellular deficit then this could manifest as a magnocellular *visual* deficit and a 'magnocellular deficit' in the *auditory* pathway (sound processing). This theory has not yet been proved, but if it is true then it suggests that a major cause of the reading difficulty in dyslexic people with an M visual deficit is likely to be attributable to phonological difficulties. Again, it seems that, although visual factors can contribute to some of the reading errors, they do not play the major causal role in dyslexia.

This conclusion is also supported by common sense. It was noted in Chapter 1 that dyslexia is defined as a *specific* difficulty with reading and spelling. Yet nearly every visual task that we perform depends on M system function.

Detecting and treating the magnocellular (M) visual pathway deficit

The tests that have been used in research to detect reliably the M deficit in dyslexia are not readily available to eyecare practitioners. So, eyecare practitioners do not test for the M pathway deficit.

Some practitioners have argued that their eye examination detects an M deficit, but this is a claim based on rather questionable assumptions. For example, some practitioners have assumed that, since binocular inco-ordination is correlated with an M deficit, if binocular incoordination is detected then this is tantamount to stating that an M deficit has been detected. But this is like saying that when children's feet are measured in a shoe shop then the assistant is measuring the person's weight. Shoe size is correlated with weight (bigger people tend to have bigger feet) but weight cannot be reliably predicted from shoe size.

An even less likely assumption is that dyslexic people who need coloured filters have an M deficit. Table 6.1 shows that detailed colour discrimination is not mediated by the M system, so this is unlikely to account for the benefit that some people receive from individually prescribed coloured filters (see Chapter 7).

There is no known treatment for the M pathway deficit. In view of the uncertainty about whether it may or may not play a causal role in dyslexia, the lack of a treatment at this time is probably not a bad thing.

Controversial theories on sensory visual function and dyslexia

Visual fields

Most measures of visual function, for example the vision as measured with a letter chart, assess the centre of our field of vision where we have the greatest ability to resolve detail. But we can also see objects, albeit coarsely, over quite a wide peripheral field of vision. This is typically tested using instruments that flash faint lights on and off at various positions in the visual field. There have been one or two suggestions in the research literature that dyslexic people may have abnormal (in one study more sensitive, in another less sensitive) vision in the periphery of their visual field. This research is very weak (Appendix 6). Many optometrists routinely assess visual fields and no clinical defects are usually reported as correlates of dyslexia. It seems unlikely that abnormal visual fields are a significant factor in dyslexia.

Another research team have evaluated the 'form resolving field', which is the ability to detect characters (e.g. letters) away from the fixation point. Dyslexic people actually seem to be better than average at detecting characters between about 5° and 12° from fixation. It has been argued that this improved ability to read outside the foveal field might be disadvantageous and these researchers investigated the effect of treatment, including reading through a mask. This was believed to be helpful but the research has been heavily criticized and the poor rigour of the experiments does not allow any confidence in interpreting the results.

Dark adaptation

Another interesting claim is that people with dyslexia have poor dark adaptation (this is the ability to adapt to reduced illumination). It has been suggested that this can be helped by a dietary supplement (DHA). This theory was disproved in a recent thorough research study (see Appendix 6).

Summary

The basic research supporting the existence of an M visual deficit in dyslexia is thorough and convincing. Evidence suggests that the M pathway deficit may be linked to some reading errors, but to what extent these contribute to an overall pattern of dyslexia is unclear. It is possible that the M deficit has no direct effect on reading but instead causes binocular instability which results in visual confusions when reading (see Chapter 3). The key points of this chapter are summarized in the box.

Summary

- About 75% of people with dyslexia appear to have a deficit of the magnocellular (M) visual system.
- The M system represents low level sensory function, and is unlikely to be linked to a 'visual' profile on psychometric testing.
- The M pathway deficit is not identified clinically and there are no treatments at present.
- The M deficit seems unlikely to be a major cause of dyslexia, so treatments seem unwarranted at present.
- The visual field is probably normal in dyslexia.
- A theory about abnormal dark adaptation and recommendation for a dietary supplement (DHA) in dyslexia has been disproved.

CHAPTER 7

Coloured filters

Coloured filters and dyslexia: historical background

Two centuries ago, when it was feasible to produce coloured glass lenses, people started to use green and blue coloured lenses of no refractive power to 'ease eyestrain from heavy reading'. In the 1980s, when plastic lenses started to become popular, the way that this new material absorbs dyes meant that coloured spectacles could be prescribed for reading, with a unique colour for each person.

An extreme case was reported in 1958 of a dyslexic child who could only read words if they were printed on coloured card. In 1980 a New Zealand teacher, Olive Meares, published a fairly detailed paper describing many cases in which children's perception of text and their reading difficulties seemed to be influenced by print characteristics. In some words the white gaps between the words and lines masked the print and caused visual distortions, such as the words blurring, doubling, and jumping. She noted that this was helped by reducing the size of print, using coloured paper, reducing the contrast, or using white print on black paper.

The Irlen system

Helen Irlen, an American psychologist, published papers in the 1980s and 1990s, and a book in 1991 which seemed to be describing the same syndrome of symptoms that Meares had outlined before. Irlen developed a treatment using coloured filters, and she stressed that different people need different colours and that the colour for each person needs to be precisely defined. Irlen stated that the condition affects 12% of the general population and 65% of those with dyslexia.

Irlen called the condition Scotopic Sensitivity Syndrome or Irlen Syndrome. The word *scotopic* refers to night vision and is probably inappropriate. More recently, in recognition of Meares' first detailed description, the term Meares-Irlen syndrome (MIS) has been used.

Symptoms

Irlen divided the symptoms into six categories, which are outlined in Table 7.1.

Table 7.1. Summary of symptoms, according to Irlen workers

Symptom	Description
Photophobia	Inability to tolerate bright light and glare. Problems with black on white
Visual resolution	Difficulty keeping an image constant. Letters move, blur, double, get darker and lighter; words flash and flicker. The page appears to swirl or 'white out'
Sustained focus	Trouble keeping the words in focus, independent of refractive error. After reading for a short time sufferers tire, their eyes water, hurt, burn or itch
Span of focus	The number of letters comprehended during a fixation pause (normally described as the perceptual span) is said to be reduced
Depth perception	This is said to be poor, not just when reading
Eyestrain	This reduces the time spent reading and causes blinking, staring, screwing eyes up, and poor concentration

Diagnosis and treatment

Irlen noted that MIS is not a learning difficulty as such, but often co-exists as a component of dyslexia or other specific learning difficulties. Irlen developed a proprietary system involving coloured overlays and lenses. Overlays are sheets of thin transparent coloured film that are placed over a page of text. Some people have experimented with reading through coloured folders that can be bought from stationery shops. But these are probably inadequate since the range of colours is small and the filters have not been designed to properly sample a full range of colours. As well as overlays, the Irlen workers use the Irlen Reading Perceptual Scale (IRPS) and the Irlen Differential Perceptual Schedule (IDPS). It is usual practice to thoroughly evaluate and publish the reliability and validity of psychometric tests, but this does not appear to be the case for the IDPS (see Appendix 7).

Although some people undergoing the Irlen treatment carry on using coloured overlays indefinitely, many progress to coloured lenses. 'Irlen

Institutes' in several countries have 'diagnosticians' who test candidates with a wide range of coloured lenses, prescribing individual tinted lenses. Although I have not found reference to this in the published scientific literature, it seems to be the case that Irlen lens wearers are periodically tested again to determine whether their optimal tint has changed.

Critique

Several aspects of the Irlen system have caused controversy. Hardly any of the Irlen personnel seem to have training in professional eyecare. Most modern spectacle lenses are made of a plastic material (CR39) which is tinted by dipping the lenses in a hot bath of dye. This is a fairly simple procedure and CR39 tinted lenses are usually inexpensive. Irlen lenses are dyed CR39, but are unusually expensive. This could be explained, at least in part, by Irlen's claims that the tint needs to be very precisely defined.

But there are also problems with some of the claims that have been made by the Irlen organization about how specific the tint needs to be. They have claimed that a lens which appeared, under a variety of light sources, to be the same colour as an Irlen lens would not be a good enough match. Scientifically, this is hard to defend. The Irlen organization has also been criticized for its tendency towards secrecy and commerciality in preference to scientific openness. Although there have been many research papers written that relate to the Irlen system, there have been very few that meet the usual standards of scientific thoroughness (see p. 9 and Appendix 7).

The science of human colour perception

Seeing beyond the rainbow

Visible light can be divided into wavelengths which make up the colours of the rainbow. Wavelengths are described in nanometres (nm). The shortest wavelength that we can detect is about 380nm and is perceived as violet. As the wavelength increases the colours progress through blue, green, yellow, orange, and red. The longest wavelength that we can perceive is a deep red of about 780nm.

The retina contains cones, which are light sensitive cells that allow us to perceive and discriminate colour. The cones contain *photo pigments* which are bleached by certain colours of light. When the photo pigments are bleached then an electrical signal is generated which is carried to the brain through the optic nerve.

Considering the colours of the rainbow, one might imagine that humans have two types of cone, one with a photopigment that is most sensitive to blue (about 380nm) and the other that is most sensitive to red (about 780nm). If this was the case and light very strongly stimulated the blue sensitive cone but not the red then the brain would be able to deduce that the colour of the light was blue. If light equally stimulated a blue and red cone then the brain could deduce that the colour of the light was in the middle of the spectrum, a yellow/green. This could be problematic, since we would be unable to discriminate whether a colour that we perceived as yellow/green really was a 'pure' yellow/green colour, or whether it resulted from a mixture of blue and red.

Fortunately, our visual system is rather more sensitive than this. We actually have three different types of cone: one with a photopigment maximally sensitive to blue, another to green, and the third to yellow/orange. The brain analyses the degree to which an object stimulates each of these three types of cone and from this obtains a perception of the colour of the object. Because there are three types of cone photopigment, our colour vision is able to discriminate a 'pure' yellow/green from a mixture of blue and red. In other words, we can perceive additional colours that are not contained within the rainbow.

Some colour vision defects are thought to result from the absence of one cone photopigment. People suffering from these defects are likely to confuse colours that other people would be able to discriminate. People with colour vision defects are often described as being *colour blind*, but this is usually a misnomer, since they are able to discriminate many colours, only confusing certain shades. Colour vision defects are common, affecting about 8% of males and 0.5% of females. True colour blindness, when people only have one type of photopigment in the retina, is exceptionally rare. Colour vision defects are not thought to be especially common in dyslexia.

The chromaticity diagram

Since a simple drawing of the colours in the rainbow will not do justice to our ability to perceive and discriminate colours, scientists have created a better method of representing human colour perception. This is called the chromaticity diagram and is illustrated in Figure 7.1.

All colours that we can see are represented on the chromaticity diagram. White is found near the centre of the diagram and the colours can be defined by three terms: *hue, saturation* and *brightness*. *Hue* is the type or shade of colour and *saturation* is the depth of colour. If you were to draw

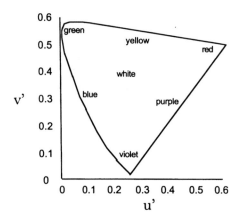

Figure 7.1. The chromaticity diagram. To be fully appreciated, this diagram needs to be drawn in colour and such a version, with approximate colours, is reproduced on the front cover of this book. See text for description.

a line straight out from the centre of the diagram then, as you moved further out from the centre along this line, the hue would remain constant but the saturation would increase. When you reached the outside edge of the diagram the colour would be a very deeply saturated colour, but the same shade (e.g. blue) as it was nearer the centre of the diagram. If you were to place the needle of a pair of compasses on the centre of the diagram and draw a circle then, as you moved around this circle, the hue would change (through every hue that the human eye can perceive) but the depth of colour (saturation) would remain constant. There is actually a third dimension to the chromaticity diagram, which you cannot see in Figure 7.1, and this represents brightness.

There are various forms of chromaticity diagram and this area of scientific research is standardized by an organization called the CIE (the Commission Internationale de l'Éclairage). The particular chromaticity diagram reproduced in Figure 7.1 is the u'v' diagram. A given distance below two colours on this diagram represents a more or less uniform difference in terms of the perceived colours.

Meares-Irlen syndrome and the chromaticity diagram

Irlen has stated that a sufferer experiences symptoms when they look at text with white light and that these symptoms are alleviated when the text is seen through a lens of a certain colour, but not through lenses of a different colour. In terms of the chromaticity diagram, it is as if there is a small ring drawn somewhere on the diagram representing the colour which alleviates that person's symptoms. Adjacent colours cause their symptoms to return.

Testing Irlen's claims

The proper way of evaluating any treatment is a double-masked randomized placebo-controlled trial (RCT; see p. 9). Some research has compared the effect of Irlen lenses with grey lenses, but this approach is flawed because the subjects would have chosen the coloured glasses so would know that they were meant to help. Hence, the trial would not be *double-masked* (p. 9) and subjects' expectations would invalidate the results. Fortunately, the invention of a new instrument, the *Intuitive Colorimeter* made a double-masked RCT possible.

The Wilkins Intuitive Colorimeter system

What is the Intuitive Colorimeter?

The Intuitive Colorimeter (Figure 7.2) was invented by Professor Arnold Wilkins who was, at the time, a scientist with the Medical Research Council (MRC) at the Applied Psychology Unit in Cambridge. The MRC is the leading government sponsored organization devoted to medical research in the UK. The MRC patented the Intuitive Colorimeter and the MRC license a company, Cerium Visual Technologies, to manufacture and market the instrument. The MRC receive a royalty based on sales of the instrument, so this is one of the rare examples of a British invention being developed in the UK and actually earning money for the UK government!

The instrument has an opening through which the subject views a page of text. The operator adjusts three controls on the side of the instrument which change the colour of light that illuminates the page. The instrument was designed according to sound principles of colour science, so that the three controls adjust independently the hue, saturation, and brightness (see above). The operator can adjust these three variables in turn, in a systematic way, to comprehensively sample a very large range of colours.

The Wilkins Intuitive Colorimeter as a research tool

When we walk into a room with a coloured light bulb then everything initially looks different. Remarkably, in an instant we adapt to the colour of the light source so that all the objects around us look more or less

Figure 7.2. The Wilkins Intuitive Colorimeter (courtesy of Cerium Visual Technologies).

normal. This is the phenomenon of *colour adaptation*. For our ancestors, colour adaptation probably served an important function, to ensure that they could correctly identify the colour of a berry regardless of whether they were in open sunlight or within the rain forest, where the illuminating light would be coloured green by overhead leaves.

It is our ability to manifest colour adaptation and the design of the Intuitive Colorimeter that made a randomized controlled trial (RCT) possible. When a person views text inside the colorimeter they adapt to the colour of the page (resulting from the colour of the illuminating light). Hence, the person does not know exactly what colour the light is. They know the general colour (e.g., a red or a blue), but not the precise shade of red or blue.

The Intuitive Colorimeter can be used to determine a colour (*the optimal colour*) which alleviates the symptoms reported by a person with Meares-Irlen syndrome (MIS). The colorimeter can also be used to determine an adjacent, similar, colour which does not alleviate the person's symptoms to the same extent (*the control colour*). Yet, because of colour adaptation the person should not be able to remember exactly what the colours looked like. If two pairs of tinted lenses are made up to match these colours (*optimal tint* and *control tint*) then the person should not be able to recall which colour it was that they had claimed alleviated their symptoms during the colorimeter testing. The person is *masked* as to which should or should not help. This meant that an RCT was at last possible and such a study was carried out in the early 1990s.

The results of this trial showed that individually prescribed coloured filters are an effective treatment for symptoms associated with MIS. As a result of this, the Intuitive Colorimeter has become a clinical tool (see next section).

Since this initial study, other research with the Wilkins system has also shown that the coloured filters can result in an improvement in the speed of reading of people with MIS. Further research, using the Irlen system, has demonstrated a sustained improvement in reading from coloured filters in MIS.

This is not to say that the coloured filters cure dyslexia, but they can in some cases make a direct contribution to improved reading performance. This is in addition to the indirect effect that they may have by reducing symptoms of eyestrain and headaches.

The research studies do show quite clearly that different people need different colours. Some researchers had claimed that a blue filter was required for all people who suffer from the condition, but the controlled studies show that this is not the case. Blue is the most popular colour, but there are many people who need other colours.

The Wilkins Intuitive Colorimeter as a clinical tool

The Intuitive Colorimeter is not just a research tool, but is now in use in several countries as a clinical tool. Professor Wilkins also invented a system of *Precision Tinted lenses* which allow a colour determined during colorimeter testing to be checked and precisely specified as a prescription for tinted lenses. Like the colorimeter, the Precision Tints are designed with due attention to the science of colour vision.

The effect of tinted lenses will vary depending on the lighting conditions. This can be important if the tint is pale and if the type of lighting is unusual. The result of testing with the Intuitive Colorimeter is usually checked by further testing with Precision Tints, which can be carried out under lighting conditions that are typical for the person who is being tested.

The Precision Tints are arranged in a geometric progression so that they can, during testing, be stacked together to obtain very fine graduations of saturation. When the tinted glasses are made up, clear plastic lenses are soaked in baths of the appropriate dyes for a given time period. The lenses can be plano (of no refractive power) or made up to correct any degree of long-sightedness, short-sightedness, or astigmatism. When the dyes are superimposed on the chromaticity diagram each dye is equally spaced from the adjacent dyes. This means that each dye only ever needs to be combined with the adjacent dye (e.g. blue is only ever combined with turquoise or purple).

This is likely to represent an advantage over the Irlen system. It seems that, with the Irlen system, lenses of complementary colours (ones that are opposite to one another on the chromaticity diagram) are sometimes combined. To a large extent, such dyes will 'cancel each other out', so that the tint becomes quite grey, and may end up being darker than necessary.

A few people do need to reduce the overall amount of light as well as to have the light coloured. The Precision Tints include greys so that the effect of varying brightness can be investigated. They also include an ultra-violet (UV) blocking filter. Although UV is not visible to adult eyes, it can be detected by children's visual systems. An infinite range of colours can be tested with the Intuitive Colorimeter and, including the grey and UV blocking filters, over 100,000 different colours can be made up from the Precision Tints (see Appendix 7).

The Precision Tints allow the optometrist to write out a prescription which specifies the dyes that need to be used by the manufacturers and the depth of each dye that is required. For example, a prescription might be Blue B4 + A5 + Purple B5. Optometrists and dispensing opticians like to check lenses that are made by manufacturing opticians to ensure that they comply with the original prescription. This is easy to do with this system.

The prescription for Precision Tinted lenses can change with time. It is usual practice to repeat the testing with the Intuitive Colorimeter and Precision Tints on a yearly basis for children, and less often for adults.

Coloured glasses can be used to view a computer screen. Some relief can also often be obtained by adjusting the settings of the computer software. A free program for this can be obtained from the website: http://essex.ac.uk/psychology/overlays

Precision Tinted contact lenses are also available, and can be popular with people who are embarrassed about wearing coloured glasses, or who have to make public appearances (e.g. musicians). However, difficulties in dyeing contact lenses mean that the precision of the colour matching for these is not always as good as with Precision Tinted spectacles. Experience with the Intuitive Colorimeter suggests that people differ in how precise their optimal colour needs to be. The Precision Tinted contact lenses may not be suitable for people who show a very precise result on the colorimeter test.

Screening for MIS: Intuitive Overlays and the Wilkins Rate of Reading Test

What is a screening tool and why is it necessary?

The Intuitive Colorimeter is an expensive instrument and the testing with it takes about half an hour. In the UK, this is not usually covered by the NHS so that a private fee has to be paid. Screening tools are commonplace in the healthcare sciences and are used to rapidly and inexpensively detect those people who may have a condition that requires further investigation or treatment.

There are two indicators that can be used to suggest that a person is particularly at risk for MIS. These are the presence of symptoms and a history of reading difficulties. Neither of these indicators is sufficiently reliable to be a screening tool.

Coloured overlays

The main screening tool for MIS is coloured overlays. These are inexpensive sheets of transparent plastic film that are placed over the page. Screening tools are always something of a compromise since they will never be as accurate as the full diagnostic process. This is true for coloured overlays, since the selection of colours that can be tested is much more restricted than the range that can be tested with the Intuitive Colorimeter. Nonetheless, with a carefully designed system of coloured overlays it should be possible to systematically sample a wide range of colours. In MIS, a colour that is similar to a person's optimal colour will generally help them more than a different colour or no colour. Therefore, it should be possible to find an overlay that will help people with MIS even if it is not their optimal colour.

Professor Wilkins has developed a range of coloured overlays (*Wilkins Intuitive Overlays*) that are designed to sample human colour space systematically, as illustrated by the chromaticity diagram (Figure 7.3, Appendix 7). The overlays are simple to use and they come with clear instructions. The Irlen organization and Cerium Visual Technologies have also developed their own ranges of overlays, but these have not been fully described in the scientific literature.

Overlays are a good screening tool, but are not usually a good long-term solution. There are several reasons for this. First, the range of colours is limited, so it is unlikely that the very best colour for a person will be found with an overlay. Overlays are not as convenient as spectacles

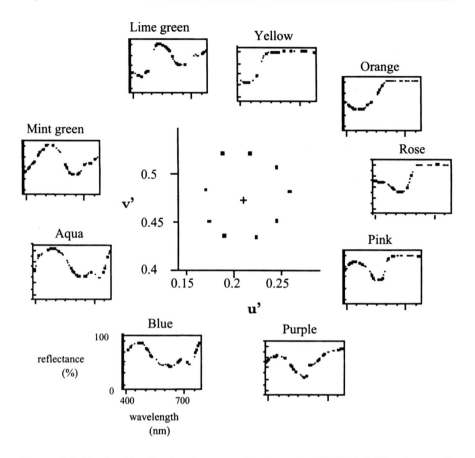

Figure 7.3. The Intuitive Overlays (courtesy of Professor Arnold Wilkins). The photograph shows the Intuitive Overlays superimposed on the chromaticity diagram of Figure 7.1.

for looking at a page of written text since they have to be moved and replaced at the end of every page. Also, overlays do not work very well for writing, viewing distance objects (e.g. a white board in class), or for computers.

People who benefit from an overlay are almost always helped more by Precision Tinted lenses. However, if a person cannot progress to coloured glasses, for example if that person would be too embarrassed to wear them, then coloured overlays can be used on a prolonged basis and are better than nothing.

Case study 7.1 is a fairly typical case who was screened with coloured overlays, tested with the Wilkins Intuitive Colorimeter and Precision Tints, and has now worn Precision Tints for eight years.

Case study 7.1: Ref. G0699

BACKGROUND: Boy, aged 11, referred to the author by a local dyslexia group.

SYMPTOMS: When tired, can only read if holds book very close. Severe headaches, about once a month, possibly more after school. Skips or omits words or lines. Family history of migraine.

CLINICAL FINDINGS: Ocular health and visual fields normal. Visual acuities and refractive error normal. Amplitude of accommodation and ocular motor balance normal. Positive response to testing with coloured overlays; issued preferred overlay (yellow).

FOLLOW-UP 3 MONTHS LATER: Overlay has helped and headache frequency has been halved. Tested with Intuitive Colorimeter and Precision Tints. Positive response. Precision Tints made up (turquoise colour).

SUMMARY OF NEXT 8 YEARS: Patient seen several times over the years. Optometric findings changed very little. Precision Tint specification changed only slightly over the years. At most recent appointment patient aged 19 years and using tints a lot with studying at university. He reports that the tints stop him losing his place and allow him to read all day (without them he can only read for about one hour). No headaches now.

COMMENT: This pleasant young man is now much more able to describe his symptoms and the benefit that he has received from the tints. He still chooses to wear them and finds that they help at university, as they did at school.

Wilkins Rate of Reading Test

Initially, the way that the Intuitive Overlays were used to screen for MIS was to see if a person reported a benefit from testing with the Intuitive Overlays and if so to issue the person with an overlay of their preferred colour to use as and when they wanted. If they used it on a voluntary basis for half to one school term, and if their parents or teachers noticed improved symptoms or reading fluency, then they were tested with the Intuitive Colorimeter.

This approach works well and is still commonly used. But an additional method of determining who benefits from an overlay has also been developed: the *Wilkins Rate of Reading Test* (Figure 7.4). Most reading tests have been developed by educationalists to assess reading skills and not to assess visual functions, so they tend to have large text and widely spaced lines. The Wilkins Rate of Reading Test was designed to assess visual factors in reading and not to be greatly influenced by reading skills.

In the Wilkins Rate of Reading Test the subject reads a passage of text made up of 15 repeated words, which were selected as being commonly encountered by young readers (see Figure 7.5). These words are repeated in random order and the subject is asked to read them out loud as quickly as possible while maintaining accuracy. The number of words correctly read in a minute is calculated. The text is small and closely spaced (Figure 7.5), so as to exaggerate the effect of any visual problems. Because the test requires little comprehension and only very basic word reading skills, performance is virtually independent of language skills. The test is produced in four versions, using the same words but in different orders. So the test can easily be used to compare the rate of reading with overlays to the rate without.

Figure 7.4. The Wilkins Rate of Reading Test (courtesy of I.O.O. Marketing Ltd).

```
come see the play look up is cat not my and dog for you to
the cat up dog and is play come you see for not to look my
you for the and not see my play come is look dog cat to up
dog to you and play cat up is my not come for the look see
play come see cat not look dog is my up the for to and you
to not cat for look is my and up come play you see the dog
my play see to for you is the look up cat not dog come and
look to for my come play the dog see you not cat up and is
up come look for the not dog cat you to see is and my play
```

Figure 7.5. An example of a passage from the Wilkins Rate of Reading Test (courtesy of I.O.O. Marketing Ltd).

Can glasses be tinted to match the colour of the overlay?

If a person finds an overlay very helpful, then why not have coloured glasses made up to match the overlay colour? This is an attractive idea since it would be an inexpensive way of prescribing coloured lenses. Unfortunately, the evidence suggests that *it is wrong to make up coloured glasses to match the colour of an overlay*. There are two reasons for this. First, the overlay colour is a compromise, since there are only a limited range of colours to choose from.

The second reason is because of *colour adaptation*. When a person looks through a coloured lens everything that they see is coloured by the lens. To the brain, it is as if the colour of the light source has changed, just as it does during testing with the Intuitive Colorimeter. Under these circumstances, the brain adapts as fully as it can to the colour. This is why when people wear coloured glasses the world does not usually look 'coloured' (unless their glasses are of an exceptionally deep colour). When a person looks at a page of text that is covered with an overlay then only the section under the overlay is coloured. Everything else on their desk, and in the room, is seen normally. Therefore, the person only partially adapts to the colour.

A recent research study supported the above comments (see Appendix 7). This study demonstrated very clearly that people read significantly slower with tinted lenses selected to match their overlay colour than with tinted lenses matching the colour determined with the Intuitive Colorimeter.

Other 'therapies' using colour

The Chromagen system

The Chromagen coloured filter system was originally developed to try to help people with a colour vision defect, but this is highly controversial (see Appendix 7). Apparently, the inventor of the Chromagen lenses, Mr Harris, noticed that a person with a colour vision defect who was also dyslexic found that a Chromagen filter eased symptoms associated with dyslexia. This led him to try Chromagen lenses with other people who have dyslexia, and he has claimed success with this approach.

There seem to be three main differences between the pre-existing systems (the Irlen system and the Wilkins system) and the Chromagen system (Table 7.2). First, although coloured lenses can be prescribed with the Chromagen system it seems that many people are fitted with contact lenses. Second, the colour for the contact lens is chosen independently for each eye: some people wear only one contact lens and others a different colour lens in each eye. Third, the colour of the filter(s) is selected from a choice of only nine colours, whereas both the Irlen and the Wilkins systems use a very wide range of colours.

I have only been able to find two pieces of research that have been published on the Chromagen system. The first appeared in a journal which does not have a reputation for publishing high quality scientific research and was described as 'an interim report'. This paper found that the Chromagen system compared favourably with the Intuitive Colorimeter. However, the research was heavily criticized, and not just by people who use the Intuitive Colorimeter, most notably because it only looked at nine subjects and the research design was poor (see Appendix 7).

The other published research study on the Chromagen system was a more rigorous study and compared the Chromagen lens with a placebo lens which only had a very pale tint. The Chromagen was found to be associated with a faster rate of reading than was obtained with the placebo lens. This finding is not surprising, since an approximate tint is probably better than no tint at all. But one wonders whether a precisely defined tint might have been better still.

Syntonics (photosyntonics)

The word *syntonic* is used in psychology to mean 'characterized by a high emotional responsiveness to the environment'. In the controversial field of behavioural optometry (see Chapter 5) the term is used to describe a form of light therapy, once called chrome-orthoptics. Syntonics has been used by a few American optometrists to 'treat' many conditions, including short-sightedness, strabismus (turning eye), amblyopia (lazy eye), headaches, visual fatigue, *reading problems*, and general binocular dysfunction (poor eye co-ordination). Syntonics involves subjects viewing a light source that is covered by a coloured filter. A treatment which appears to be similar has been practised in Europe as the *Downing Technique*. Recently, I have heard of a couple of optometrists practising syntonics (photosyntonics) in the UK.

Treatment is said to result in improved ('normalized') visual fields. The theory behind this therapy seems tenuous and the experimental evidence is not very convincing. It was noted in Chapter 6 that there is no strong evidence in the research literature to suggest that abnormal visual fields are a common feature of dyslexia. Visual field testing is highly subjective and performance improves with practice. If a child fails a visual field test then the test should be repeated using a different test method. If there is a repeatable visual field defect then the child ought to be referred to a consultant eye surgeon since sometimes (rarely) a visual field loss can be a sign of a serious eye or brain disease. However, the most common type of visual field defect in children is thought to be psychological in origin, since no cause can be found and it usually spontaneously improves with time or when the child become more emotionally settled (e.g. adjusts to a new sibling, settles in a new class at school, etc.). Another explanation is that the span of visual attention might be reduced, and this is discussed in Chapter 8.

Comparison of systems

The Irlen, Wilkins, and Chromagen systems all seem to be treating the same condition and are compared in Table 7.2. Another, very recent, approach uses a 'trichromatic light' in the form of a desk lamp to mix colours. This 'Optim-Eyes' system awaits scientific evaluation, the influence of colour adaptation may be a problem. Syntonics is very different and seems to be much more questionable.

Table 7.2. Table contrasting the Irlen, Wilkins, and Chromagen systems. The systems are listed in chronological order

Feature	Irlen	Wilkins	Chromagen
Nomenclature	Scotopic Sensitivity Syndrome or Irlen Syndrome	Meares-Irlen syndrome	Meares-Irlen syndrome
Symptoms	Light sensitivity Trouble dealing with high contrasts Problems resolving print Difficulty reading groups of letters, numbers, or words Inability to maintain concentration	Visual fatigue/discomfort Too bright, hurts eyes Visual perceptual distortions Movement, blur, aware of spaces Deterioration in reading fluency Poor concentration	Blurring of text Movement of words or letters Distracting patterns from spaces between words and lines
Screening	Questions about symptoms when reading Performance at a range of tasks that are thought to detect visual perceptual difficulties Testing with coloured overlays	Questions about symptoms when reading Testing with coloured overlays Effect of coloured overlays at Wilkins Rate of Reading Test	Not clearly stated, but seems to be presence of dyslexia and symptoms
Diagnostic criteria	Positive response from screening stage Positive response to diagnostic assessment with Irlen filters (tinted lenses)	Sustained benefit from coloured overlays or improvement of at least 5% at Wilkins Rate of Reading Test with chosen coloured overlay, and Positive response to testing with Intuitive Colorimeter, and Positive response to testing with Precision Tints	Improvement with Wilkins Rate of Reading Test

(contd)

Table 7.2. (contd)

Feature	Irlen	Wilkins	Chromagen
Treatment	Irlen tinted lenses individually prescribed on the basis of testing with a large range of trial tints	Precision Tints individually prescribed on the basis of testing with the Intuitive Colorimeter and Precision Tints trial set	Chromagen contact lenses, prescribed monocularly (one lens only or two of same or different colour)
Range of tints	Very large range	Over 100,000	Nine
Prevalence	Acknowledge that there is a continuum About 12% of general population mildly affected Affects 46% of those with reading difficulties	Acknowledge that there is a continuum About 11% of general population show a sustained (10 month) voluntary use of overlays Affects 46% of those with reading difficulties	Not specified
Research	Many studies, one RCT (may be double-masked)	Several studies, one RCT (double-masked)	Two small controlled studies (may be double-masked)

Meares-Irlen syndrome: relationship with other visual factors

A problem with MIS is that the symptoms are non-specific: they could be caused by a variety of eye problems other than MIS. For example, blurring, doubling, and moving of text are all symptoms of binocular instability which, like MIS, is known to be common in dyslexia (see Chapter 3). Research suggests that when optometrists encounter dyslexic people with these symptoms, sometimes they find conventional optometric problems, in other cases they find MIS, and in some cases they find a combination of these conditions. There is some debate over the proportion of dyslexic children who fall into each of these categories (see Appendix 7).

Case study 7.2 is a child who had been given a coloured overlay to use at school because he had reading difficulties and reported some visual symptoms and frequent headaches. The symptoms are typical of people with MIS and no-one would blame the teacher for trying a coloured overlay. However, an eye examination revealed long-sightedness, and glasses to correct this eliminated his symptoms. When wearing the glasses, he no longer needed any coloured filters and he reported that the glasses were more helpful than the overlay. A similar case was described in Chapter 3 (Case study 3.2, p. 41) in which a child had been given an overlay but really needed eye exercises. In contrast there are other cases where children had seen optometrists who had not specialized in dyslexia and who had declared that nothing was amiss. It was only when someone (often a teacher) tried an overlay that MIS was discovered.

Case studies 3.2 (p. 41) and 7.2 illustrate why it is important for people with dyslexic difficulties to see an eyecare practitioner who has specialized in vision and dyslexia and who is aware of the need to look for conventional eye problems and MIS. Such a practitioner will need to search for and treat any significant problems in a logical sequence, and this is discussed in Chapter 8.

Case study 7.2: Ref. F5035

BACKGROUND: Boy, aged 12, referred to the author because of reading difficulties at school for which the child was receiving extra teaching. No psychological assessment. No previous eye examinations, just the usual screening tests. Child was using a coloured overlay at school that he had been given by a teacher.

SYMPTOMS: After a few seconds words 'go fidgety'. Severe headaches, approximately two a month, bilateral, for which the GP had prescribed analgesics. Frequently rubs eyes, blinks excessively, uses finger as marker, confuses letters and words, reads slowly.

CLINICAL FINDINGS: Visual acuities normal. Ocular health and visual fields normal. Refractive error (objective) without cycloplegic: R = L = +1.25DS; with cycloplegic: R = L = +1.50DS. Amplitude of accommodation slightly low (8D in each eye). Ocular motor tests reveal small alternating esotropia at distance and near, with unstable suppression (see Chapter 3).

MANAGEMENT: Explained prescription is low, but try glasses to investigate effect on symptoms and esotropia (see Chapters 2 and 3).

FOLLOW-UP 2 MONTHS LATER: No symptoms. 'Glasses have completely stopped jumbling up of words'. Does not experience any perceptual distortions and does not now find any coloured overlays to be helpful. No more headaches since received glasses. Clinical findings essentially as above, but esotropia slightly reduced and sensory status (suppression) more stable.

COMMENT: It is unusual for a refractive error this slight to be significant, but in this case it was causing problems. If he had not consulted an eyecare professional he might have been inappropriately prescribed a coloured filter.

Appendix 7 also cites some evidence suggesting that certain ocular motor problems (poor eye co-ordination and poor focusing; see Chapter 3) may be more common in dyslexic people with MIS than in dyslexics without MIS. One theory is that the MIS causes unstable or unclear images from each eye which may be harder for the brain to fuse together. But the opposite hypothesis is also possible: that it is the ocular motor problem that causes the MIS, although this is certainly not always the case (see Case study 7.3). It is even possible that the two are non-causal correlates (neither causes the other).

At the moment, it is recommended clinical practice to treat any conventional optometric anomalies first and, only once their function is within normal limits, then to treat MIS, if present (see Case study 7.3 and Chapter 8). It will require further research to discover whether this turns out to be a case of 'the cart leading the horse'.

Case study 7.3: Ref. F4050

BACKGROUND: Boy, aged 8 at first appointment, referred to me by teacher because of specific learning difficulties.

SYMPTOMS: Words 'jump around on the page' and eyestrain after reading for 20 mins when he has trouble 'following the line'. No headaches. Skips or omits words or lines and light sensitive.

CLINICAL FINDINGS: Normal: ocular health, visual acuities, refractive error (low long-sightedness), accommodative function. Large decompensated exophoria at near (see Chapter 3).

MANAGEMENT: Given eye exercises to improve his ability to overcome the exophoria.

FOLLOW-UP 2 MONTHS LATER: Exercises done, but make eyes hurt and symptoms unchanged. Ocular motor status had improved and exophoria was now compensated. Tested with coloured overlays and showed consistent response, so issued coloured overlay.

FOLLOW-UP 3 MONTHS LATER FOR TESTING WITH INTUITIVE COLORIMETER: Overlay definitely helps: less 'hurting eyes' and less movement of text. Consistent response to testing with Intuitive Colorimeter and Precision Tints. Precision Tints prescribed.

FOLLOW-UP 9 MONTHS LATER: Precision Tints used voluntarily for reading, writing etc. No symptoms, as long as wears glasses. Refraction, ocular motor tests, ocular health and visual fields all normal. Colorimeter checked and new tint found which further improved perception. This was prescribed.

FOLLOW-UP 24 MONTHS LATER: No symptoms as long as wears tints. Reading and spelling: 'improved a lot'. Refraction, ocular motor tests, ocular health, visual fields all normal. Colorimetry checked and no change to tint required. Advised routine check every year.

COMMENT: In this case correction of the ocular motor problem had no effect on symptoms, which originate from Meares-Irlen syndrome. The required tint initially changed, but now appears to have stabilized.

Why do coloured filters help?

Several theories have been proposed to explain the underlying mechanism behind the symptoms and the benefit from coloured filters in Meares-Irlen syndrome (MIS). Of course, there may be several explanations for the benefit from tints, with one or more explanations applying to a given individual.

Placebo effect

Two randomized controlled trials (RCTs), by different research teams in different parts of the world, have demonstrated that individually prescribed tinted lenses really do help for reasons that cannot be solely attributed to a placebo effect (see Table A7.1 in Appendix 7). But a positive RCT does not mean that a placebo effect cannot operate, just that it is not the whole explanation. It seems very likely that there are some children who have been wrongly diagnosed as having MIS and who use tinted lenses (and even find them beneficial) solely for placebo reasons. But it also seems likely that there are a great many who really do need them.

Ocular motor anomalies

If MIS cannot be explained away by the placebo effect, then what is the cause of this condition? It was noted above that people with MIS often have ocular motor anomalies, particularly poor binocular co-ordination and poor accommodation. This has led some people to conclude that everyone who has been diagnosed with MIS really needs vision therapy. But this theory does not fit the facts.

The randomized controlled trials (see Appendix 7) demonstrate that some people are very precise about the colour they need. Binocular incoordination can sometimes cause glare, but this would be alleviated by a grey tint and would not need to have a very specific colour.

Many people with MIS have completely normal ocular motor function. A few only have one eye (e.g. an eye was lost in an accident), so binocular incoordination cannot account for their symptoms. Many people with MIS are elderly, past the age where there is any accommodation, so poor accommodation cannot account for their symptoms.

It has been suggested that saccadic eye movements might account for MIS, but this seems unlikely. It was noted in Chapter 3 that saccadic dysfunction does not seem to be a strong correlate of dyslexia and it is hard to see how this could explain the need for specific colours.

There certainly are some cases who are misdiagnosed as having MIS when in fact they have an ocular motor problem and all they really need is to have this treated (see Case study 3.2). But these people appear to be the exception rather than the rule. These cases will be detected by the clinical protocol outlined in Chapter 8.

Fluorescent lighting

Offices and schools are often illuminated by fluorescent lamps which flicker, and research has demonstrated that even when we cannot consciously perceive this flicker it is still being registered by a subconscious part of our brains that controls eye movements. It has been suggested that this flickering causes visual discomfort and that this is why coloured filters appear to help.

Some people with MIS do report that their symptoms are worse under fluorescent lighting, especially when the light levels are high, as in many supermarkets. But most people with MIS also report symptoms when text is illuminated by other light sources. Typically, children report their symptoms in summer, when classrooms are lit by daylight, as well as during the winter terms, when fluorescent lights may be in use.

Pattern glare

Striped patterns, like that in Figure 7.6, can cause discomfort and many people have noticed this, for example when ironing striped shirts. Apart from discomfort, certain patterns can cause people to perceive illusions of shape, motion, and colour. A great deal of research has been carried out into this *pattern glare* and it turns out that the symptoms of pattern glare are very similar to those of MIS.

Figure 7.6. A pattern that may cause *pattern glare*, especially when viewed at a distance of about 50cm. Do not stare at the pattern if you suffer from epilepsy or migraine.

Lines of text on a page form a striped pattern and research has shown that text can cause pattern glare. Research studies that have attempted to find the mechanism for MIS have demonstrated that pattern glare is a very strong correlate of MIS. Indeed, it seems possible that the underlying cause of MIS might be a heightened sensitivity to pattern glare, and this is discussed further in the next section and in Chapter 8.

Pattern glare and tinted lenses

If pattern glare seems likely to account for the symptoms of MIS then could it also explain the treatment? To answer this, we need to look at what is happening when a person experiences pattern glare. The full answer to this is not known, but it seems that high contrast striped patterns can be a very strong signal for the visual part of the brain (*visual cortex*). For some people, the visual cortex seems to be over sensitive (*hyperexcitable*) and a very strong signal can cause a sort of 'overload'. Cells that would normally signal movement, for example, are caused to fire inappropriately, giving rise to perceptual distortions. The result of the overload is pattern glare: visual perceptual distortions, discomfort, and headaches.

Cells in the visual cortex, including those that process shapes and movement, respond differently according to the colour of the stimulus. This sensitivity to colour differs from one cell to another, so coloured filters will influence the response of these cells and may thus alleviate pattern glare. Although this theory seems to make sense, it has yet to be fully investigated.

If MIS is explained, or partially explained, by pattern glare then it might be possible to help people with MIS by using devices which cover or mask the lines above and below the line which is being read. One such device, the Dex frame, included a magnifier and a limited range of coloured filters. Another recent device, the VTM magnifier, does not incorporate any coloured filters, just a mask and magnifier. Both these devices restrict the field of view and this may be a limitation on their usefulness (see Appendix 7).

Why might people with dyslexia experience more pattern glare?

Most reports suggest that people with dyslexia are more prone to MIS and to pattern glare. This may be because people with dyslexia have innate cortical hyper-excitability. The underlying cause for dyslexia (e.g. p. 5) may result in a predisposition to a hyper-excitable visual cortex. An alternative explanation, relating to a link with *visual attention*, is proposed in Chapter 8.

The link with migraine and epilepsy

Long before it was ever suggested that dyslexic people may be particularly prone to pattern glare, research identified a link between pattern glare and migraine. People with migraine tend to experience more pattern glare than people who don't suffer from migraine. Similarly, some people with epilepsy are also particularly prone to pattern glare. Recent research studies show that people in both of these groups can also benefit from Precision Tinted lenses.

Tinted lenses are not going to be a panacea for migraine. They are only likely to help people whose migraine has a visual trigger, or who experience symptoms related to certain visual tasks. In many cases, migraine has nothing to do with vision, and in these people visual treatments will not help.

Similarly, only a small percentage of people who suffer from epilepsy are likely to benefit from coloured filters. Again, they will only help people whose fits are triggered by light or patterns, or who experience symptoms related to visual tasks.

There is evidence to suggest that many of the dyslexic children with MIS experience frequent headaches, which can sometimes be diagnosed as migraine. It is reassuring to note that epilepsy, which is of course much rarer than headaches, has not been suggested to be much more common in dyslexia than in good readers.

Other theories about why coloured filters help

Other theories (see Appendix 7) have been proposed to explain the benefit from coloured filters in MIS, including a retinal defect and the magnocellular (M) visual system deficit. A retinal defect seems unlikely and it is also hard to see how an M deficit could account for the benefit from *individually prescribed* filters of a *specific* colour. This is because the M system is not sensitive to specific colours (see Chapter 6 and Appendix 7). A possible indirect involvement of the M system is discussed in Chapter 8.

Summary

The key points of this chapter are summarized in the box. Although this book is about the specific learning difficulty of dyslexia, it should be noted in passing that there have been reports of people with other learning difficulties, especially ADD and autism, benefiting from coloured filters.

Summary

- Syntonic photo-therapy is a controversial approach that lacks objective scientific evidence.
- Some people with dyslexia have Meares-Irlen syndrome (MIS);
  - this causes visual distortions, eyestrain and headaches;
  - treatment is individually prescribed coloured filters.
- The most likely explanation for MIS is pattern glare.
- The symptoms of MIS can result from other optometric problems, so a detailed eye examination is required.
- Overlays can be used to screen for MIS, but the colour of required overlay is different to the colour of required tinted lens.

Chapter 8
Conclusions

Summary of visual correlates of dyslexia

Earlier chapters in this book have discussed the many visual factors which have been claimed to be correlates of dyslexia. Only some of these alleged correlates have been substantiated by objective research. Even fewer are likely to contribute to reading difficulties, and these are unlikely to be major causes of dyslexia. These issues are summarized in Table 8.1, which also includes comments on the availability of treatments.

Linking the visual deficits

It would make a lot of sense if the various visual correlates of dyslexia were linked to one another. It would make even more sense if associations between variables were causal (i.e. one caused another), but this is hard to prove and such relationships remain speculative.

We do know that the magnocellular (M) visual processing deficit (Chapter 6) is associated with binocular instability (Chapter 4). Also, we know that an unstable reference eye on the Dunlop test (Chapter 3) is associated with both binocular instability and with the M deficit. It seems quite likely that the Dunlop test is measuring a form of binocular instability, although the Dunlop test is not very reliable. The M system is likely to play a major role in the control of binocular co-ordination, so it is tempting to reason that the M deficit causes binocular instability in dyslexia.

There is some evidence that both the M deficit and binocular instability (as detected with the Dunlop test) are associated with an increased occurrence of visual confusions when reading. So the M deficit may cause binocular instability which could contribute to dyslexic difficulties directly, through visual confusions, and indirectly through asthenopia

Table 8.1. Summary of visual correlates of dyslexia (N/A, not applicable; RCTs, randomized controlled trials)

Visual factor	Is it a correlate of dyslexia?	Does it contribute to the reading difficulty?	Is there a treatment?
Eye disease	No	N/A	N/A
Visual acuity	Possibly	No, except in very rare cases	Depends on cause (e.g. refractive error)
Refractive errors	Long-sightedness may be a weak correlate	No, except in rare cases	Correct any significant refractive errors
Accommodative insufficiency	Yes	Rarely. Not a major cause	Refractive correction or exercises
Strabismus	No	Possibly, very rarely	Yes, depending on type
Heterophoria	No, except for possibly near exophoria	Rarely, if decompensated. Not a major cause	Eye exercises
Binocular instability	Yes	Occasionally. Probably not a major cause	Eye exercises
Convergence insufficiency	Possibly	No, unless decompensated exophoria	Eye exercises
Amblyopia	No	N/A	N/A
Saccadic eye movement dysfunction	Probably not	Probably not	Probably not (controversial)
Abnormal ocular dominance	Probably not	Probably not	Controversial (patching)
Visual perceptual skills deficit	Unknown: lack of RCTs	Probably not	Unknown: lack of RCTs
Cerebello-vestibular dysfunction	Possibly	Possibly	Controversial (seasickness medication)
Abnormal visual fields	Probably not	N/A	N/A
Abnormal dark adaptation	No	N/A	N/A
Magnocellular deficit	Yes	Possibly (maybe via binocular instability)	No
Meares-Irlen syndrome	Yes	Yes	Individually prescribed coloured filters
Weakened visual attention	Possibly	Unknown	Unknown

(eyestrain and headaches). This is summarized in Figure 8.1. Eye exercises that increase fusional reserves improve a person's ability to overcome binocular instability and may, therefore, improve their ability to cope with this possible effect of an M deficit.

The M system is also likely to play a major role in the control of saccadic and pursuit eye movements. It is possible that a similar link to that in Figure 8.1 could also be used to explain the claims of some researchers that saccadic eye movements may be abnormal in dyslexia. However, it was noted in Chapter 3 that the evidence for saccadic dysfunction in dyslexia is equivocal.

A low amplitude of accommodation is present in some cases of dyslexia (Chapter 3). The M system is not sensitive to blur and is unlikely to be directly associated with low accommodation. It is possible that, at least in some cases, the low amplitude of accommodation may be a consequence of binocular instability, but this remains speculative.

Concerning Meares-Irlen syndrome (Chapter 7), the strongest correlate of this appears to be pattern glare. People with Meares-Irlen syndrome sometimes manifest subtle signs of binocular instability and accommodative dysfunction. Some authors have suggested that the M deficit directly explains the benefit from colour in Meares-Irlen syndrome, but there is no experimental evidence to support this idea. Furthermore, the M system is unable to discriminate hues so is unlikely to explain the need for individually prescribed coloured filters. Nonetheless, it would be appealing if the M deficit was somehow associated with

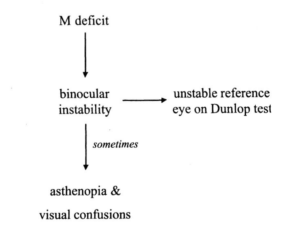

Figure 8.1. Hypothesized link between the magnocellular (M) deficit, binocular instability, Dunlop test result, and some cases of reading problems. See text for more details.

Meares-Irlen syndrome, since this might explain the correlation between Meares-Irlen syndrome and binocular instability. A theory for such a relationship is described in the next section.

The role of attention: a unifying theory?

Attentional deficits may underlie the various visual correlates of dyslexia. Attention is needed to help us cope with large quantities of information. It is the process whereby we attend to the most relevant detail so that information is sampled in an orderly and efficient way.

There are several types of attention. These are summarized in Appendix 8, but the main types are *selective attention* and *sustained attention*. *Selective attention* is when a person selectively attends to some information source in preference to others. An example of selective attention is *visual attention*, which can be thought of as a 'spotlight' in the mind which excludes peripheral detail that is not pertinent to the task in hand. For example, when driving in rain a person might be carefully watching a car on a side road in case it pulls out. Their spotlight of visual attention may be so strongly focused on the car that they are unaware of the windscreen wipers sweeping across in front of their nose. A non-visual example of selective attention is hearing one voice among many in a crowd.

The other main type of attention is *sustained attention*, or *vigilance*, which requires attention to be directed to one or more sources of information for a sustained period. For example, a driver may be attending to a red traffic light at road works waiting for some time to pull away as soon as it changes. If they have a lapse of attention then they may look away and miss the moment when it changes.

Attention deficit disorder (ADD) is characterized by inattention, impulsivity, poor vigilance, motor impersistence, and sometimes hyperactivity. ADD is often present in people with dyslexia and is commonly associated with a deficit of sustained attention. I have been unable to find any research investigating visual attention in ADD, but people with dyslexia have been found to have a weakened spotlight of visual attention (see Appendix 8).

Attention and ocular motor factors

People with ADD may not fully attend to optometric tests. For example, when measuring the near point of convergence (p. 16) the patient is asked to follow an approaching target until one eye is seen to deviate. If the patient has poor sustained attention then they may look away and a false result is recorded. Additionally, a feature of ADD is *motor impersistence*: the inability to sustain movement. This could influence performance at many ocular motor tasks.

Even if the patient does not manifest such obvious attentional difficulties, it is possible that a weakened spotlight of visual attention may reduce the ability to 'lock' both eyes on to the target.

It was also noted in Chapter 3 that ADD may account for the results of some studies which have argued that saccadic dysfunction may occur in dyslexia. When saccades are tested, people with ADD may make more erratic saccades as they become distracted from the test target. There is also evidence to suggest that before saccadic, pursuit, or vergence eye movements occur the visual attention needs to be shifted to the new position to which the eyes will move. A deficit of visual attention can influence ocular motor skills in this way.

Attention and Meares-Irlen syndrome

I have hypothesized that a weakened spotlight of visual attention may cause some dyslexic people to notice peripheral distortions resulting from pattern glare. It is even possible that people with dyslexia may not be innately more prone to pattern glare. They might just notice the pattern glare which other non-dyslexic people suppress because it is peripheral to their spotlight of attention. According to this theory, heightened sensitivity to pattern glare results from a deficit of visual attention.

An alternative theory is that some dyslexic people are more sensitive to the global pattern of text which may produce greater attention to this feature of the page (see Appendix 8). According to this theory, the underlying problem is pattern glare which alters the distribution of attention across the page.

Attention and the magnocellular (M) deficit

The M system is likely to provide the dominant input to visual attention (see Appendix 8). Hence, an M deficit in dyslexia might be the underlying cause of a weakened spotlight of visual attention. This theory, which remains speculative, is discussed further in the next section.

As with ocular motor factors, it is possible that ADD might have influenced the outcome of some research studies on the M deficit in dyslexia. Thorough research often uses a method called *two alternative forced choice* where subjects are forced to choose between two alternatives. For example, they might be asked to select which of two targets is flickering. By forcing them to choose, the scientist overcomes differences in the criteria that different subjects might use. However, two alterative forced choice methods do not control for other variables that might cause some subjects to respond differently. When asked to carry out an essentially boring task it seems likely that people with ADD will attend less well to the task than other subjects. This difference in performance might not be predicted from IQ test results, because these intellectual tasks may be more likely to capture the interest of the subject. So it is possible that some of the experimental results supporting the M deficit hypothesis could be explained by ADD. However, this is unlikely to apply to all such experiments, since some had control conditions where the parvocellular (P) function was assessed using a similar method to the M function, and yet no P deficit was found.

Synthesis

The optometric correlates of dyslexia are reproduced in Figure 8.2. Those for which there is greatest evidence are drawn in bold. Possible relationships between variables are drawn as arrows, again with those that seem (to the author) to be most likely drawn in as thicker lines.

The M deficit is a strong correlate of dyslexia and is associated with binocular instability, possibly causing binocular instability. As described above, the M deficit may also cause impaired visual attention, which in turn may contribute to binocular instability. Similar arguments may apply to saccadic dysfunction, but since this is a less well established correlate (see Chapter 3), this box and associated lines are fainter in Figure 8.2.

A deficit of visual attention might cause pattern glare or vice versa, so this arrow in Figure 8.2 points in both directions. It was concluded in Chapter 7 that pattern glare is the most likely explanation for Meares-Irlen syndrome. The visual perceptual distortions from pattern glare represent an unstable image that is likely to make accurate binocular and saccadic control more difficult. In severe cases impaired binocular and saccadic control could cause a merging of adjacent words into one another, which could contribute to pattern glare. Hence the arrows linking binocular instability and saccadic dysfunction with pattern glare in Figure 8.2 also point in both directions.

It must be stressed that Figure 8.2 is a diagram of possible interactions between factors that have been suggested as visual correlates of dyslexia. A great deal more research is required before it is known whether the hypothesized links are correct and it is very unlikely that everything in the diagram will be found to be accurate! But it is hoped that this analysis might be useful for further discussion and research in this area.

In the appendices of this book a distinction is drawn between studies that have and have not controlled for the intelligence quotient (IQ). To an intelligent dyslexic child, an IQ test can be an interesting challenge and this may help to maintain their interest. In contrast, optometric tests are generally designed to be very simple and are unlikely to maintain the interest of an intelligent but inattentive person. Perhaps, in the future the most rigorous studies will be those that do not just control for IQ, but also for attentional factors.

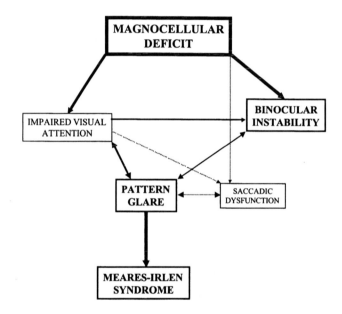

Figure 8.2. Diagram of possible interactions linking the visual correlates of dyslexia. The most likely correlates and links have been drawn as bolder lines and boxes. See text for more details.

Detecting visual problems in dyslexia

Screening

The evidence seems to suggest that, although visual problems are probably not major causes of dyslexia, they can contribute to the overall difficulty in some cases. This contribution may be direct, through causing some reading errors, or indirect through causing eyestrain or headaches which make a person more reluctant to read. It therefore seems desirable to seek out visual problems in people with dyslexia. What is the best way of doing this?

It was noted in Chapter 1 that long-standing symptoms, particularly in children, are often accepted by the child as being 'normal'. Hence, we cannot rely upon children (or even adults) telling us when they need an eye examination by complaining of problems.

Another point that was made in Chapter 1 is that the 'visual' (dyseidectic) sub-type of dyslexia, which might be diagnosed by an educational psychologist, does not relate to the type of visual problems that are described in this book. Indeed, some of the visual correlates of dyslexia may be more likely to be present in dyslexic people who also have phonological difficulties. The results of psychometric testing cannot be used to reliably determine the cases who will benefit from optometric investigation. The term 'visual dyslexia' is vague and is best avoided.

Children in some schools are occasionally screened for visual problems. The most common test appears to be visual acuity (p. 18), which would *not* detect most of the visual factors outlined in this book. Some schools include additional tests by orthoptists, typically cover testing (p. 15), which greatly improves the ability of the screening programme to detect strabismus. Detecting strabismus is important, but is not particularly relevant to dyslexia.

Occasionally, schools use instruments to screen for visual problems. These typically include some tests of binocular co-ordination, but are not usually sensitive enough to detect the ocular motor correlates of dyslexia described in Chapter 3. An exception is a new computerized screening instrument, which seems to be a cost-effective method of screening for refractive and orthoptic problems in school-children (see Appendix 8). Unfortunately, this is not yet in widespread use.

In summary, there is no validated screening system in common use in the UK that screens for refractive errors, ocular motor problems, and Meares-Irlen syndrome. The only way to be sure of detecting these problems is for all children with difficulties at school to be examined by an eyecare practitioner who has specialized in dyslexia. Usually, this will be an optometrist (see pp. 10–11). Such an eye examination will take much longer (about 40–60 minutes) than an NHS eye examination and will require tests that are not typically included in NHS eye examinations. Unfortunately, the current method by which the NHS remunerates primary care optometrists in the UK does not facilitate the NHS paying for additional tests, so a private fee is usually charged.

Regrettably, many dyslexic children are statemented under the 1993 Education Acts as having special educational needs without ever receiving a proper eye examination. Sometimes, the statement includes a comment that vision is 'normal', solely based on an assessment of visual acuity (p. 18). This is a cause of concern because such a test will not detect the most common visual correlates of dyslexia (see Case study 8.1). A statement that vision is normal when visual function has not been adequately assessed may cause the parents to neglect to have vision properly investigated.

Case study 8.1: Ref. F5342

BACKGROUND: Boy, aged 11, saw the author following recommendation by a friend of the parents. The child had been statemented as having special educational needs (reading at 2nd percentile but average IQ) and the statement included the comment 'Vision: normal'. Apparently, the vision had only been assessed with a letter chart test and the child had never seen an eyecare professional.

SYMPTOMS: Blurring, double vision, about two headaches a month, and tendency to rub eyes and skip lines when reading.

CLINICAL FINDINGS: Ocular health and visual fields normal. Visual acuities R6/9+, L6/6. Refractive error: R +3.25/–0.75 x 180 = 6/6 L +2.00/–0.50 x 170 = 6/5. Large decompensated esophoria (without refractive correction) at distance and near.

MANAGEMENT: The patient was prescribed glasses to correct the long-sightedness.

COMMENT: The refractive error was likely to be causing the esophoria and the symptoms. But it would not be expected to cause significantly reduced visual acuity, so would not be detected with a letter chart test. The severe reading difficulty was probably not solely the result of the refractive error. However, it seems likely that his visual symptoms would have made reading more strenuous and unpleasant than it ought to have been.

Finding a suitable eyecare practitioner

At the moment, the best way of finding an eyecare practitioner who has specialized in dyslexia is by word of mouth. Teachers and educational psychologists often know of practitioners in an area who have the appropriate specialist skills. A code of conduct for such practitioners is currently being prepared and it is hoped that a list of practitioners who have undertaken to adhere to this will be available, which will be held on or linked to the following website: http://privatewww.essex.ac.uk/~arnold/vpu%20 main.htm

In the longer term, the College of Optometrists has shown interest in setting up a higher qualification in the subject of learning difficulties, which will include dyslexia. It is hoped that in due course practitioners will be able to gain this qualification as a recognition of their expertise and this will help the public to find an appropriate optometrist.

Usually, a special eye examination to detect visual factors in dyslexia will result in a report summarizing the findings. It is helpful if the practitioner, or the parent, distributes this report to other relevant professionals (e.g. teachers, educational psychologists, paediatricians etc.).

A sequential approach

Since many of the visual correlates of dyslexia appear to be related to one another, it is not surprising that sometimes more than one of these correlates are present in a given dyslexic person. If treatment is required then the question arises as to which correlate should be treated first. The usual approach is outlined in Figure 8.3. This places conventional factors, such as refractive errors, before more recent developments, such as the investigation and treatment of Meares-Irlen syndrome. It was noted earlier in this chapter that a great deal of research still needs to be carried out before the relationships between the visual correlates of dyslexia are fully understood. The sequence in Figure 8.3 will probably need to be refined in line with research findings in the future.

Footnote: profound learning disabilities

Profound learning disabilities (e.g. Down's syndrome) are very different to the specific learning difficulties (e.g. dyslexia) which are discussed in this book. There is convincing evidence for a link between profound learning disabilities and many visual factors, including reduced visual acuity, refractive errors, poor accommodation and strabismus (see Appendix 8). It is important that people with profound learning disabilities receive professional eyecare from a young age.

Concluding remarks

Dyslexia is a common condition which often goes undetected. The history of research on visual factors in dyslexia has included extreme opinions, ranging from 'there are no visual factors in dyslexia' to 'visual factors are the major cause of dyslexia'. The former view is now unten-

SEQUENTIAL MANAGEMENT PLAN

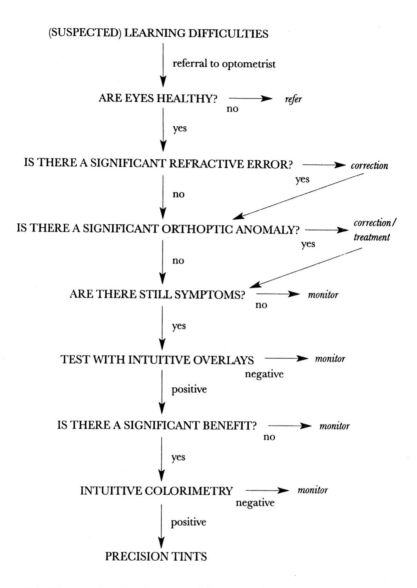

Figure 8.3. Diagram showing the sequential optometric management of people with dyslexia. Modified after Lightstone and Evans (1995, Ophthalmic and Physiological Optics 15, 507–12).

able: there is overwhelming evidence for the existence of visual correlates of dyslexia. But the second view is also untenable: there is also overwhelming evidence for phonological (sound decoding) factors being a major cause of dyslexia.

Dyslexia is a complex condition, and has been compared elsewhere in this book to the common condition of headache. Nobody would argue that red wine is the sole cause of headache, yet nor can it be denied that excessive red wine can cause headaches.

Visual problems do not seem to be a major cause of dyslexia, but they can contribute to the reading problem. In occasional cases, visual factors may contribute directly to dyslexia through causing visual confusions. Perhaps more commonly, visual problems cause eyestrain and headaches which can contribute to a reluctance to read. However, it should also be stressed that many cases of dyslexia do not have any visual problems and in other cases the visual problems are so subtle that they do not require treatment.

All people who under-achieve at school, whether formally diagnosed as dyslexic or not, should be referred to an eyecare professional who has specialized in dyslexia. This should happen when the under-achievement is first suspected, so that any visual factors can be addressed sooner rather than later.

Some of the visual factors and treatments that have been associated with dyslexia have been very poorly researched and are not sufficiently proven to warrant their inclusion in clinical practice. Resources, both in terms of time and money, are never limitless and members of the public should not be asked to pursue poorly validated 'remedies'. An exception to this is when such approaches are offered as part of a research study, in which case their experimental nature should be made clear to the public.

Even when visual problems are detected in dyslexia, the person still has an educational problem and will need specialist teaching. Dyslexic children benefit from a co-ordinated approach from several professionals, the most important of whom are their parents and teachers. Eyecare practitioners should be a part of this team, and communication with the other members of this team is essential if the best interests of the child are to be served.

Summary

- The main visual correlates of dyslexia are binocular instability, a magnocellular deficit, and Meares-Irlen syndrome.
- These correlates may be related, possibly through the common link of a deficit of visual attention.
- The psychometric profile of a person with dyslexia does not indicate whether they are likely to have the visual correlates of dyslexia.
- Commonly used screening methods do not detect many of the visual problems that need to be sought in dyslexic people.
- All people who under-achieve at school should see an eyecare practitioner who has specialized in this subject

Introduction

Overview of specific learning difficulties

Dyslexia

Several authors have discussed the definition,[1-5] prevalence,[2] and early diagnosis[6] of dyslexia. Dyslexia often runs in families,[7-11] usually persists throughout life,[12] but the diagnosis is not always constant over time.[13] It has been found in many,[2] but not all,[13,14] studies to be more common in males than females.

Contrary to the conventional view,[2] it has been argued that IQ data should not be used in the diagnosis of dyslexia.[15,16] The distinction between *specific* reading difficulty and *non-specific* (general) reading backwardness has also been criticized.[17]

Although the term *dyslexia* has been criticized, it has several advantages.[18] This book deals with developmental dyslexia: the rarer acquired dyslexia is not discussed.[19] In North America people with specific learning difficulties or dyslexia are often described as *learning disabled.*[20]

Attention deficit disorder (ADD)

Several authors have discussed the definition,[21] diagnosis,[22-25] aetiology,[26-28] classification,[29,30] and treatment[22] of attention deficit disorder (ADD) and have discussed the relationship with dyslexia.[21,31-33] Key features of ADD include impaired vigilance[34] (vigilance is the same as sustained attention),[35] inattention,[26] motor impersistence,[26] and often hyperactivity.[36]

Other specific learning difficulties

Dyscalculia, or specific arithmetic difficulty, usually co-exists with dyslexia.[37] Authors have discussed the definition of dyspraxia,[38] and the subject has been reviewed.[39]

Causes of dyslexia

A complete review of research on the aetiology of dyslexia is beyond the scope of this book, but a few typical references are cited here.[40-48] There is some debate over whether dyslexia represents a 'hump' at the lower end of the distribution of reading ability,[49] or whether dyslexia is just the lower tail of a normal distribution of reading ability.[13,17]

The overwhelming evidence for deficiencies in storing and retrieving the names of printed words lying at the heart of dyslexia has led some authors to adopt the 'no visual deficit hypothesis'.[50-51] This hypothesis is, in essence, that dyslexia is exclusively caused by a low level phonological processing deficit.[51]

The role of visual problems and therapies in dyslexia

An early paper noted the existence of separate sight and phonemic vocabularies[52] and several authors have outlined models of the reading and spelling processes.[53] Most attempts to classify dyslexia[54-56] can be re-conceptualized within the framework outlined by Boder,[57,58] whose classification has attracted considerable support,[37,59,60] although with a few exceptions.[41,61,62] Not all authors agree that dyslexia is readily sub-typed,[17,63] and a 'continuity model of dyslexia' has been advocated.[17] The model in Figure 1.1 is a simplified version of published work.[53]

Optometrists do not treat dyslexia, but treat visual problems which sometimes co-exist with dyslexia.[64] The arguments for and against various visual factors causing and contributing to dyslexia are reviewed in the appendices discussing these visual factors.

The evidence-based approach and its application in this book

The placebo effect can be very large and can influence so-called objective measures.[65] Randomized placebo-controlled trials are just as important for 'complementary' activities as they are for 'conventional' healthcare practices.[66] Yet, some optometric texts[67] fail to stress the importance of randomized controlled trials.

Some authors have outlined the particular difficulties involved in researching vision and dyslexia and have offered useful advice for researchers.[68-71]

In these appendices, most of the papers under review studied groups of children who were diagnosed as having dyslexia or specific learning difficulties. Pertinent studies of children with less clearly defined learning difficulties are included, where it seems likely that most of the children in the relevant studies had dyslexia.

As a general rule, papers will only be cited if they have been published in the public domain and are retrievable by readers. Previous reviews of the literature are cited when these are comprehensive and balanced.

The main reasons why studies on the optometric correlates of dyslexia were excluded from these appendices are:

1. inadequate diagnostic techniques or criteria for establishing whether 'the dyslexic group' had dyslexia;
2. absence of a control group that was at least matched for age and preferably also for IQ;
3. small subject numbers (e.g. one study investigated five dyslexic children, one control child, and one control adult);[72]
4. inappropriate scaling of optometric variables. For example,[73,74] some studies arbitrarily classified continuous variables (e.g. visual acuity) into binary classification (e.g. pass/fail), using criteria that are inappropriate for the reading process.

Research on the optometric correlates of dyslexia should control for intelligence by matching the IQ of the control group to that of the experimental group. This is important because the variables under investigation may be correlated with IQ (e.g. people with higher IQ tend to be more myopic) and intelligence may influence the ability of subjects to carry out optometric tests. It is probably not adequate to state that the IQ of both groups was within the normal range. In these appendices, studies that control for IQ will be listed separately and greatest weight should be attached to these studies. It is hoped that in future the influence of other psychometric factors will also be investigated (see Chapter 8 and Appendix 8).

Ideally, the experimenters should be masked (blind) as to whether a subject belongs to the dyslexic or control group. However, very few studies have achieved this and there are real difficulties with dyslexic children since their difficulties so often become apparent during the course of testing (e.g. when they reverse letters on a letter chart). When studies are reviewed that have been particularly rigorous and masked then this is noted.

One problem with research in this field is the tendency to treat various optometric factors in isolation and ideally research should consider the interaction between different optometric factors (e.g. refractive errors, accommodation, binocular co-ordination, and sensory factors) rather than treating them in isolation.[75]

The main reasons why studies on the effect of optometric interventions on dyslexia were excluded from these reviews are:

1. absence of a control treatment;
2. failure to randomize the allocation of subjects to treatment or control groups;
3. absence of a masked (blind) protocol.

Some of the studies which were excluded from the present review, for the reasons given above, are summarized in an earlier review by the author.[76] Web-based literature searches for this book have used Medline[77] and a CD-ROM bibliography has also been used (Silver Platter Ophthalmology database).[78] The references cited by these papers have in turn led to the discovery of other relevant publications.

Professionals who help people with dyslexia

Typically, dyslexia is diagnosed by educational psychologists,[45] and it is widely recognized that the best therapy for dyslexia is extra teaching.[50]

Structure of the eye and basic visual functions

A distinction has been drawn between low level (peripheral) and higher level (central) functions.[79]

Visual symptoms

Excessive reversals when reading have been claimed to be significant in dyslexia, but are nowadays thought to be the result of the reading problem, not the cause.[50] One study has argued that visual symptoms are not especially prevalent in dyslexia,[80] although other studies have found the opposite.[81–84] A review has discussed potential causes for unusual visual symptoms.[85]

Ocular health and refractive errors

Research studies are included in this review if they meet certain basic requirements of scientific rigour, which are outlined on p. 112–114. Many of the papers in this review, and some that have been excluded, are described in more detail elsewhere.[1] It has been noted that refractive factors are linked to ocular motor status, and ideally these interactions should be considered rather than studying individual variables in isolation.[2]

Ocular health

There is no evidence to suggest that eye or brain diseases are especially common in developmental dyslexia.[3-6] Although not specifically relating to developmental dyslexia, several authors have investigated the effect of eye diseases[7,8] and brain diseases[9-11] (e.g. from tumours or strokes) on reading. Visually impaired children do not usually exhibit the characteristics of dyslexia.[12]

Refractive errors, vision, and visual acuity

For comfortable reading, text has to be 2–8 times larger than threshold visual acuity.[13] Literature reviews and research studies on visual acuity and dyslexia are summarized in Table A2.1. It has been suggested that apparent poor visual acuity in dyslexia might simply result from a high level naming deficit, and this notion has some experimental support.[14]

The prevalences[24] of refractive errors in Chapter 2 are approximate because prevalence varies with age, nationality, and race.[24] Induced blur has an adverse effect on reading comprehension as well as reducing accuracy and rate, and people with a higher IQ are better able to overcome these problems.[25]

Research on the relationship between refractive errors and dyslexia is summarized in Table A2.2. There appears to be a weak relationship whereby myopes tend to have a higher IQ than hypermetropes,[26-28] and this may account for some of the findings in Table A2.2. Studies, which

Table A2.1. Summary of literature reviews and controlled research on visual acuity and dyslexia. The numbers refer to the publications listed in the notes to this appendix

Parameter	Literature reviews	Studies controlling for IQ	Studies not controlling for IQ
Dyslexia *is* correlated with reduced distance visual acuity		5, 6	
Dyslexia *is not* correlated with reduced distance visual acuity	15, 16	17–21	
Dyslexia *is* correlated with reduced near visual acuity	22	5, 6	23
Dyslexia *is not* correlated with reduced near visual acuity			

Table A2.2. Summary of literature reviews and controlled research on refractive errors and dyslexia. The numbers refer to the publications listed in the notes to this appendix

Parameter	Literature reviews	Studies controlling for IQ	Studies not controlling for IQ
Dyslexia *is* correlated with increased myopia			
Dyslexia *is not* correlated with increased myopia	31, 32	5, 6, 17	33–35
Dyslexia *is* correlated with increased hypermetropia	15, 16, 22, 33, 36	19	35, 37
Dyslexia *is not* correlated with increased hypermetropia	31, 32	5, 6	33
Dyslexia *is* correlated with increased astigmatism		38	
Dyslexia *is not* correlated with increased astigmatism	31, 32	5, 6	
Dyslexia *is* correlated with increased anisometropia			
Dyslexia *is not* correlated with increased anisometropia	31, 32	6, 18	

did not control for IQ, found that hypermetropes have significantly worse visual perceptual skills than emmetropes and myopes,[29] and younger correction of hypermetropia was associated with the development of better visual perceptual skills.[30]

Some studies have found that, despite the lack of evidence of a higher prevalence of refractive errors in dyslexia, an unusually high proportion of people with dyslexia have been prescribed glasses.[18,6] The finding appears to result from a well-intended tendency to prescribe low power spectacles for dyslexic people as an 'experimental correction', in the hope that they may be of some help;[18,39] this practice has been criticized by some authors.[40]

APPENDIX 3

Ocular motor factors

Research studies are included in this review if they meet certain basic requirements of scientific rigour, which are outlined on p. 112–114. Many of the papers in this review, and some that have been excluded, are described in more detail elsewhere.[1] It has been noted that ocular motor factors are linked to refractive status, and ideally these interactions should be considered rather than studying individual variables in isolation.[2]

Accommodative function (focusing)

The normal data for amplitude of accommodation in Table 3.1 are derived from the Hofstetter formulae.[3] More information for eyecare practitioners on the diagnosis and treatment of accommodative anomalies can be found in a previous book by the author.[4] Another author reviewed the symptoms and efficacy of treatment of accommodative anomalies.[5]

There have been few comprehensive reviews of the literature on accommodation and dyslexia, but these suggest a relationship between accommodative dysfunction and dyslexia.[6]

Some authors have noted the many variables that can confound the measurement of accommodative facility,[7] and this may account for reports of apparent accommodative infacility in dyslexia.[8] Research on accommodative function in dyslexia is summarized in Table A3.1.

Binocular co-ordination (eye teaming)

More information for eyecare practitioners on the diagnosis and treatment of binocular incoordination can be found in another book by the author.[4] The prevalence of binocular anomalies is about 5%.[18] It has been argued that the vergence system is the most vulnerable ocular motor

Table A3.1. Summary of research on accommodation and dyslexia. The numbers refer to the references listed in the notes to this appendix

Parameter	Studies controlling for IQ	Studies not controlling for IQ
Dyslexia *is* correlated with low amplitude of accommodation	8, 9	10
Dyslexia *is not* correlated with low amplitude of accommodation	11, 12	13
Dyslexia *is* correlated with increased accommodative lag	14	
Dyslexia *is not* correlated with increased accommodative lag	8	
Dyslexia *is* correlated with accommodative infacility		15, 16
Dyslexia *is not* correlated with accommodative infacility	8	10, 17

system and that problems with binocular control can cause unstable visual perceptions during reading.[19]

Several reviews of the literature have concluded that binocular inco-ordination could contribute to dyslexia;[20-27] others felt that it did not.[28-30] The few studies that have evaluated ocular motility in dyslexia have found this to be normal.[8,9,12]

Strabismus and its sensory adaptations (suppression and HARC) have been reviewed in another publication by the author.[4] Most studies that have controlled for the effect of IQ[8,11] and most that have not[31] agree that manifest strabismus is not a correlate of dyslexia. An early study that did not control for IQ and may have included people with general reading difficulties rather than dyslexia did report an increased occurrence of strabismus in poor readers.[32] A few papers have claimed, anecdotally, that strabismus is less common in dyslexia.[33-35] Induced esotropia in the Maya Indians was discussed by Trachtman.[36]

Some studies that have controlled for IQ and have evaluated the size and type of heterophoria in dyslexia have found increased heterophoria in dyslexia,[37-39] but others have not.[8,11] Studies that have not controlled for IQ have similarly sometimes supported[31,32,40,41] and other times not supported[42] a relationship between dyslexia and heterophoria. Interestingly, the studies that do indicate an increased prevalence of heterophoria fail to agree on the type, with most finding more exophoria,[32,38,41] and some esophoria.[39]

The diagnosis of decompensated heterophoria is not straightforward, but the presence of an aligning prism on the Mallett fixation disparity test is a good indicator of decompensation.[4] Most studies have not found the presence of an aligning prism to be a correlate of dyslexia, whether they controlled for IQ[8] or not.[43] The few exceptions did not control for IQ.[17,44]

Binocular instability is characterized by low fusional reserves and an unstable heterophoria.[4] Studies that have evaluated binocular instability, fusional reserves, and/or stability of heterophoria in dyslexia are summarized in Table A3.2. Binocular instability in dyslexia is associated with the symptom of doubling.[8]

A distinction needs to be drawn between *convergence insufficiency* (literally, a remote near point of convergence) and *convergence weakness exophoria* (a decompensated exophoria at near, but not at distance).[47] Confusingly, the North American literature sometimes refers to both conditions as

Table A3.2. Summary of research on binocular instability, the components of binocular instability, and dyslexia. Fusional amplitude is the sum of convergent and divergent fusional reserves. One study[12] obtained equivocal results relating to divergent fusional reserves. The numbers refer to the references listed in the notes to this appendix

Parameter	Studies controlling for IQ	Studies not controlling for IQ
Dyslexia *is* correlated with low convergent fusional reserve	8	40
Dyslexia *is not* correlated with low convergent fusional reserve	11, 12, 45	42
Dyslexia *is* correlated with low divergent fusional reserve	8, 45	40
Dyslexia *is not* correlated with low divergent fusional reserve	11	42
Dyslexia *is* correlated with low fusional amplitude	8, 13, 38, 46	
Dyslexia *is not* correlated with low fusional amplitude	11	
Dyslexia *is* correlated with an unstable heterophoria	8	
Dyslexia *is not* correlated with an unstable heterophoria		
Dyslexia *is* correlated with binocular instability	8, 46	42
Dyslexia *is not* correlated with binocular instability		

convergence insufficiency. This term is used in this book simply to describe a remote near point of convergence. A few studies that have controlled for the effect of IQ have found convergence insufficiency to be correlated with dyslexia,[9,39] although others have not.[8,48] Similarly, a study that did not control for IQ found a correlation between convergence insufficiency and dyslexia,[41] but another study did not.[10] Some of the studies of near point of convergence have used cut-offs for defining normal or abnormal convergence, sometimes at inappropriate levels,[48] when it might have been more appropriate to treat the near point of convergence as a continuous variable.

I know of no studies which have suggested that amblyopia is a correlate of dyslexia, although one that controlled for IQ suggested that amblyopia is not especially prevalent in dyslexia.[49]

Of the studies that have controlled for IQ, one study has[45] found a correlation between dyslexia and stereopsis, but most have not.[8,11,12,50] A less clear-cut picture emerges from studies that have not controlled for the effect of IQ: some studies suggest a relationship[16,42] and others do not.[31] One study, which did not control for IQ, found that foveal suppression, as assessed with the 4Δ base out test,[4] was correlated with dyslexia. A study that did control for IQ found a similar prevalence of foveal suppression in dyslexia as in good readers.[8] The literature on aniseikonia and dyslexia has been reviewed[1] but is now quite dated, although methods are still available to measure aniseikonia.[51]

Treatment

Many of the problems of ocular motor co-ordination that are described above are amenable to treatment with eye exercises,[4] or occasionally with 'exercise glasses',[4] or prisms.[4] The efficacy of eye exercises to train fusional reserves has been demonstrated in randomized controlled trials,[4] and the author has developed a form of these exercises that are suited to dyslexic children and can be used at home.[47,52] A retrospective survey found that about 20% of people referred to an optometric SpLD clinic required eye exercises to train convergence or convergent fusional reserves.[53]

The multi-factorial nature of dyslexia makes it difficult to evaluate the effect of eye exercises on dyslexia, although one study which controlled for intelligence but not for the placebo effect found a beneficial effect of optometric treatment on reading performance.[54] Another study suggests that treatment of low fusional reserves is effective at reducing eyestrain and headaches in children with reading difficulties, and can also improve reading performance.[35] However, the use of orthoptic exercises in children with dyslexia has been criticized.[55] A distinction has been drawn between validated exercises (e.g. to train fusional reserves) as described above and more controversial approaches that are typical of behavioural optometry (see Appendix 5).[56]

Additional comments

Some authors have criticized tests that are carried out during brief periods of static viewing, as being unlikely to reflect the situation during the prolonged dynamic task of reading.[39,57,58] However, it has also been suggested that performance at dynamic visual tasks can be predicted from results measured on standard static clinical tests.[59] One small study used an ingenious design to look at vergence in a dynamic task and did not find a deficit in dyslexia, but the small subject numbers limit the conclusions.[60]

One study noted that, although accommodative insufficiency and binocular instability appeared to be correlates of dyslexia, when present these are usually mild and unlikely to be major causes of the reading difficulty.[8] Data from a simulated reading visual search task supported this conclusion.[8] This study also used a reading-age matched paradigm to demonstrate that these ocular motor correlates of dyslexia did not result from lack of reading experience.[8]

Some authors have suggested that attentional problems might confound the assessment of binocular co-ordination in dyslexia.[41,61] A controlled study noted that binocular instability in dyslexia is correlated with a magnocellular deficit (see Appendix 6) and this study also investigated the interaction between binocular instability and some psychometric factors.[62]

Many authorities who have concluded that specific ocular motor anomalies are not correlated with dyslexia have nonetheless observed that these visual factors could contribute to poor reading in individual cases and that eye examinations are an important part of the management of reading disability.[11,28,63]

In northern continental Europe a controversial method of investigating binocular co-ordination, the Zeiss Polatest,[64,65] tends to result in excessive[66,67] prescribing of prisms[66–68] or surgery.[66,67]

Eye movements (eye tracking)

Several authors have provided detailed reviews of the nature of the different types of eye movements,[69–71] and specifically those during reading.[72–75]

A seminal study half a century ago showed that intelligence was strongly correlated with saccadic eye movement parameters, and that the saccadic eye movement characteristics of six-year-old children were similar to those of older children but showed a much larger inter-subject variation.[76] A review of early research on eye movements in reading noted that eye movement habits have become fairly stable by the age of nine years and, if intelligence was controlled for, good readers made fewer fixations and regressive movements per line and demonstrated a greater accuracy of the return sweep to the beginning of the succeeding line than poor readers.[77]

Research studies support the notion of 'top-down' processing whereby eye movements are under the moment-to-moment control of cognitive processes,[78] although 'bottom-up' (low level) automatic control may predominate for simple text.[79]

Reviews can also be found on the requirements and characteristics of different methods of measuring eye movements.[80]

The vagueness of the term *tracking* has been criticized as it has been used to describe vergence, pursuit, and saccadic eye movements.[81] Pursuit eye movements are discussed in the section below on the role of attention. Fixation stability appears to be normal in dyslexic and backward readers.[45]

Saccadic eye movements and dyslexia

There is overwhelming evidence from the research literature (including many of the studies described below) demonstrating that when dyslexic people read they tend to make excessive saccades (fixations and regressions). As noted in Chapter 3, this is not surprising since their dyslexia means that they have trouble understanding the text and they will therefore need to 're-trace their steps' more often than good readers. Other explanations are that they might have saccadic dysfunction *causing* their dyslexia, or they may have saccadic dysfunction which is a non-causal correlate of the dyslexia. Research to investigate these hypotheses has used one of three paradigms.

1. Studies have assessed the reading eye movements of groups of dyslexic people when they read material of a level set at the reading age of the dyslexic subjects (i.e. well below their chronological age). This is a questionable approach, since it is possible that years of difficulty in coping with text could have caused dyslexic people to develop the habit of making more fixations, even when they are reading material that they find easy.

2. Some studies have compared the pattern of saccadic eye movements in dyslexia with those of younger controls who read at the same reading age as the dyslexics (the *reading-age match* paradigm). This paradigm is not without its critics.[45]

3. The third paradigm is to have subjects make reading-like eye movements but in a non-reading task. Most studies that have used this approach have had their subjects fix a series of LEDs in a horizontal line that are sequentially illuminated.

Studies that have assessed saccadic eye movements in dyslexia using these three paradigms are summarized in Table A3.3. A fourth paradigm, rapid serial visual presentation (RSVP), presents two to three words at a time in the same place on a screen so that eye movements are not required.[82] One review found that this does not improve reading speed.[83] Some poorer readers do perform better with RSVP, but this does not necessarily suggest saccadic dysfunction since the advantage could be through 'dividing text into smaller idea units'.[82]

Table A3.3. Summary of research on saccadic eye movements and dyslexia. Most of the studies which found abnormal saccadic eye movements in dyslexia detected an excessive number of regressions. The numbers refer to the references listed in the notes to this appendix

Parameter	Studies controlling for IQ	Studies not controlling for IQ
APPROPRIATE READING MATERIAL		
Dyslexia *is* correlated with saccadic dysfunction	14	72, 84
Dyslexia *is not* correlated with saccadic dysfunction		85
READING-AGE MATCHED PARADIGM		
Dyslexia *is* correlated with saccadic dysfunction		72, 86
Dyslexia *is not* correlated with saccadic dysfunction		
NON-READING TASKS		
Dyslexia *is* correlated with saccadic dysfunction	87, 46, 88	89, 72
Dyslexia *is not* correlated with saccadic dysfunction	14, 108, 90–92	

As discussed in Chapter 3, it is not yet known whether the King-Devick and DEM[93,94] tests detect saccadic dysfunction or to what degree they are influenced by other confounding variables (e.g. digit naming and cognitive skills).[95] One study found that results with the King-Devick test were not associated with reading achievement.[10] Results at the DEM test demonstrate poor repeatability,[96] do not correlate with reading age[97] or optometric factors,[95] but do show a significant correlation with the Wide Range Achievement Test results,[93] which might suggest that the DEM test result is confounded by intelligence. People who do poorly at the DEM test seem to do progressively worse as they work through the test, and it has been hypothesized that this may be linked to inattention.[98]

The effect of attention

The orienting of visual attention (see Appendix 8) to the target position for saccadic and pursuit eye movements may be an essential feature of these eye movements.[99]

In an early report, choreiform (fine, jerky, and irregular) movements in muscles of the tongue, face, neck, trunk and eyes were described as being associated with poor school performance, behavioural problems, and restlessness.[100] It seems likely that these children would nowadays be described as having ADD.

Poor performance at saccadic eye movement tasks by people with dyslexia may be linked to attentional factors.[87,101,102] Saccadation of pursuit eye movements in hyperactive children[103–105] is attributable to poor sustained attention rather than an ocular motor deficit,[103] and responds to treatment by medication combined with other methods.[105] Poor sustained attention is a consistent feature of attention deficit disorder (ADD), which is a strong correlate of dyslexia.[106] Other authors[92,107] have suggested that an attentional deficit might account for the finding[72] of excessive fixations and regressions in some dyslexic subjects. The finding of abnormal (saccadation of) pursuit eye movements in dyslexia[17,108–110] could also be explained by an attentional deficit.[107] A study which did not support this hypothesis[46] used a method of diagnosing ADD which may, by itself, be invalid.[111] Pursuit eye movements are not usually used during reading.[112] Motor impersistence, a feature of ADD, may cause fixation instability as well as unstable eye movements.[113]

One study found a possible effect of diet on reading eye movements of dyslexic people.[114] The authors felt that diet, specifically sugar, might influence the neurological system, possibly affecting eye movements and attention. Unfortunately, this study suffered from methodological limitations.[1]

It is interesting to note that, although eye movement control may be particularly prone to the influence of lapses of attention, none of the studies in Table A3.2 appears to have controlled adequately for attentional deficits. Attentional factors might account for differences in saccadic parameters in different dyslexic subgroups.[115]

An alternative hypothesis is that the magnocellular visual system, which is often deficient in dyslexia (see Appendix 6), plays a major role in the control of saccadic and pursuit eye movements and fixation control.[116] This theory may be linked with the attentional hypothesis outlined above and this is discussed in Chapter 8 and Appendix 8.

Additional comments

Most of the rigorous research on saccadic eye movements and dyslexia seems to support the conclusions of an earlier review,[117] that abnormal eye movements do not contribute to dyslexia,[30,118] but a different pattern of eye movements during reading may be the result of abnormal reading development and/or a lack of disciplined reading experience.[74,83] Even researchers who have concluded that there is a saccadic eye movement deficit in dyslexia have often argued that this is a reflection of the underlying 'pathophysiology that causes dyslexia'[119] (e.g. difficulty with sequential tasks),[72] with few thinking that it may be a cause of the reading difficulty.[87]

Although most evidence seems to suggest that eye movement abnormalities are not a general cause of dyslexia, this remains a possibility for a few individuals.[118,102] One thorough case study describes an ambidextrous dyslexic who showed an almost irrepressible tendency to read from right to left.[120]

Vergence drifts have been shown to occur during reading eye movements,[79,121] but these studies have not related their findings to clinical measures of binocular co-ordination.

In view of the failure to establish saccadic dysfunction as a clear correlate of dyslexia, it is not surprising that attempts to train saccadic eye movements do not appear to be an effective intervention for dyslexia[75] and have been criticized.[55] An exception is a research group who recently found impaired voluntary saccadic control in dyslexia[88] which correlated with poor dynamic perception[122] and improved with treatment, in a partially controlled experiment.[123] It is hoped that fully randomized controlled trials of this treatment will investigate whether it has an effect on reading.

Ocular dominance

Research studies are included in this review if they meet certain basic requirements of scientific rigour, which are outlined on pp. 112–114. Many of the papers in this review, and some that have been excluded, are described in more detail elsewhere.[1]

General research on ocular dominance

Several authors have attempted to define[2,3] ocular dominance and many have supported the concept of different types of ocular dominance,[4–8] with some attempting to classify these, principally into sighting, sensory, and motor dominance.[1,9–12] Many researchers have produced evidence suggesting that the dominant eye varies according to the way that it is tested,[10,12,13,14] although one study has found that the dominant eye remains constant with different tests.[15] It has also been noted that different types of dominance may interact with one another.[10–12] Some authors have noted a lack of research on the reliability of tests of ocular dominance,[12] and the reliability of the Keystone screening instrument has been specifically questioned.[16]

Hemispheric dominance has been quite widely researched,[17] and its possible role in dyslexia has been the subject of detailed reviews.[1,18,19]

Methods of measuring sensory ocular dominance include suppression,[20,21] visual acuity, retinal rivalry,[12,22,23] and the phi test.[14,12,24] It has been recommended that research with retinal rivalry should reverse the monocular targets over several trials.[1]

Fixation disparity has been advocated as a test of motor ocular dominance for some time,[15,20] as has the eye to break during fusional reserve or near point of convergence testing,[20] and the difference in movement of the eyes on changing fixation.[25,26] Most research on motor ocular dominance has used the Dunlop test to assess populations of people with dyslexia and this is described below.

For many decades, researchers have noticed that different tests of sighting dominance give varying results[27] and many authorities have advocated using a battery of tests to assess sighting dominance.[37] Sighting dominance may only start to develop at the age when children start to sight (e.g. through tubes);[28] and objects appear larger to the most dominant eye.[29] Methods of assessing the sighting eye should stimulate both eyes,[30] and are likely to find that the egocentre (cyclopean eye) lies somewhere between the two eyes.[31,32] The relationship between sighting dominance and physiological diplopia is not widely recognized, although a few researchers have made this connection.[8,9,33,34]

Ocular dominance and dyslexia

Sighting dominance and crossed dominance

Some reviews have concluded that sighting dominance is not related to dyslexia,[35,36] although others have reached the opposite conclusion,[37,38] or have been equivocal.[39]

Research studies on sighting dominance and dyslexia are summarized in Table A4.1. One research team initially claimed, in a non-controlled study, that dyslexia was associated with crossed, mixed, and incomplete dominance.[40] Further analysis of their data led them to question many of their initial conclusions.[36] In view of the equivocal nature of these papers, they are not included in Table A4.1.

The view is sometimes stated that the sighting dominant eye should not have worse visual acuity than the non-dominant eye,[3] although I have been unable to find any studies supporting this contention. Similarly, the notion that crossed dominance causes reversals is supported only by anecdotal claims[37] and very limited research,[41] but not by rigorous research and this idea has been criticized.[42] The belief[43] that reversals are the result of a general laterality problem has also been criticized; the current view tends to be that reversals in dyslexia are a result of the reading problem, not the cause.[44] There is also little evidence[36] to support the practice of 'treating' (reversing) crossed dominance, and this practice has been criticized by several authors.[35,45]

Annett and co-workers have carried out a considerable amount of research supporting their elaborate theory that people with dyslexia are very strongly right or left handed.[46,58] This work is not without its critics.[59]

Table A4.1. Summary of research on sighting dominance and dyslexia. Additional references are cited in the text. The numbers refer to the references listed in the notes to this appendix

Parameter	Studies controlling for IQ	Studies not controlling for IQ
Dyslexia *is* correlated with left handedness		46
Dyslexia *is not* correlated with left handedness	47–49	12, 50, 45, 51
Dyslexia *is* correlated with left eye dominance		52, 53
Dyslexia *is not* correlated with left eye dominance		12, 48, 54, 45
Dyslexia *is* correlated with crossed dominance		55, 52
Dyslexia *is not* correlated with crossed dominance	48	12, 45, 54, 56, 57

Sensory ocular dominance

Of the few studies that have assessed sensory ocular dominance in dyslexia, most have not found a correlation,[36,48] although there are a few exceptions.[12] Only one of these studies investigated the effect of intelligence.[48]

Motor ocular dominance and the Dunlop test

Theories about the Dunlop test (see box on p. 58) have changed over the years.[1] Initially, the test was used to detect a form of crossed dominance,[7] or crossed and unstable dominance,[60,61] which was said to be associated with 'the mirror reversals of dyslexia'.[62] The initial treatment that was recommended for an abnormal response with the test was occlusion and eye exercises.[63,64] A small controlled study did not support this practice,[65] and a larger well-controlled study suggested that, as long as steps were taken to control for subjects' intelligence, neither unstable nor crossed dominance with the Dunlop test was correlated with poor reading.[47]

The Stein and Fowler version of the test involved repeating the testing 10 times to detect an unstable reference eye,[66] which was said to reflect poor visuomotor control,[67] a deficit of the right posterior parietal cortex,[68,69] impaired vergence control,[69] unstable binocular control,[70,71] and binocular instability.[72] One study found that reading difficulties were not associated with crossed dominance on the Dunlop test but were associated with an unstable reference eye.[57] The hypothesis that two-thirds of dyslexic people have a deficit of the right posterior parietal lobe was not supported by a controlled research study using a line bisection task.[73] It has been claimed that up to half of dyslexic children have 'visual dyslexia', as detected with the Dunlop test.[74]

The first version of the Dunlop test used convergence and divergence to induce a fixation disparity.[7] Later versions just diverged the eyes beyond parallel,[61] which gives different results to converging.[47] Anecdotal comments also suggest that the eye in which a fixation disparity may occur often varies at different testing distances.[75,76] Divergence beyond parallel is an unnatural act, which is hard to relate to reading, and the synoptophore which is used in the Dunlop test has also been criticized for creating artificial test conditions.[77] Some authors have used alternative methods of creating a fixation disparity which better simulate conditions during reading,[78–80] and one of these methods has been shown to produce similar results to the synoptophore Dunlop test.[80] Many authors[47,81,82] have commented on the unreliability of the synoptophore Dunlop test, which is possibly influenced by attentional disorders,[80,83] and alternative versions may demonstrate better reliability.[78] A recent study found that many subjects with an unstable reference eye spontaneously develop a stable reference eye and suggested that this might be related to the use of coloured filters (see Chapter 7), but these authors only used one colour.[72]

Controlled research studies that have attempted to determine whether an unstable reference eye is a correlate of dyslexia are summarized in Table A4.2. Two of the studies in Table A4.2 included a reading-age matched control design.[78,84] Crossed dominance detected by the Dunlop test results has been associated with heterophoria,[7,60,61,64] remote near point of convergence,[7,60,61] and poor stereo-acuity.[60,61] An unstable reference eye has been associated with poor spatial discrimination,[85] low fusional reserves (if small targets are used),[86,87] reduced stereo-acuity,[88] fixation instability,[89] and a low spatial frequency contrast sensitivity deficit.[90] Hence, the clinical correlates of an unstable reference eye suggest that this diagnosis may be related to the conventional clinical meaning of binocular instability.[1,91] A recent study found that occlusion of people with an unstable reference eye seemed to help reading even in cases who did not develop a fixed reference eye,[72] which could be explained by the patching addressing an underlying binocular incoordination. There is also evidence that an unstable reference eye may be associated with the magnocellular visual deficit,[90] and a similar association has been found between binocular instability and the magnocellular visual deficit (see Chapter 6 and Appendix 6).[92]

An initial double masked randomized controlled trial (RCT) demonstrated that patching children with an unstable reference eye made the reference eye more stable and was associated with improved reading performance.[67] The methods and statistics in this study were criticized,[83]

Table A4.2. Summary of research, that included a control group, on the reference eye and dyslexia. It has been suggested that some of the positive studies may have suffered from a referral bias. The numbers refer to the references listed at the end of this appendix

Parameter	Studies controlling for IQ	Studies not controlling for IQ
Dyslexia *is* correlated with an unstable reference eye	78, 93	81
Dyslexia *is not* correlated with an unstable reference eye	80, 84, 94, 95	79, 82, 96

and the criticism was responded to.[98] A later RCT partially supported the initial results,[72] but there have been no independent replications.

No controlled studies have investigated whether binocular instability, as detected by the Dunlop test, might be better treated with orthoptic exercises, although an early paper suggested that unstable dominance on the Dunlop test should be treated with patching combined with eye exercises.[63] A later paper recommended that poor vergence control, as detected by the Dunlop test, might be best treated in older children with exercises based on physiological diplopia,[69] and one form of these exercises has been developed by the present author.[99,100]

One approach to the issue of causality is to investigate the type of reading and spelling errors that are made by people with an unstable reference eye. People with an unstable reference eye make a significantly greater proportion of reading[101,102] and spelling errors[103] that suggest visual confusions than people who have a stable reference eye; and occlusion reduces the visual reading errors in children with an unstable reference eye.[102]

Behavioural optometry and other controversial visual approaches

Research studies are included in this review if they meet certain basic requirements of scientific rigour, which are outlined on pp. 112–114. Many of the papers in this review, and some that have been excluded, are described in more detail elsewhere.[1]

Behavioural optometry and developmental vision therapy

What is behavioural optometry?

The history and theoretical approach of behavioural optometry (BO) are outlined by some thorough reviews, both written from a behavioural optometrist's (BO's) perspective,[2,3] and from a more sceptical approach.[4,5]

At the conservative end of the spectrum, the BO practised by some optometrists[6] is only slightly more 'adventurous' than many of the more proven approaches outlined in this book. An advantage of BO is that it generates interest within optometry in providing care for people with specific learning difficulties. It is also commendable that BOs advocate a careful consideration of the interaction between psychological factors and visual symptoms and signs.[7]

Some BOs argue that the majority of people with dyslexia need 'vision therapy',[8] and may treat pursuit and saccadic eye movements, myopia, and visual perceptual skills.[9,10] Other controversial activities include training visual information processing (including visual imagery and visualization)[11] in individuals who do not appear to have a specific ocular or vision defect.[2,12] One reviewer noted that 'treatment of binocular function in patients without any binocular problems is not likely to produce any significant effects'.[13] Some BOs also carry out psychometric testing to diagnose and classify dyslexia.[14] Another unproven[15] use of BO is to improve sporting performance.

Some reviews of studies on BO adopt an unquestioning stance and concentrate on papers supporting BO;[3,16] others take up the opposite bias and concentrate on studies that do not support BO;[17–19] but most balanced reviews have been critical of the lack of objective evidence for BO.[4,5,20,21]

In North America, where there is fierce competition between optometrists and ophthalmologists, the debate about BO often divides the professions. The ophthalmologists argue that BO is unproven and does not adhere to standard scientific methods of investigation:[22–25] the optometrists claim that it is a valid and effective approach.[26,27]

Claims by some BOs that vision training can treat dyslexia has led authorities to criticize all eye exercises,[28] although others have noted the difference between conventional orthoptics and BO vision therapy.[19,21] Although the former has received more validation,[21] orthoptic eye exercises are not a treatment for dyslexia, just for dyslexic people with a visual anomaly. Some reviews do not draw a distinction between these two types of treatment and do not emphasize the importance of randomized controlled trials.[3]

The evidence for the effect of behavioural optometry in dyslexia

Myopia control does not specifically relate to dyslexia, although this is sometimes given as an explanation to dyslexic children's parents as to why their children need low powered plus glasses, bifocals, or varifocals. Near work plays a minimal role as a risk factor in juvenile onset myopia[29] and large scale controlled studies suggest that bifocals have no significant effect on the progression of myopia,[30] apart from a very small effect at reducing myopia in children who are esophoric at near.[31] These cases might in any event be prescribed bifocals by conventional practitioners to alleviate any symptoms from the esophoria (p. 37). A high lag of accommodation does not appear to be a cause of myopia.[32] Controlled studies also suggest that vision therapy is 'of no value in curing myopia',[33,34] although there was 'a psychological change in the patients to their handicap'.[33]

A literature search was carried out to identify any randomized controlled trials of several key BO interventions: the use of low plus glasses and yoked prisms, the training of pursuit or saccadic eye movements, and visual perceptual skill training.[35] No randomized controlled trials were identified, and this concurs with a recent very thorough and balanced review of the literature.[5] This review concluded that 'It seems to me unlikely that present behavioural optometry can satisfy evidence-based scrutiny, indeed there must be concern that groups of optometrists following idiosyncratic management strategies within areas traditionally associated with other professions might hinder the credibility and development of optometry as a whole.'

Despite the lack of randomized controlled double-masked studies, two controlled studies have obtained particularly interesting results. One suggests that perceptual and visual training may in some cases be beneficial, although the absence of a masked design and of details of the treatment limit these conclusions.[36] The other study, although not by BOs, was a large-scale investigation of the effect of visual training on saccade control in dyslexia.[37] Daily training improved perceptual capacity and voluntary saccade control. Although the study did not employ a full randomized controlled design, the protocol did suggest that the improvement may not be fully attributable to placebo effects. It is not clear whether the training had any effect on reading or other everyday tasks.

A meta-analysis has demonstrated that about 14% of the variance in reading skills can be accounted for by visual perceptual skills,[38] although this does not imply causality. It is quite common in the literature on BO to assume that a correlation implies causality. For example, a study found that perceptual-motor test results in kindergarten children correlated with 'readiness to read'.[39] However, this does not imply that training perceptual-motor skills will help children, since the study did not control for IQ and the result could simply be explained as achievers in one field (reading) achieving better in another field (perceptual-motor skills).

Some research on BO methods has noted the effect on children's self-confidence and one author has discussed the role of attention.[40]

Neuro-developmental and neuro-physiological retraining (patterning)

The theories and methods of neuro-developmental and neuro-physiological retraining (patterning) have been criticized[41] and I have been unable to find any double-masked randomized controlled trials of these activities, despite a literature search.[42]

Cerebello-vestibular dysfunction

An initial report, which contained few details and no control group, claimed that 97% of dyslexic children have cerebello-vestibular (C-V) dysfunction which caused subclinical nystagmus resulting in 'letter and word scrambling'.[43] A later paper described these patients as 'dysmetric dyslexics and dyspractics', and gave a little more detail of the diagnosis and treatment of the 'condition'; but still contained no details or statistical analysis.[44] A further paper contained more claims, but again very little in the way of data,[45] and a later paper also contained no control group.[46]

A thorough study of an eye movement measure of C-V function found no significant difference between a group of boys with dyslexia and age and IQ matched controls.[47] Although a later study did find reduced C-V function in dyslexia, the groups were small (only six in each group) and were not matched for intelligence, which may well have influenced the results.[48]

More recently, research studies have identified psychophysical indicators[49,50] of cerebellar dysfunction and two imaging studies have provided direct evidence of the involvement of the cerebellum in dyslexia.[51,52] The role of the cerebellar dysfunction in reading, if any, remains to be determined.

Ocular lock and chiropractic treatment

The theory behind ocular lock and chiropractic treatment of dyslexia has been summarized.[53] I have been unable to find any controlled trials of this intervention.[54] Applied kinesiology[19] seems to be very similar to cranial osteopathy.

Visual processing

Research studies are included in this review if they meet certain basic requirements of scientific rigour, which are outlined on p. 112–114. Many of the papers in this review, and some that have been excluded, are described in more detail elsewhere.[1]

Low level versus high level visual function

Several authors have drawn a distinction between low level (peripheral) and high level (central) sensory visual function.[2] Some have noted that the ocular motor deficits and the low level sensory visual deficits described below[3] bear little relation to the high level visual functions assessed in psychometric evaluations.[2] This is discussed in more detail below and in Chapter 8.

The magnocellular visual deficit and dyslexia

Magnocellular (M) and parvocellular (P) function

There have been several excellent reviews[4–6] of magnocellular (M; transient) and parvocellular (P; sustained) parallel pathways, some stressing the anatomical[7–9] and others the functional characteristics.[10–14] Many authors have stressed that there are anatomical and functional overlaps between the two sub-systems.[14–16]

Evidence for an M deficit in dyslexia

Most reviews of the literature[17,18] have concluded that there is over-whelming psychophysical evidence for an M pathway deficit affecting

75% of cases of dyslexia, and only 8% of controls;[17] although some reviews have noted weaknesses in the literature.[19,20] Controlled research studies investigating the M deficit in dyslexia are summarized in Table A6.1. Some of these studies involved small group sizes,[21,22] and the methodology of visual persistence experiments has been criticized.[23] Most studies involve children, although the M deficit in dyslexia seems to persist beyond childhood.[24] Some of the contradictions in the literature might be explained by differences in the language spoken by research subjects in different countries.[25] Two studies investigated the relationship between different tests designed to measure M function and showed them to be only loosely related.[26,27]

An early theory about a P pathway deficit in dyslexia[49] has rather been discredited by studies demonstrating normal functioning of the P visual system in dyslexia.[17] An exception is a study which suggested a P system deficit in dyseidectic (surface) developmental dyslexics.[25] The reason why

Table A6.1. Summary of controlled research on the M deficit in dyslexia. SF, spatial frequency; TF, temporal frequency. The numbers refer to the references listed in the notes to this appendix

Parameter	Studies controlling for IQ	Studies not controlling for IQ
Dyslexia *is* correlated with reduced ability to perceive high TF flicker	26–30	
Dyslexia *is not* correlated with reduced ability to perceive high TF flicker	31	
Dyslexia *is* correlated with reduced ability to detect low SF	21, 26, 32–34	
Dyslexia *is not* correlated with reduced ability to detect low SF	35	
Dyslexia *is* correlated with prolonged visual persistence	3, 34, 36–39	40, 41
Dyslexia *is not* correlated with prolonged visual persistence	31, 42	22
Dyslexia *is* correlated with abnormal metacontrast/ backward masking	39, 43, 44	40
Dyslexia *is not* correlated with abnormal metacontrast/ backward masking		
Dyslexia *is* correlated with impaired perception of fine motion	27, 30, 34, 35, 45–48	
Dyslexia *is not* correlated with impaired perception of fine motion	31	22

some workers[50,51] have concluded that there is no visual deficit in dyslexia may be because they have been investigating visual function mediated by the P system.[52]

Most electrophysiological studies have provided weak evidence for an M pathway deficit in dyslexia,[53-59] others have been equivocal,[60] and some have found no such evidence.[61,62] A functional MRI study provided support for the M deficit hypothesis.[46] One anatomical study found evidence of changes to the magnocellular layers of the lateral geniculate nucleus in dyslexia.[54,55] However, this study has been criticized,[63] and analogous anatomical observations resulting from deprivation experiments occurred without a physiological correlate.[5]

Role of the M deficit in dyslexia

Many authors have assumed that the M deficit is a cause of dyslexia,[64-66] although others have noted that there is no direct evidence of causality,[17,59,67] and that the M visual deficit is less likely to be a cause of dyslexia than another known correlate, poor phonological processing.[63-68] A few authors have noted that the M deficit appears to be subtle,[26,46,69] requiring special experimental conditions for it to be detected,[69] including lower luminance levels than are typically used for reading.[29,35,60] Indeed, the M visual deficit in dyslexia must be subtle or dyslexia would be a *general*, not a *specific*, disability.[26]

One study of the M deficit found, using a simulated reading visual search task, that the M deficit was unlikely to be a major cause of dyslexia.[26] Nonetheless, a study that has evaluated reading errors in unselected children suggested that the M deficit may play a causal role in some reading errors.[70] In adults, those who are 'poor motion detectors' tend to be worse at letter position encoding.[71]

It has been suggested that the M pathway deficit might result from a failure to learn to read,[72] although experimental evidence suggests that this is not the case.[26,73] It has been argued that the psychophysical correlates outlined above are not necessarily commensurate with the M deficit explanation.[74]

The M visual deficit is a low level sensory deficit,[3,75] and some studies have hypothesized about possible higher level[75] perceptual consequences of an M pathway deficit.[76] Dyslexic populations have been found to have deficits in some of these functions, including perceptual grouping,[77,78] sluggish foveal temporal processing (small subject numbers),[79] lack of inhibitory processes in peripheral visual processing,[80] spatial localization discrepancies,[81] impaired visual temporal order judgements,[72] improved visual search with target blurring,[82,83] and impaired visual search when distractors are present.[67] It has been suggested that the beneficial effect from coloured filters in dyslexia might be a perceptual consequence of the M deficit,[84,85] and this hypothesis is discussed in Appendix 7. Surprisingly, none of these studies have investigated low level M function to determine whether these high level deficits are in fact linked to the M deficit.

One study suggests that the M deficit, but only when detected at low luminance levels, might be related to an advantage for single word as opposed to full line reading, although the researchers noted that their result could be attributable to other factors, including attentional differences.[29]

Breitmeyer's saccadic suppression theory[86,87] was presented as a hypothesis, yet has been assumed by some authors to be an *explanation* for an assumed causal role of the M deficit in dyslexia.[85,88] Although the saccadic suppression (iconic persistence) theory has gained some indirect experimental support,[89–91] a recent study and other research[92] raises major doubts by demonstrating that the M system is not primarily responsible for saccadic suppression. An alternative hypothesis is that the M visual system plays a major role in the control of saccadic (and pursuit) eye movements and fixation stability.[93]

Several authors have hypothesized that an M pathway deficit may be correlated with binocular incoordination (see Appendix 3) in dyslexia,[94,95] and this has been demonstrated in a well-controlled research study, which noted that a causal relationship had not been proven.[96] This relationship may account for a research study that only included subjects with normal binocular co-ordination and failed to find evidence of an M pathway deficit in poor readers.[97] Another study found that an unstable reference eye on the Dunlop test (see Appendix 4) was correlated with an M deficit.[98] Several authors seem to have assumed that the presence of an ocular motor anomaly[85] or Meares-Irlen syndrome[66,85] is synonymous with an M deficit, despite the lack of evidence of a causal relationship.

Some studies have found that dyslexic subjects with an M visual deficit (see below) are likely to have phonological decoding deficits,[3,48,99] which are also associated with a reduced sensitivity to detecting rapidly changing auditory stimuli.[48] The ability to process rapidly changing auditory stimuli is associated with phonological skills[100,101] and the ability to process rapidly changing visual stimuli is associated with orthographic skills.[101] It has been suggested that the underlying deficit in dyslexia may be a reduced ability to process very rapid stimuli,[46,48,102,103] a generalized magnocellular deficit in visual and other senses,[72] linking the M visual deficit with a phonological decoding deficit.[46,48,103] The M deficit is not likely to be a feature of the dyseidectic subgroup of dyslexia,[17,25,34,104,105] but preliminary studies with small group sizes suggest that it may be a feature of dysphoneidectic (mixed) and possibly dysphonetic dyslexia.[34,105]

Controversial theories on sensory visual function and dyslexia

A theory about cerebello-vestibular dysfunction in dyslexia is discussed in Chapter 5.

Visual fields

One research team (Grosser and Spafford) suggested that there is reduced visual field sensitivity,[106] particularly in the upper field, in dyslexia which is linked to the M deficit and to a hypothesized reduced number of rods[106] and excessive number of cones,[106,107] but this research suffered from several weaknesses, including small subject numbers. An earlier paper by these authors found evidence of better visual fields in a dyslexic than in a control group.[108] A recent paper found little effect of coloured filters on visual field thresholds in dyslexia, but there were only four subjects in each group.[109]

Another controversial line of research, carried out by Geiger and Lettvin, has looked at visual acuities at different retinal eccentricities in dyslexia and at lateral masking. Initial claims, that a dyslexic group was worse at identifying letters within 5° of fixation and better than controls between 5° and 12° from fixation,[110] have been criticized for design flaws,[111,112] including small group size (five in each group), questionable diagnosis of dyslexia, and no matching of groups by IQ. A similar research study later interpreted the results in terms of lateral masking or a crowding effect and proposed a treatment using a masking device,[113] which was not subjected to a randomized controlled trial. The effect of masking was later investigated in more detail;[114] and a small study with many methodological weaknesses evaluated the effect of various treatments, including reading through coloured masks.[115] It has been suggested that these findings, of peripheral objects interfering with the perception of central objects, might be a manifestation of the M deficit which could interfere with perception during reading.[35] In another study, a sample of children (few selection criteria were given) who received the Geiger and Lettvin treatment improved more than a control group; but this could be attributable to a placebo effect because the control group received no treatment.[116] These authors noted that their data did not fully support the Geiger and Lettvin theory.[116]

A study that attempted to investigate the theories of Geiger and Lettvin and Grosser and Spafford did find evidence of enhanced letter and colour peripheral recognition in dyslexia, although their groups were small and were not matched.[117] Other studies have failed to support Geiger and Lettvin,[43,118] and argued that their results may be accounted for by a failure to control for fixation and attention.[43] Word recognition in different eccentricities may vary in the dyslexic subgroups.[119]

Other research on form visual fields, used to justify *syntonic* treatment, is described in Appendix 7. An early review of the literature suggested that visual fields are normal in dyslexia.[120]

Dark adaptation

An initial claim that people with dyslexia had poor dark adaptation and might benefit from a dietary supplement (DHA)[121] was made with only very limited evidence,[122] and was supported by a poorly controlled and methodologically unsound study of children with Meares-Irlen syndrome (see Chapter 7 and Appendix 7). A study found reduced dark adaptation in the peripheral, but not the central field, in dyslexia,[123] but this study suffered from some methodological limitations. The dark adaptation and DHA hypothesis was disproved by a subsequent detailed controlled investigation, which evaluated both psychophysical and electrophysiological measures.[124]

Coloured filters

Research studies are included in this review if they meet certain basic requirements of scientific rigour, which are outlined on pp. 112–114. Many of the papers in this review, and some that have been excluded, are described in more detail elsewhere.[1,2] Several studies in this area which are sometimes cited are unpublished and are not readily retrievable. These have not been included in the present review (see pp. 112–114), but are summarized in other reviews.[1–4]

Coloured filters and dyslexia: historical background

Blue and green coloured lenses were used over 200 years ago to ease eyestrain when reading.[5] But for the first half of the last century, the prevailing medical view was that tinted lenses may be useful from a cosmetic standpoint but should not be promoted for the relief of photophobia, 'nor promulgated upon the basis of any physiologic advantages such as reducing difficulty associated with fluorescent lighting, improving the acuity, or similar claims'.[6] Another reason for caution in using tints to relieve photophobia was the possibility that the photophobia may result from ametropia.[7] A British Standard specifies the properties of sun glare filters that are considered safe for detecting traffic signals.[8] It has been suggested that some people wear tinted glasses due to neuroses,[9] and some experimental evidence supports this contention.[10]

A case study reported in 1958 demonstrated a benefit from colour in dyslexia.[11] The first detailed description of the symptoms of Meares-Irlen syndrome (MIS) was by Olive Meares[12] and the first detailed treatment outlined by Helen Irlen.[13]

The Irlen system

Supporters of the Irlen system argue that a wide range of coloured filters are required,[14] and that the required tint for a person is both idiosyncratic and highly specific.[15] Irlen called the condition Scotopic Sensitivity Syndrome[13] or Irlen Syndrome.[16] Precedents in the medical literature suggests that the name ought to include the first person to clearly describe the syndrome, so the term Meares-Irlen syndrome (MIS) seems most appropriate.[17] Irlen claims that her filters have an effect on scotopic vision,[16] which may relate to a presumed retinal dysfunction;[18] but scotopic[19] refers to vision at light levels that are too low for reading and I am unaware of any evidence linking MIS with stationary night blindness, a loss of scotopic sensitivity.[20]

The symptoms were first described by Meares,[12] and then by Irlen workers.[18] The Irlen organization used coloured overlays[21] to test for the condition, together with proprietary screening instruments, the IRPS[22] and IDPS.[18,22] An analysis of the Irlen overlays found that they did not systematically sample colour space and lacked a purple;[23] and the Irlen range of overlays was subsequently modified. The IDPS has been criticized because of the lack of published reliability and validity data,[24] and may be unreliable.[25]

Irlen has stated that the condition affects 12% of the general population and 65% of people with dyslexia.[15] She has acknowledged that her treatment is not a cure for dyslexia,[26] which still needs a multi-disciplinary approach.[14] A preliminary study raised the possibility that the condition may be genetically based.[27]

The Irlen methods have been criticized for a lack of openness[28] and excessive cost.[29] Research on the Irlen method, although voluminous, has been criticized for a lack of scientific rigour.[28,30-35]

The science of human colour perception

There are thorough reviews of the physical and chromatic properties of light,[36] of photometry,[36] human colour perception,[36,37] and colour vision defects.[37] Children can perceive shorter wavelength light than can adults, extending their range into the ultra-violet.[38] Colour vision defects do not appear to be correlated with dyslexia,[11] although they may be more prevalent in children with non-specific learning difficulties.[39]

The Intuitive Colorimeter system

The literature contains detailed descriptions of the Wilkins Intuitive Colorimeter,[40] Precision Tints,[41] Intuitive Overlays,[23] and Wilkins Rate of Reading Test.[42] The range of colours available from Precision Tints is over 100,000.[43]

Many authors have noted that coloured filters should not be expected to cure dyslexia: they will only help any visual symptoms resulting from MIS.

A clinical protocol for the use of the Intuitive Overlays and Intuitive Colorimeter as a part of primary eyecare has been outlined, and a clinical audit demonstrates this protocol in practice,[44] although it has not been followed in all studies.[45] Studies have also demonstrated the use of the Intuitive Overlays and Wilkins Rate of Reading Test in screening programmes.[46]

Theoretical predictions suggest that the optimal colour of overlay cannot be used to predict the required colour of tinted lens,[47] and controlled studies confirm this.[48,49]

It is generally recommended that colorimetry is repeated on a yearly basis,[44] although not all authors have recommended this.[50]

Other 'therapies' using colour

The Chromagen system was originally developed to 'treat' colour vision defects, although this is highly controversial.[51] The initial research study into the use of the Chromagen in dyslexia[52] was heavily criticized,[53,54] but a more recent controlled study suggests that the Chromagen lenses may be better than a placebo.[55] The use of a monocular tint or a different tint in each eye is not popular but neither is it unique to the Chromagen system.[16,56]. There are no published evaluations of the Optim-Eyes light.

It has been claimed that syntonic photo-therapy can treat a wide range of conditions.[57] The theory involves the inferior accessory optic tract and relates to the effect of secretions from the pineal gland on the autonomic nervous and endocrine systems.[58,59] The experimental evidence, which mostly consists of small uncontrolled studies, has been criticized.[30]

A recent paper claimed that many children have visual fields that are 'often less than 2.5 degrees' which can be treated with syntonics associated with vision therapy.[60] One study supporting a positive effect of syntonics on visual fields[57] did have a control group but involved small subject numbers, poor group matching, an unmasked design, and lack of random allocation of subjects to groups. In another controlled study[59] supporting syntonics, the groups were not matched for intelligence, there was no masking, and the control group did not receive any treatment, so a placebo effect could account for the results. I have been unable to find any rigorous randomized controlled trials of syntonic therapy,[61] or any controlled trials of the Downing technique.[62]

Summary of 'controlled' trials relating to MIS

Table A7.1 summarizes research studies investigating the efficacy of coloured filter treatments. Only one study,[63] and possibly two others, appear to be fully randomized double-masked placebo controlled trials (RCTs); and these trials have validated the use of individually prescribed coloured filters in dyslexia. Other, less well-controlled, studies have been included in the table to illustrate the limitations of much research in this field and because some of the studies provide clues as to possible mechanisms. Only studies that looked at long-term continued use or that have included some form of control conditions have been included.

Studies which investigated the immediate effect of coloured filters can be criticized because the benefit from filters may only be apparent after reading for 10–15 minutes.[64] Many studies only used a limited range of coloured filters (e.g. overlays) and are therefore unlikely to have investigated the optimal filter for each subject.[65] Several studies used the Neale Analysis of Reading Ability which uses widely spaced lines and might therefore minimize the symptoms of MIS (see pp. 94 and 152) and thus reduce the ability of the study to detect a benefit from filters.

Meares-Irlen syndrome: relationship with other visual factors

The symptoms of MIS are non-specific,[87] and could also indicate refractive, accommodative and binocular dysfunctions, as well as other aetiologies. At least one form of binocular incoordination is characterized by photophobia.[88]

Children who are selected in schools as being likely to benefit from coloured filters often have conventional optometric anomalies that have not been detected by screening or by the statementing process.[89]

Several publications,[30,90–92] including Irlen's patent,[16] have suggested a link between MIS and ocular motor factors. A small research study claimed that most people with MIS in fact need vision therapy,[71] but acknowledged that there was a subgroup who genuinely needed coloured filters.[71] Later research suggested that, although ocular motor factors are a correlate of MIS, they are not usually the cause of the symptoms.[93,94]

It is possible that binocular or accommodative anomalies might be the result of unstable perception from MIS. Nonetheless, current clinical guidelines are to treat conventional factors first.[95]

Why do coloured filters help?

Papers citing evidence for and against several suggested mechanisms for MIS are summarized in Table A7.2 and are reviewed elsewhere.[96,97] Chromatic aberration is unlikely to play a significant role[2] because the spectral sensitivity of the eye minimizes the effect of ocular chromatic aberration.[98] Flicker from fluorescent lights and VDUs has been shown to cause symptoms[99,100] and accommodative[101] and saccadic[102,103] anomalies. Although several studies in Table A7.2 conclude that their data support the hypothesis that a magnocellular (M) deficit accounts for the benefit from coloured filters, none of these studies included a rigorous measure of M function and an M deficit could not directly account for the specific nature of the required tint.[1,2,104]

Table A7.1. Summary of research studies investigating the efficacy of coloured filters for MIS. The sole rigorously double-masked study is in bold italics and two other studies that attempted to be double-masked are in italics. SpLD, specific learning difficulties; WRRT, Wilkins Rate of Reading Test. The numbers in the first column refer to the references listed in the notes to this appendix

Study	System	Type of study	Limitations of study	Results
21	Irlen	Timed visual task with preferred, random, or clear overlay	Not double-masked. No optometric data. Limited colours	Best performance with chosen overlay
66	Irlen	Timed visual search task with Irlen lenses and plano grey and clear lenses and no lenses. Attempted to generate a placebo effect with claims about control conditions	Not fully double-masked. No optometric or psychometric data. No details of lighting or text characteristics	No significant difference between conditions

67	None	Reading and letter identification tasks in peripheral and central field with transparency, polarized lens, no lens	No masking, only 11 dyslexics and 11 controls, colour selected from only six options	No significant effect of coloured filters
68	None	21 disabled readers and 33 controls; investigated reading comprehension on white and grey paper	Only looked at contrast (investigating claims by Meares).[12] Groups not well-defined or matched. Not masked	Experimental group significantly better with grey; no effect in control group
69	Irlen	20 disabled readers who had used tints for 6 months cf reading age and chronological age controls	Groups not matched for IQ or gender. Not placebo control-led or masked. No optometric details	Tinted lens group bene-fited more from teacher instruction
48	None	24 children diag-nosed as dyslexic randomly assigned to two matched groups, one of which wore tints for one term, then controls fitted with tints	Single masked. No optometric details. Tints selected from range of 20. Almost half the original experimental group dropped out. 54% excluded because of asthma. Used Neale analysis of reading	No significant effect of tints on reading, but made anecdotal comment that they feel there is a subgroup who benefit
70	Irlen	92 children classified with IDPS as MIS or not. Randomly assigned to six groups using coloured overlays or clear overlays. Determined reading performance	No masking. Groups not matched for IQ. Improvement in reading was equivocal	Reading of MIS group improved with preferred overlay, not with other overlays and no improve-ment for controls
71	Irlen	30 Irlen candidates randomly given Irlen filters, vision therapy (VT), no treatment	No masking. Small groups (N = 11, 11, 8)	Improvements in filter and VT groups. One subgroup achieved most benefit from filters and VT
72	Irlen	44 Irlen lens users had Neale test and psychometric tests at 3, 6 and 12 months after given tints. Placebo lenses were worn for 3 months	No masking. No optometric data, no control group. Neale test. Likely practice effect with repeated Neale tests	Neale accuracy and comprehension, but not rate, significantly improved. Greater improvement with placebo over a 3 month period than with tints

(contd)

Table A7.1. (contd)

Study	System	Type of study	Limitations of study	Results
73	Irlen	60 children with dyslexia, 38 with MIS diagnosed by IDPS. Compared performance with tinted lenses/plain lenses/random colour/no lenses at: Neale, eye–hand co-ordination, stereo-acuity, personality	Used Neale test. Not masked	No significant difference on tests except personality tests showed MIS group to be more neurotic
74	None	Used spatial task to identify best and worst overlays. Measured contrast sensitivity with best, worst, grey and clear filters in dyslexic group and compared with age-matched controls	Groups not IQ matched. Design not masked. Limited range of colours	Above 1.6 cpd, dyslexics had worse contrast sensitivity with preferred overlay. Controls showed no such effect
75	None	Reading of 18 normal readers and 18 dyslexic assessed with blue, green, red, grey and clear overlays	Limited range of colours, few details. Not masked. Looked at average results, rather than individual improvements with best colour	Overlays improved reading comprehension and speed in 80% of dyslexics. On average, best colours were blue and grey
76	None	24 dyslexic children, reading speed measured with blue, green, red, yellow, grey filters	Limited range of colours, research design unlikely to detect individual differences, spacing of lines of reading test not specified	No significant difference on average and no individual correlation with preferred colour
77	Wilkins	55 patients with variety of conditions including visual discomfort prescribed precision tints with colorimeter	Not controlled, only looked at patient characteristics and long-term use	82% were still using precision tints after 6 months
65	Irlen	29 subjects with MIS, cf 31 controls, fairly well matched	No placebo treatment. Not masked. Neale test	MIS group showed significant improvement in Neale reading rate and comprehension

78	None	Compared 18 attention disordered and 18 controls, matched for age, gender, IQ. Assessed cognitive flexibility and attention shifting skills with different colours	Limited range of colours, no details	Colour does not affect mechanisms underlying impulsivity and behavioural control, but does affect attentional and memory processing
79	None	110 pupils with SpLD who chose overlays; cf 185 pupils who did not have access to overlays	No data on refractive errors. Only four colours. Not masked	Reading of group with overlays improved significantly more than control group
63	*Wilkins*	*36 children with MIS wore tints selected with the Intuitive Colorimeter as optimal or slightly sub-optimal. Each worn for 1 month in random order. True double-masked RCT with optometric and photometric data*	*Trial started with 68 children, but 32 dropped out*	*Significantly fewer symptoms on days when optimal tints were worn. Subjects were shown to be unaware of which tints were optimal*
50	Irlen	Survey of 267 filter users to evaluate long-term (6 years) reported usage	Only 43% responded	94% of respondents reported that tints had been of 'some' or 'large' help
80	None	Compared letter naming accuracy and visual spatial judgements of 18 poor and 18 good readers at various eccentricities with blue, yellow, and no filters, with and without diffusion	Poor subject selection criteria. Assume magnocellular deficit. Not masked	Some results supported hypothesis, others did not
64	Irlen	Subjects choosing an Irlen overlay performed search task after reading for 5, 10 and 15 minutes	Did not specifically control for the placebo effect, but the 5 and 10 minute conditions to some extent acted as controls	Poor readers more likely to choose an overlay. For the last 5 minutes of the 15 minute sessions, subjects faster with overlay than without
42	Wilkins	77 unselected children, 49% choose an overlay, 40% continue to use for 8 weeks. Used WRRT	No optometric data. Not masked	WRRT predicts those who continue to use overlay with sensitivity and specificity of 65%

(contd)

Table A7.1. (contd)

Study	System	Type of study	Limitations of study	Results
46	Wilkins	152 unselected children offered overlays; 53% choose one, 22% (11% of all) still using after 10 months. Study effect on WRRT	No optometric data. Not masked	Choice of overlay colour is more consistent than chance. WRRT predicts those who will continue to use overlay, who read significantly faster (8%) with overlay
81	None	Saccadic function during reading of 27 poor readers compared with 27 controls with clear, grey, blue filters	Not masked. Very limited range of filters	Blue filters significantly improved eye movement parameters
82	Irlen	Matched groups of reading disabled subjects who were positive or negative to Irlen screening tests. Assessed rate of reading with high and low contrast and blue, red and grey conditions on a monitor	No optometric or photometric details. Not double-masked. Limited range of colours and did not look for individual responses	For high contrast text, students with signs of MIS read as fast with red as grey but slower with blue
83	Irlen	113 children with MIS and 35 controls did DEM tracking tasks with optimal or control filter (similar to optimal) or blue tint	No optometric or photometric details, not clear to what degree subjects were masked	(Only) one task supported hypothesis: greatest improvement for optimal tint
55	Chromagen	47 dyslexic children, 9 of whom had a colour vision deficiency had WRRT with Chromagen contact lenses and with control contact lens and with no tint	No details of diagnosis of dyslexia or optometric details. Study attempted to be double-masked, but unclear whether subjects were truly masked	Read significantly faster with Chromagen than with placebo or without, for those who reported distortions
84, 85	Irlen	113 children with MIS placed in four groups: optimal tint, placebo (similar colour to optimal), blue, no tint. Reading with Neale assessed over 18–20 months. Crossover and claimed to be double-masked	No optometric or photometric data. Stated that placebo and optimal tints were very similar, but unclear how well subjects were masked. Groups not closely matched for initial reading age	Reading accuracy and comprehension improved most with optimal tint. No effect on Neale rate of reading or on reading strategies

44	Wilkins	Audit of 323 patients seen in an optometric SpLD clinic, including a telephone survey	Not a controlled study, only about half of the subjects could be reached by telephone	48% were given a conventional optometric intervention, 50% overlays, some both. Of those given overlays, 32% were ultimately prescribed Precision Tints. More than 80% of these were still wearing them regularly after 18 months
49	Wilkins	17 children with MIS tested with Intuitive Overlays and Colorimeter. WRRT with lenses to match preferred overlay v. lenses to match colorimeter result	Limited optometric data	WRRT significantly improved with coloured overlay and with lenses matching the colorimeter setting. Worse with lenses to match overlay
86	Irlen	49 adults with MIS (33 completed) randomly given tinted lenses, or had supply of lenses delayed	Not placebo controlled or masked	Reading rate, accuracy, and comprehension improved significantly once they had received the tints

Table A7.2. Summary of papers citing evidence for and against suggested mechanisms for MIS. The numbers refer to the references listed in the notes to this appendix

Hypothesized mechanism	Supportive papers	Critical papers
Placebo (see Appendix 1) or novelty/attributional/ externalized	63, 66	55, 63, 84, 85
Retinal anomaly	21	105
Magnocellular deficit (see Appendix 6)	22, 75, 106, 107	46, 82, 93, 94, 108
Accommodative dysfunction		93, 94, 109
Binocular incoordination (see Appendix 3)	71, 110	47, 93, 94
Saccadic deficit (see Appendix 3)	110	
Fluorescent lighting	47	
Iconic persistence (see Appendix 6)	111	
Pattern glare	47, 93, 94	

Extensive reviews[96,112–114] describe pattern glare, which can be triggered by text,[115,116] as a neuro-physiological basis for visual discomfort. In addition to causing visual discomfort, pattern glare can slow performance at visual tasks.[114] It is believed to result from cortical hyperexcitability,[112] and can sometimes be treated successfully by monocular occlusion[117,127] (see Chapter 4). The symptoms and some other features of MIS and pattern glare are very similar,[1,2] and pattern glare may be reduced with coloured filters[118] by reducing focal cortical hyperexcitability in colour specific areas of the visual cortex.[96,106] Any link between pattern glare and visual attention[119] remains speculative (Appendix 8), but it has been noted that dyslexic people often focus on irrelevant features on the page,[120] and poor visual selective attention in those with reading difficulties might cause peripheral detail on the page to interact with the perception of text.[121] One study of attention disordered children did find that colour may affect attentional and memory processing.[78]

Pattern glare is a correlate of MIS, headaches[112,122] (especially[122] migraine),[112,123] and photosensitive epilepsy.[124–128] In migraine sufferers, pattern glare can be influenced by colour.[129] A survey[130] and an open and randomized controlled trial[131] have shown that Precision Tinted lenses can help patients whose migraines have a visual trigger. Migraine is often under-diagnosed in children.[132] Individually prescribed tinted lenses have been used as a treatment for photosensitive epilepsy for some time,[133,134] and an open trial has shown a benefit from Precision Tinted lenses in photosensitive epilepsy.[135] It should be noted that although 'reading epilepsy' can occur, this is different from the *photosensitive epilepsy*[136] that may benefit from coloured filters.

Typoscopes have been shown to alleviate pattern glare in epilepsy[137] and two devices have been advocated for use in dyslexia which magnify text and mask adjacent lines of text. One of these, the Dex frame, was not found to help dyslexic children in a small controlled trial,[138] and it was suggested that larger sheets of overlays might be more use.[89] The other, the VTM magnifier,[139] has not been subjected to published RCTs, but research has shown that magnifiers reduce reading speed.[140]

Some studies suggest that reducing the high contrast[74] of text (black on white) may improve performance at visual search,[141,142] and possibly improve reading comprehension[68] and make reading faster and more comfortable.[143] However, a series of studies concluded that 'contrast per se does not appear to be a crucial mechanism' for MIS[46] and a thorough recent study showed that changes in contrast (from 100% to 2%) affected the reading performance of dyslexic and normal readers similarly.[144]

APPENDIX 8
Conclusions

Optometric correlates: which are validated?

As a general rule, treatment is likely to help the visual correlates that cause symptoms[1] and treatment will not take away the need for help from educational professionals.[1] Binocular instability is associated with the M deficit[2] and with Meares-Irlen syndrome, although in a non-causal way (see Appendix 7). It is also noted in Appendix 7 that an M pathway deficit is unlikely to be a direct cause of Meares-Irlen syndrome. There is a need for more research to consider the relationship between different visual factors.[3]

Many of the optometric correlates of dyslexia may also be present in people with non-specific learning difficulties.[4,5] It is therefore not necessary for children to have dyslexia formally diagnosed before having a thorough eye examination.

Linking the visual deficits

Supporters of the Dunlop test now argue that an unstable reference eye ('binocular instability') is caused by the M visual system deficit.[6] Saccadic suppression is frequently discussed, and suppression during vergence eye movements also occurs.[7]

Recent research links a deficit of magnocellular processing in the visual system with a deficit of magnocellular processing in the auditory system,[8] possibly resulting from an adverse immunological influence in utero.[9] The authors of the latter paper argue that the M visual deficit causes binocular and fixation instability and saccadic dysfunction in dyslexia.

Attention: a possible unifying theory

Nearly every task that we do is accomplished through the use of both automatic and control processes.[10] Although attention is involved during automatic processing,[11,12] attention plays a much greater role in control than in automatic processes.[10] With practice, tasks that initially require conscious control may become automatized,[10] and it has been suggested that there may be an automaticity deficit in dyslexia.[13]

Attentional skills can be classified[14] and the nervous pathways involved in visual attention have been reviewed.[15] *Selective attention* is when the person selectively attends to some information source in preference to others.[10] Selective attention can be sub-classified into *focused attention* on one stimulus or *divided attention* between two or more stimuli.[14] There are many ways of investigating selective attention, including visual search. Spatial attention is one type of selective attention,[15] and is sometimes used to describe *visual selective attention* or just *visual attention*, which has been likened to a spotlight highlighting the object of regard at the expense of the rest of the visual field.

Sustained attention is assessed with vigilance tasks which require attention to be directed to one or more sources of information over periods of time that are long (seconds to hours)[16] and generally unbroken. Selective and sustained attention may be influenced by IQ, personality, gender, and cognitive style.[14] A third category of attention, intensity of attention, has been related to the concept of 'paying attention'.[12]

Some authors have argued that sustained and selective attention are largely independent.[14] However, selective attention has at least three components (selectivity, resistance to distraction, and switching or shifting)[14] and resistance to distraction seems likely to be related to sustained attention. Studies have shown that even low level reflexive features of visual attention are influenced by general attentional state (state of arousal).[15]

Given the wide distribution of attentional processes, it is not surprising that children diagnosed as having attentional deficits show considerable diversity in symptoms and aetiology.[17] Many authors differentiate between ADD with hyperactivity (ADDH) and ADD without hyperactivity (ADDnoH)[17] and motor impersistence is significantly more likely to be present in ADDnoH than ADDH.[18] Motor impersistence is a deficit of sustained motor control[19] and people with ADDH have also been found to have abnormalities of sustained attention.[18] But I have been unable to find any studies investigating whether people with ADD exhibit impaired visual attention.[20] Nonetheless, visual attention deficits have been found in dyslexia (see below), which has a high co-morbidity with ADD.[21]

The M system provides the dominant input to visual attention.[22-24] A small study suggests that the 'spotlight' of visual attention may be narrower in dyslexia and the authors speculated that this might be linked to an M deficit and an hypothesized eye movement deficit, which they assumed may be a cause of dyslexia.[25] Further evidence of a deficit of visual attention in dyslexia suggests that there is a specific difficulty in orienting and focusing visual attention.[26] Two studies have used search task data to suggest that reading difficulties might be associated with a weakened spotlight of visual attention and hypothesized that this could be associated with an M pathway visual deficit.[27,28] However, these studies did not measure visual selective attention or M function directly.

If dyslexia is associated with impaired visual attention then this could account for ocular motor dysfunction in dyslexia. Before a saccadic or pursuit eye movement occurs, visual attention needs to be oriented to the target position,[29] and shifts in visual attention may also be an important feature of vergence eye movements.[30] The posterior parietal cortex, which receives most of its input from the M system, plays an important role in the influence of visual attention on saccadic, pursuit, and vergence eye movements[15,31] and may be dysfunctional in dyslexia.[31] It is therefore possible that a deficit of visual attention in dyslexia might cause eye movement dysfunction (see Appendix 3).

An alternative, or complementary, hypothesis linking attentional deficits to eye movement dysfunction in dyslexia is through impaired sustained attention in ADD.[15] Motor impersistence, a feature of ADD, may cause fixation instability as well as unstable eye movements.[32]

Concerning Meares-Irlen syndrome, it has been hypothesized that a weakened spotlight of visual attention could cause some dyslexic people to notice peripheral distortions resulting from pattern glare.[33] An alternative theory is that some dyslexic people manifest an increased sensitivity to the global pattern of text, which may produce greater attention to this percept, so contributing to the induction of unpleasant side effects from the page.[34] A link with colour may be implicated by the finding that the requirement to perform a difficult visual discrimination causes neurons in the visual cortex (V4) to respond more strongly and to be more sharply tuned for colour and orientation.[15]

One author suggested that vision therapy might improve visual attention.[35] Some of the claims that visual fields are reduced in dyslexia (see Chapter 6 and pp. 140–141) or of a decreased perceptual span may also relate to a narrow spotlight of visual attention.

Detecting visual problems in dyslexia

The psychometric profile of a child cannot be used to predict how likely they are to have visual problems: ocular motor problems and deficiencies of phonemic awareness can co-exist.[4,5,36,37] Phonological and decoding deficits are not alternatives to the visual deficits discussed in this book: rather, they interact with one another.[2,8,38] Low level (peripheral) visual deficits do not necessarily cause high level (central) visual dysfunction.[39] It has even been argued that the M deficit precedes and causes phonological language deficiency.[40]

Several studies have noted the inadequacies of the usual[41] visual screening methods that are used in schools and the process of statementing for detecting optometric anomalies.[42] A new method of computerized visual screening improves upon the current methods.[43] The process of obtaining a statement of special educational needs is described in information available from the Department for Education.[44]

A protocol has been suggested for the optometric management of patients with dyslexia.[45] The application of this protocol has been reviewed in a study of over 300 cases.[46]

Footnote: Profound learning disabilities

Profound learning disabilities, such as Down's syndrome, can be associated with several visual anomalies, some of which may have a dramatic effect on quality of life.[47–49]

Useful addresses

The Dyslexia Institute has local Institutes throughout the UK offering private psychological assessments & teaching. They can be contacted at:

Head office:
133 Gresham Road
Staines
TW18 2AJ
Tel: 01784 463851

The British Dyslexia Association provides support for people with dyslexia and can provide advice on how to pursue an educational assessment through the state system. They can be contacted at:

98 London Road
Reading
RG1 5AU
Tel: 0118 966 2677

Cerium Visual Technologies hold a list of optometrists (over 100) throughout the UK who have a Wilkins Intuitive Colorimeter and can prescribe Precision Tinted lenses. They can be contacted at:

Appledore Road
Tenterden
Kent TN30 7DE
Tel: 01580 765211

A list of optometrists who have access to the Chromagen system can be obtained from:

Cantor and Nissel
Market Place
Brackley
Northamptonshire NN13 7DP
Tel: 01280 702002

The Irlen organization has several centres in the UK and can be contacted at:

24 Lofting Road
Barnsbury
London N1 1ET
Tel: 020 7609 7435

I.O.O. Marketing Ltd supply the Wilkins Intuitive Overlays, the Wilkins Rate of Reading Test, the IFS eye exercises, and other equipment for eyecare professionals. They can be contacted at:

56–62 Newington Causeway
London SE1 6DS
Tel: 020 7378 0330

Notes to Appendices

1 Introduction

1 Critchley, M. (1970) *The Dyslexic Child*, Thomas, Springfield, Illinois.

2 Rutter, M. (1978) Prevalence and types of dyslexia. In Benton, A.L. and Pearl, D. *Dyslexia, an appraisal of current knowledge*, pp. 5–28, Oxford University Press, New York.

3 Stanovich, K.E. (1991) The theoretical and practical consequences of discrepancy definitions of dyslexia. In *Dyslexia: Integrating Theory and Practice* (ed M. Snowling and M. Thomson), pp. 125–43, Whurr, London.

4 Rack, J.P. (1995) Steps towards a more explicit definition of dyslexia. *Dyslexia Review* **7**, 11–13.

5 Miles, E. (1995) Can there be a single definition of dyslexia. *Dyslexia* **1**, 37–45.

6 Muter, V. (1995) Predictors of beginning reading: their role in early identification. *Dyslexia Review* **6**, 4–7.

7 Pennington, B.F. and Smith, S.D. (1983) Genetic influences on learning disabilities and speech and language disorders. *Child Development* **54**, 369–87.

8 Duane, D.D. (1991) Neurobiological issues in dyslexia. In *Dyslexia: Integrating Theory and Practice* (eds M. Snowling and M. Thomson), Whurr, London, 21–30.

9 McManus, I.C. (1991) The genetics of dyslexia. In. *Vision and Visual Dysfunction* **Vol. 13**, (ed. J Cronly-Dillon), Macmillan Press, London, pp. 94–112.

10 Rack, J.P. (1995) The biological bases of reading ability: (1) Evidence from behaviour-genetic studies. *Dyslexia Review* , 7–11.

11 Smith, S.D., Kimberling, W.J., Pennington, B.F., Lubs, H.A. (1983) Specific reading disability: Identification of an inherited form through linkage analysis. *Science* **219**, 1345–47.

12 Ingram, C.F., Dettenmaier, L. (1987) LD college students and reading problems. *Academic Therapy* **22**, 513–18.

13 Shaywitz, S.E., Escobar, M.D., Shaywitz, B.A., Fletcher, J.M., Makuch, R. (1992) Evidence that dyslexia may represent the lower tail of a normal distribution of reading ability. *N. Engl. J. Med.* **326**, 145–50.

14 Guerin, D.W., Griffin, J.R., Gottfried, A.W., Christenson, G.N. (1993) Concurrent validity and screening efficiency of the dyslexia screener, *Psychological Assessment* **5**, 369–73.

15 Siegel, L.S. (1989) IQ is irrelevant to the definition of learning disabilities. *J. Learn. Disab.* **22**, 469–78.

16 Stanovich, K.E. (1991) Discrepancy definitions of reading disability: has intelligence led us astray?. *Reading Research Quarterly* **26**, 7–29.

17 Wright, S.F., Groner, R. (1993) Dyslexia: issues of definition and subtyping. In. *Facets of Dyslexia and its Remediation* , S.F. Wright and R. Groner (Eds.), North-Holland, Amsterdam, pp. 437–53.

18 Anon (1995) Why call them "dyslexic". *Dyslexia 2000* , 5.

19 Riddoch, J. (1990) Neglect and the peripheral dyslexias. *Cognitive Neuropsychology* **7**, 369–389.

20 Keys, M.P., Silver, L.B. (1990) Learning disabilities and vision problems: are they related?. *Pediatrician* **17**, 194–201.

21 Shaywitz, B.A., Shaywitz, S.E. (1991) Comorbidity: a critical issue in attention deficit disorder. *J. Child Neurol. (supp.)* **6**, S14–S22.

22 Voeller, K.K.S. (1991) Clinical management of attention deficit hyperactivity disorder. *J. Child Neurol. (supp.)* **6**, S51–S67.

23 American Psychiatric Association (1987) Diagnostic and Stastical Manual of Mental Disorders (DSM-III-R). *3rd ed., revised,* American Psychiatric Association, Washington DC, pp. 50–3, 94–5.

24 Epstein, M.A., Shaywitz, S.E., Shaywitz, B.A., and Woolston, J.L. (1991) The boundaries of attention deficit disorder. *J. Learn. Disab.* **24**, 78–86.

25 Cohen, M., Becker, M.G., Campbell, R. (1990) Relationships among four methods of assessment of children with attention deficit-hyperactivity disorder. *J. School Psychol.* **28**, 189–202.

26 Heilman, K.M., Voeller, K.K.S., Nadeau, S.E. (1991) A possible pathophysiologic substrate of attention deficit hyperactivity disorder. *J. Child Neurol. (suppl.)* **6**, S74–S9.

27 Swanson, J.M., Posner, M., Potkin, S., Bonforte, S., Youpa, D., Fiore, C., Cantwell, D., Crinella, F. (1991) Activating tasks for the study of visual-spatial attention in ADHD children: a cognitive anatomic approach. *J. Child Neurol. (suppl.)* **6**, S117–S125.

28 Colby, C.L. (1991) The neuroanatomy and neurophysiology of attention. *J. Child Neurol. (suppl.)* **6**, S88–S116.

29 Hynd, G.W., Lorys, A.R., Semrud-Clikeman, M., Nieves, N., Huettner, M.I.S., Lahey, B.B. (1991) Attention deficit disorder without hyperactivity: a distinct behavioral and neurocognitive syndrome. *J. Child Neurol. (supp.)* **6**, S37–S43.

30 Lahey, B.B., Carlson, C.L. (1991) Validity of the diagnostic category of attention deficit disorder without hyperactivity: a review of the literature. *J. Learn. Disab.* **24**, 110–20.

31 Cantwell, D.P., Baker, L. (1991) Association between attention defecit-hyperactivity disorder and learning disorders. *J. Learn. Disab.* **24**, 88–95.

32 Dykman, R.A. and Ackerman, P.T. (1991) Attention deficit disorder and specific reading disability: separate but often overlapping disorders. *J. Learn. Disab.* **24**, 96–103.

33 Richards, I. (1994) ADHD, ADD and dyslexia.. *Therapeutic Care and Education* **3**, 145–58.

34 Weinberg, W.A., Emslie, G.J. (1991) Attention deficit hyperactivity disorder: the differential diagnosis. *J. Child Neurol. (supp.)* **6**, S23–S36.

35 Parasuraman, R. (1984) Sustained attention in detection and discrimination. In. *Varieties of Attention* (eds. R. Parasuraman and D.R. Davies), Academic Press, London, 243–271.

36 Taylor, E. (1994) Hyperactivity as a special educational need. *Therapeutic Care and Education* **3**, 131–44.

37 Spreen, O., Haaf, R.G. (1986) Empirically derived learning disability sub-types: a replication attempt and longitudinal patterns over 15 years. *J. Learn. Disab.* **19**, 170–79.

38 Macdonald Critchley (1986) Butterworths Medical Dictionary, *2nd edition* Butterworths, 148.

39 Chu, S. (1997) Dyspraxia. *Dyslexia Review* **8**, 24–7.

40 Orton, S.T. (1943) Visual functions in strephosymbolia. *AMA Archives of Ophthalmology* **30**, 707–17.

41 Naidoo, S. (1972) *Specific Dyslexia: The Research Report of the ICAA Word Blind Centre for Dyslexic Children*, Pitman, London.

42 Vellutino, F.R. (1977) Alternative conceptualizations of dyslexia: evidence in support of a verbal-deficit hypothesis. *Harvard Educational Review* **47**, 334–54.

43 Chasty, H.T. (1979) Functional asymmetry of the brain in normal children and dyslexics. *Dys Rev.* **2**, 9–12.

44 Ellis, N.C. and Miles, T.R. (1978) Visual information processing in dyslexic children. *Dyslexia Review* **1**, 10–12.

45 Singleton, C.H. (1988) The early diagnosis of developmental dyslexia. *Support for Learning* **3**, 108–21.

46 Bradley, L. and Bryant, P.E. (1983) Categorizing sounds and learning to read – a causal connection. Nature (London) **301**, 419–20.

47 Geschwind, N. and Galaburda, A.M. (1985) Cerebral lateralization biological mechanisms, associations, and pathology: I a hypothesis and a program for research. *Arch. Neurol.* **42**, 429–57.

48 Galaburda, A.M. (1988) The Pathogenesis of Childhood Dyslexia. In *Language, Communication, and the Brain (ed. F. Plum)* **Raven Press**, 129–37.

49 Rutter, M. and Yule, W. (1975) The concept of specific reading retardation. *J. Child Psychol. Psychiat.* **16**, 181–97.

50 Vellutino, F.R. (1987) Dyslexia. *Scientific American* **256**, 20–7.

51 Shaywitz, S.E. (1996) Dyslexia. *Scientific American* **November**, 78–84.

52 Shepherd, E.M. (1956) Reading ability of 809 average school children (the effect of reversal on their performance). *Am. J. Ophthalmol.* **41**, 1029–39.

53 Singleton, C.H. (1987) Dyslexia and cognitive models of reading. *Support for Learning*, **2**, 47–55.

54 Johnson, D.J. and Myklebust, H.R. (1967) Disorders of reading. In *Learning Disabilities: Educational Principles and Practices*, pp. 147–73, Grune and Stratton, New York.

55 Jordan, D.R. (1972) *Dyslexia in the classroom*. Merrill, Columbus.

56 Christenson, G.N., Griffin, J.R., and Wesson, M.D. (1990) Optometry's role in reading disabilities: resolving the controversy. *J. Am. Optom. Assoc.* **61**, 363–72.

57 Boder, E. (1971) Developmental dyslexia: prevailing diagnostic concepts and a new diagnostic approach. In *Progress in Learning Disabilities* (ed. H.R. Myklebust), pp. 293–21, Grune and Stratton, New York.

58 Flynn, J.M., Boder, E. (1991) Clinical and electrophysiological correlates of dysphonetic and dyseidectic dyslexia. In. *Vision and Visual Dysfunction* **Vol. 13**, (ed. J Cronly-Dillon), Macmillan Press, London, pp. 121–31.

59 Flynn, J.M. and Deering, W.M. (1989) Topographic brain mapping and evaluation of dyslexic children. *Psychiatry Research* **29**, 407–8.

60 Duffy, F.H., Dencla, M.B., McAnulty, G.B., Holmes, J.A. (1988) Neurophysiological studies in dyslexia. In. *Language, Communication, and the Brain* , (Ed. F. Plum), Raven Press, New York, pp. 149–70.

61 Hicks, C., Spurgeon, P. (1982) Two factor analytic studies of dyslexic sub-types. *Br. J. Educ. Psychol.* **52**, 289–300.

62 Brown, G.D.A. (1988) Cognitive analysis of dyslexia. *Perception* **17**, 695–8.

63 Nicolson, R., Fawcett, A.J. (1995) Dyslexia is more than a phonological disability. *Dyslexia* **1**, 19–36.

64 Solan, H.A. (1993) Dyslexia and learning disabilities: an overview. *Optom. Vis. Sci.* **70**, 343–7.

65 Richardson, P. (1995) Placebos: their effectiveness and modes of action. Chapter 3 in:. *Health Psychology* , Broome, A. (Ed.), London, Croom Helm, pp. 34–56.

66 Ernst, E., Sewing, K.Fr., Joyce, C.R.B. (1995) Letters: Placebos in medicine. *Lancet* **345**, 65–6.

67 Griffin, J.R., Christenson, G.N., Wesson, M.D., Erickson, G.B. (1997) . *Optometric Management of Reading Dysfunction*, Butterworth-Heinemann, Boston.

68 Robinson, H.M. and Huelsman, C.B. (1953) Visual efficiency and progress in learning to read. In Robinson, H.M. (Ed.) *Clinical studies in reading II*. Supplementary educational monograms number 77, pp 31–63, University of Chicago Press, Chicago.

69 Hartlage, L.C. (1976) Vision deficits and reading impairment. In *Basic Visual Processes and Learning Disability* (ed. G. Leisman), Charles C Thomas, Illinois, pp. 151–62.

70 Pierce, J.R. (1977) Vision therapy and academic achievement: part 1. *Review of Optometry* June 1977, 48–63.

71 Peli, E., Garcia-Perez, M.A. (1997) Contrast sensitivity in dyslexia: deficit or artifact?. *Optom. Vis. Sci.* **74**, 986–90.

72 Elterman, R.D., Abel, L.A., Daroff, R.B., Dell'Osso, R.F., and Bornstein, J.L. (1980) Eye movement patterns in dyslexic children. *J. Learn. Disab.* **13**, 16–21.

73 O'Grady, J. (1984) The relationship between vision and educational performance; a study of year 2 children in Tasmania. *Austral. J. Optom.* **67**, 126–40.

74 Helveston, E.M., Weber, J.C., Miller, K., et al. (1985) Visual function and academic performance. *Am. J. Ophthalmol.* **99**, 346–55.

75 Park, G.E. and Burri, C. (1943) The effect of eye abnormalities on reading difficulty. *J. Educ. Psychol.* **34**, 420–30.

76 Evans, B.J.W. (1991) *Ophthalmic factors in dyslexia*. PhD Thesis, Aston University, Birmingham, UK.

77 http://igm.nlm.nih.gov/

78 available from SilverPlatter Information Ltd., 0208 585 6400.

79 Seymour, P.H.K., Evans, H.M. (c. 1994) The visual (Orthographic) processor and developmental dyslexia. Chapter 16 in. , 347–76.

80 Goulandris, N., McIntyre, A., Snowling, M., Bethel, J., Lee, J.P. (1998) A comparison of dyslexic and normal readers using orthoptic assessment procedures. *Dyslexia* **4**, 30–48.

81 Evans, B.J.W., Drasdo, N., Richards I.L. (1994) Investigation of accommodative and binocular function in dyslexia. *Ophthal. Physiol. Opt.* **14**, 5–19.

82 Eden, G.F., VanMeter, J.W., Rumsey, J.M., Maisog, J.M., Woods, R.P., Zeffiro, T.A. (1996) Abnormal processing of visual motion in dyslexia revealed by functional brain imaging. *Nature* **382**, 66–9.

83 Stein, J.F., Richardson, A.J., Fowler, M.S. (2000) Monocular occlusion can improve binocular control and reading in dyslexics. *Brain* **123**, 164–70.

84 Baraas, R.C., Demberg, A. (1999) Clinical research note: The prevalence of optometric anomalies and symptoms in children receiving special tuition. *Ophthal. Physiol. Opt.* **19**, 68–73.

85 Wright, J. (1999) Visual complaints from healthy children. *Survey Ophthalmology* **44**, 113–21.

2 Ocular health and refractive errors

1 Evans, B.J.W. (1991) *Ophthalmic factors in dyslexia*. PhD Thesis, Aston University, Birmingham, UK.

2 Suchoff, I.B. (1981) Research on the relationship between reading and vision – what does it mean?. *J. Learn. Disab.* **14**, 573–6.

3 Evans, B.J.W. and Drasdo, N. (1990) Review of ophthalmic factors in dyslexia. *Ophthalmic Physiol. Opt.* **10**, 123–32.

4 Evans, B.J.W., Drasdo, N., Richards, I.L. (1994) Refractive and sensory visual correlates of dyslexia. *Vision Research*. **34** (14), 1913–26.

5 Ygge, J., Lennerstrand, G., Axelsson, I., Rydberg, A. (1993) Visual functions in a Swedish population of dyslexic and normally reading children. *Acta Ophthalmologica* **71**, 1–9.

6 Evans, B.J.W., Drasdo, N., Richards, I.L. (1994) Refractive and sensory visual correlates of dyslexia. *Vision Research* **34**, 1913–26.

7 Cummings, R.W., Whittager, S.G., Watson, G.P., and Budd, J.M. (1985) Scanning characters and reading with a central scotoma. *Am. J. Optom. Phys. Opt.* **62**, 833–43.

8 Bailey, I.L., Bullimore, M.A., Hall, A., and Orel-Bixler, D.A. (1989) Reading characteristics in age-related maculopathy. *Invest. Ophthal. Vis. Sci.* **30** (suppl.), 400.

9 Kinsbourne, M. and Warrington, E.M. (1962) A variety of reading disability associated with right hemisphere lesions. *J. Neurol. Neurosurg. Psychiat.* **25**, 339–44.

10 Bodis-Wollner, I. (1972) Visual acuity and contrast sensitivity in patients with cerebral lesions. *Science* **175**, 769–71.

11 Ciuffreda, K.J., Kenyon, R.V., and Stark, L. (1985) Eye movements during reading : two further case reports. *Am. J. Optom. Phys. Opt.* **62**, 844–52.

12 Corley, G., Pring, L. (1993) Reading strategies in partially sighted children. *Internat. J. Rehab. Res.* **16**, 209–20.

13 Lovie-Kitchin, J., Oliver, N.J., Bruce, A., Leighton, M.S., Leighton, W.K. (1994) The effect of print size on reading rate for adults and children. *Clin. Expt. Optom.* **77**, 2–7.

14 Latvala, M-L., Korhonen, T.T., Penttinen, M., Laippala, P. (1994) Ophthalmic findings in dyslexic schoolchildren. *Br. J. Ophthalmol.* **78**, 339–43.

15 Shearer, R. (1966) Eye findings in children with reading difficulties. *J. Ped. Ophthalmol. Strabismus* **3**, 47–53.

16 Robinson, H. M. (1969) Visual maladjustments as a cause of reading disability. In *Why Pupils Fail in Reading*, pp. 7–33, University of Chicago Press, Chicago.

17 Eames, T.H. (1959) Visual handicaps to reading. *Boston University J. Educat.* **141**, 1–36.

18 Norn, M.S., Rindziunski, E., and Skydsgaard, H. (1969) Ophthalmologic and orthoptic examination of dyslexics. *Acta Ophthal.* **47**, 147–60.

19 Drasdo, N. (1972) The ophthalmic correlates of reading disability. In *Transactions of the international ophthalmic optics congress 1970*, pp 97–106, British Optical Association, London.

20 Bedwell, C.H., Grant, R., and McKeown, J.R. (1980) Visual and ocular control anomalies in relation to reading difficulty. *Brit. J. Educat. Psychol.* **50**, 61–70.

21 Aasved, H. (1987) Ophthalmological status of schoolchildren with dyslexia. *Eye* **1**, 61–8.

22 Grisham, J.D. and Simons, H.D. (1986) Refractive error and the reading process: a literature analysis. *J. Am. Optom. Assoc.* **57**, 44–55.

23 Johnson, R., Zaba, J. (1994) Vision and illiteracy: the link. *J. Behavioral Optometry* **5**, 41–3.

24 Borish, I.M. (1975) *Clinical Refraction*, The Professional Press Inc., Chicago.

25 Dickinson, C.M. and Rabbitt, P.M.A. (1991) Simulated visual impairment – effects on text comprehension and reading speed. *Clin. Vis. Sci.* **6**, 301–8.

26 Hirsch, M.J. (1959) The relationship between refractive state of the eye and intelligence test scores. *Am. J. Optom. Arch. Am. Acad. Optom.* **36**, 12–21.

27 Young, F.A. (1963) Reading, measures of intelligence and refractive errors. *Am. J. Optom. & Arch. Am. Acad. Optom.* **40**, 257–64.

28 Grosvenor, T. (1970) Refractive state, intelligence test scores, and academic ability. *Am. J. Optom. & Arch. Am. Acad. Optom.* **47**, 355–61.

29 Rosner, J., Gruber, J. (1985) Differences in the perceptual skills development of young myopes and hyperopes. *Am. J. Optom. Vis. Sci.* **62**, 501–4.

30 Rosner, J., Rosner, J. (1986) Some observations of the relationship between the visual perceptual skills development of young hyperopes and age of first lens correction.. *Clin. Exp. Optom.* **69**, 166–8.

31 Witty, P.A. and Kopel, D. (1936) Studies of eye muscle imbalance and poor fusion in reading disability: and evaluation. *J. Educ. Psychol.* **27**, 663–71.

32 Critchley, M. (1964) *Developmental dyslexia,* Whitefriars, London.

33 Pierce, J.R. (1977) Vision therapy and academic achievement: part 1. *Review of Optometry* June 1977, 48–63.

34 Adler, P.M. and Grant, R (1988) Literacy skills and visual anomalies. *Optometry today* 2nd Jan.

35 Taylor, E.A. (1937) Physiological defects and eye discomfort among schoolchildren. In *Controlled Reading: a correlation of diagnostic, teaching, and corrective techniques,* University of Chicago Press, Illinois, pp. 161–201.

36 Simons, H.D., Gassler, P.A. (1988) Vision anomalies and reading skill: a meta-analysis of the literature. *Am. J. Optom. Physiol. Opt.* **65**, 893–904.

37 Eames, T.H. (1948) Comparison of eye conditions among 1,000 reading failures, 500 ophthalmic patients, and 150 unselected children. *Am. J. Ophthal.* **31**, 713–6.

38 Fendrick, P. (1935) *Visual characteristics of poor readers.* Bureau of publications, Teachers college, Columbia University, New York City, New York.

39 Dunlop, P. (1979) Orthoptic management of learning disbility. *Brit. Orth. J.* **36**, 25–35.

40 Grosvenor, T. (1977) Are visual anomalies related to reading ability? *J. Am. Optom. Assoc.* **48**, 510–7.

3 Ocular motor factors

1 Evans, B.J.W. (1991) *Ophthalmic factors in dyslexia.* PhD Thesis, Aston University, Birmingham, UK.

2 Suchoff, I.B. (1981) Research on the relationship between reading and vision – what does it mean?. *J. Learn. Disab.* **14**, 573–6.

3 Reading, R. (1988) Near point testing. In *Optometry,* (eds. K. Edwards and R. Llewellyn), Butterworths, London, pp. 150–60.

4 Evans, B.J.W. (1997) *Pickwell's Binocular Vision Anomalies: Investigation and Treatment.* Third edition, Butterworth-Heinemann, Oxford.

5 Rouse, M.W. (1987) Management of binocular anomalies: efficacy of vision therapy in the treatment of accommodative deficiencies. *Am. J. Optom. Physiol. Opt.* **64**, 415–20.

6 Evans, B.J.W., Drasdo, N. (1990) Review of ophthalmic factors in dyslexia. *Ophthalmic Physiol. Opt.* **10**, 123–32.

7 Kedzia, B., Pieczyrak, D., Tondel, G., Maples, W.C. (1999) Factors affecting the clinical testing of accommodative facility. *Ophthal. Physiol. Opt.* **19**, 12–21.

8 Evans, B.J.W., Drasdo, N., Richards I.L. (1994) Investigation of accommodative and binocular function in dyslexia. *Ophthal. Physiol. Opt.* **14**, 5–19.

9 Evans, B.J.W., Drasdo, N., and Richards I.L. (1992) Optometric correlates of reading disability. *Clinical and Experimental Optometry 75 (5),* 192–200 **95**, 192–200.

10 Hall, P.S., Wick, B.C. (1991) The relationship between ocular functions and reading achievement. *J. Ped. Ophthalt Strab.* **28**, 17–19.

11 Ygge, J., Lennerstrand, G., Axelsson, I., Rydberg, A., Wijecoon, S., Pettersson, B.M. (1993) Visual functions and oculomotor functions in a Swedish population of 9-year-old dyslexics and normal readers. A preliminary report. *Acta Ophthalmol.* **71**, 10–21.

12 Goulandris, N., McIntyre, A., Snowling, M., Bethel, J., Lee, J.P. (1998) A comparison of dyslexic and normal readers using orthoptic assessment procedures. *Dyslexia* **4**, 30–48.

13 Bettman, J.W., Stern, E.L., Whitsell, W.J., and Gofman, H.F. (1967) Cerebral dominance in developmental dyslexia. *Arch. Ophthal.* **78**, 722–9.

14 Poynter, H., Schor, C., Haynes, H., and Hirsch, J. (1982) Oculomotor functions in reading disability. *Am. J. Optom. Physiol. Opt.* **59**, 116–27.

15 Buzzelli, A.R. (1991) Stereopsis, accommodative and vergence facility: do they relate to dyslexia?. *Optom. Vis. Sci.* **68**, 842–846.

16 Kulp, M.T., Schmidt, P.P. (1996) Visual predictors of reading performance in kindergarten and first grade children. *Optom. Vis. Sci.* **73**, 255–62.

17 Sucher, D.F., Stewart, J. (1993) Vertical fixation disparity in learning disabled. *Optom. Vis. Sci.* **70**, 1038–43.

18 Stidwill, D. (1997) Clinical survey: epidemiology of strabismus. *Ophthal. Physiol. Opt.* **17**, 536–539.

19 Stein, J.F., Richardson, A.J., Fowler, M.S. (2000) Monocular occlusion can improve binocular control and reading in dyslexics. *Brain* **123**, 164–70.

20 Vernon, M.D. (1957) *Backwardness in Reading*. Cambridge University Press, London.

21 Shearer, R. (1966) Eye findings in children with reading difficulties. *J. Ped. Ophthalmol. Strabismus* **3**, 47–53.

22 Robinson, H. M. (1969) Visual maladjustments as a cause of reading disability. In *Why Pupils Fail in Reading*, pp. 7–33, University of Chicago Press, Chicago.

23 Drasdo, N. (1972) The ophthalmic correlates of reading disability. In *Transactions of the international ophthalmic optics congress 1970*, pp 97–106, British Optical Association, London.

24 Pierce, J.R. (1977) Vision therapy and academic achievement: part 1. *Review of Optometry* June 1977, 48–63.

25 Barnard, N.A.S. (1983) Screening by optometrists. *Ophthal. Physiol. Opt.* **3**, 365–8.

26 Simons, H.D. and Grisham, J.D. (1987) Binocular anomalies and reading problems. *J. Am. Optom. Assoc.* **58**, 578–87.

27 Simons, H.D., Gassler, P.A. (1988) Vision anomalies and reading skill: a meta-analysis of the literature. *Am. J. Optom. Physiol. Opt.* **65**, 893–904.

28 Witty, P.A. and Kopel, D. (1936) Studies of eye muscle imbalance and poor fusion in reading disability: and evaluation. *J. Educ. Psychol.* **27**, 663–71.

29 Critchley, M. (1964) *Developmental dyslexia*, Whitefriars, London.

30 Lennerstrand, G., Ygge, J. (1992) Dyslexia: ophthalmological correlates. *Acta Ophthalmol. (Copenh.)* **70**, 3–13.

31 Cassin, B. (1975) Strabismus and learning disabilities. *American Orthoptic Journal* **25**, 38–45.

32 Eames, T.H. (1959) Visual handicaps to reading. *Boston University J. Educat.* **141**, 1–36

33 Dunlap, E.A. (1965) Role of strabismus in reading problems. *Transact. Pennsylvania Acad. Ophthal. Otolaryngology* **18**, 9–15.

34 Norn, M.S., Rindziunski, E., and Skydsgaard, H. (1969) Ophthalmologic and orthoptic examination of dyslexics. *Acta Ophthal.* **47**, 147–60.

35 Atzmon, D., Nemet, P., Ishay, A., Karni, E. (1993) A randomized prospective masked and matched comparative study of orthoptic treatment versus conventional reading tutoring treatment for reading disabilities in 62 children. *Binocular Vision and Eye Muscle Surgery Qtrly.* **8**, 91–106.

36 Trachtman, J.N. (1976) The cross-eyed Maya: an interesting note. *Am. J. Optom. Physiol. Opt.* **53**, 807–8.

37 Fendrick, P. (1935) *Visual characteristics of poor readers.* Bureau of publications, Teachers college, Columbia University, New York City, New York.

38 Park, G.E. and Burri, C. (1943) The effect of eye abnormalities on reading difficulty. *J. Educ. Psychol.* **34**, 420–30.

39 Moseley, D. and Lane, D. (1986) Children's binocular efficiency in relation to competence in reading. *Educational Child Psychology* **3**, 90–102.

40 Taylor, E.A. (1937) Physiological defects and eye discomfort among schoolchildren. In *Controlled Reading: a correlation of diagnostic, teaching, and corrective techniques,* University of Chicago Press, Illinois, pp. 161–201.

41 Latvala, M-L., Korhonen, T.T., Penttinen, M., Laippala, P. (1994) Ophthalmic findings in dyslexic schoolchildren. *Br. J. Ophthalmol.* **78**, 339–43.

42 Bedwell, C.H., Grant, R., and McKeown, J.R. (1980) Visual and ocular control anomalies in relation to reading difficulty. *Brit. J. Educat. Psychol.* **50**, 61–70.

43 Mohindra, I. and Schieman, M.M. (1976) Fixation disparity and learning disability. *Brit. J. Physiol. Opt.* **30**, 128–31.

44 Silbiger, F. and Woolf, D. (1968) Fixation disparity and reading achievement at college level. *Am. J. Optom. & Arch. Am. Acad. Optom.* **45**, 734–42.

45 Eden, G.F., Stein, J.F., Wood, M.H., Wood, F.B. (1995) Verbal and visual problems in reading disability. *J. Learning Disabilities* **28**, 272–90.

46 Eden, G.F., Stein, J.F., Wood, H.M., Wood, F.B. (1994) Differences in eye movements and reading problems in dyslexic and normal children. *Vision Res.* **34**, 1345–58.

47 Evans, B.J.W. (2000) Decompensated exophoria at near, convergence insufficiency and binocular instability. *Optician* **219**, 20–8.

48 Létourneau, J.E., Lapierre, N., and Lamont, A. (1979) The relationship between convergence insufficiency and school achievement. *Am. J. Optom. & Physiol. Optics* **56**, 18–22.

49 Evans, B.J.W., Drasdo, N., Richards, I.L. (1994) Refractive and sensory visual correlates of dyslexia. *Vision Research* **34**, 1913–26.

50 Felmingham, K.L., Jakobson, L.S. (1995) Visual and visuomotor performance in dyslexic children. *Exp. Brain Research* **106**, 467–74.

51 Romano, P.E. (1999) Aniseikonia. *Binocular Vision & Strabismus Quarterly* **14** (3), 173–6.

52 Evans, B.J.W. (2000) An open trial of the Institute Free-space Stereogram (IFS) exercises. *British Journal of Optometry & Dispensing* **8**, 5–14.

53 Evans, B.J.W., Patel, R., Wilkins, A.J., Lightstone, A., Eperjesi, F., Speedwell, L., Duffy, J. (1999) A review of the management of 323 consecutive patients seen in a specific learning difficulties clinic. *Ophthal. Physiol. Opt.* **19**, 454–466.

54 Bedwell, C.H. and Grant, R. (1985) Improvement of reading age with treatment of anomalies of ocular control. *Remedial Education* **20**, 118–22.

55 Vellutino, F.R. (1987) Dyslexia. *Scientific American* **256**, 20–7.

56 Worrall, R.S., Nevyas, J. (1993) The eye exorcisors. In. *The Health Robbers: A Close Look at Quackery in America* , (Eds. S. Barrett and W.T. Jarvis, pp. 347–54.

57 Taylor, E.A. (1976) Ocular-motor processes and the act of reading. Chapter 9 in. *Basic Visual Processes and Learning Disability* , Thomas, Illinois, pp. 163–216.

58 Gruber, E. (1962) Reading ability, binocular co-ordination, and the ophthalmograph. *Arch. Ophth.* **67**, 280–288.

59 Holland, K.C. (1987) The treatment of dynamic visual problems. *The Optician* **24 Jul**, 13–17.

60 Moores, E., Frisby, J.P., Buckley, D., Reynolds, E., Fawcett, A. (1998) Vergence control across saccades in dyslexic adults. *Ophthal. Physiol. Opt.* **18**, 452–62.

61 Richman, J.E. (1999) The influence of visual attention and automaticity on the diagnosis and treatment of clinical oculomotor, accommodative, and vergence dysfunctions. *J. Optom. Vision Development* **30**, 132–41.

62 Evans, B.J.W., Drasdo, N., Richards, I.L. (1996) Dyslexia: the link with visual deficits. *Ophthal. Physiol. Opt.* **16**, 3–10.

63 Aasved, H. (1987) Ophthalmological status of schoolchildren with dyslexia. *Eye* **1**, 61–8.

64 Cagnolati, W. (1991) Qualification and quantification of binocular disorders with Zeiss Polatest. *European Society of Optometry Communications* **134**, 9–12.

65 Pestalozzi, D. (1986) Treatment of legasthenics with heterophoria and fixation disparity by fully prismatic correciton. *Klin. Monatsbl. Augenheilkd.* **188**, 471–3.

66 Lang, J. (1992) The treatment of legasthenia with occlusion of prisms. *Klin. Monatsbl. Augenheilkd.* **200**, 596–8.

67 Lang, J. (1994) The weak points of prismatic correction with the Polatest. *Klin. Monatsbl. Augenheilkd.* **204**, 378–80.

68 Fletcher, R. (1993) Piles and piles of prisms? *Optom. Today* **May 3rd**, 12–13.

69 Young, L.R. and Sheena, D. (1975) Survey of eye movement recording methods. *Behav. Res. Meth. Instrum.* **7**, 397–429.

70 Tinker, M.A. (1946) The study of eye movements in reading. *Psychol. Bulletin* **43**, 93–120.

71 Robinson, D.A. (1981) Control of eye movements. In *Handbook of Physiology. Section 1: The Nervous System. Volume II, Part 2*, (eds. J.M. Brookhart and V.B. Mountcastle), American Psychological Society, Maryland, pp.1275–320.

72 Pavlidis, G.Th. (1981) Sequencing eye movements and the early objective diagnosis of dyslexia. In *Dyslexia research and it's application to education* (eds. G.Th. Pavlidis and T.R. Miles), John Wiley and Sons, Chichester, pp 98–165.

73 Stark, L.W., Giveen, S.C., Terdiman, J.F. (1991) Specific dyslexia and eye movements. In. *Vision and Visual Dysfunction* **13**, (ed. J Cronly-Dillon), Macmillan, London, pp. 203–32.

74 Morris, R.K., Rayner, K. (1991) Eye movements in skilled reading: implications for developmental dyslexia. In. *Vision and Visual Dysfunction* **13**, (ed. J Cronly-Dillon), Macmillan, London, pp. 233–42.

75 McConkie, G.W., Zola, D., Grimes, J., Kerr, P.W., Bryant, N.R., Wolff, P.M. (1991) Children's eye movements during reading. In. *Vision and Visual Dysfunction* **Vol. 13**, (ed. J Cronly-Dillon), Macmillan Press, London, pp. 251–62.

76 Gilbert, L.C. (1953) Functional motor efficiency of the eyes and it's relation to reading. *Univ. Calif. Pub. Educ.* **11**, 159–232.

77 Tinker, M.A. (1936) Eye movements in reading. *J. Educat. Research* **30**, 241–77.

78 Underwood, G., Bloomfield, R., and Clews, S. (1988) Information influences the pattern of eye fixation during sentence comprehension. *Percep.* **17**, 267–78.

79 Heller, D., Radach, R. (1999) Eye movements in reading: are two eyes better than one? In. *Current Oculomotor Research: Physiological and Psychological Aspects* , (Eds. W. Becker, H. Deubel, T. Mergner), Plenum, New York.

80 Haines, J.D. (1980) Eye movement recording using optoelectronic devices. In *Techniques in Psychophysiology*, (eds. I. Martin and P. Venables), Wiley, Chichester, pp. 309–27.

81 Evans, B.J.W. (1993) Dyslexia: eye movements, controversial optometric therapies, and the transient visual system. *Optometry Today.* **33** (14), 17–21.

82 Juola, J.F., Haugh, D., Trast, S., Ferraro, F.R., Liebhaber, M. (1987) Reading with and without eye movements. In. *Eye Movements: From Physiology to Cognition* , (eds. J.K. O'Regan and A. Levy-Schoen), Elsevier, Holland, pp. 499–508.

83 Stark, L.W., Krischer, C.C. (1989) Reading with and without eye movements. In. *Brain and Reading* , (Eds. C. von Euler, I. Lundberg, and G. Lennerstrand), Stockton Press, New York, pp. 345–55.

84 Solan, H.A., Ficarra, A., Brannan, J.R., Rucker, F. (1998) Eye movement efficiency in normal and reading disabled elementary school children: effects of varying luminance and wavelength. *J. Am. Optom. Assoc.* **69**, 455–64.

85 Goldberg, H.K. and Arnott, W. (1970) Ocular motility in learning disabilities. *J. Learn. Disab.* **3**, 40–2.

86 Pavlidis, G.Th. (1985) Eye movement differences between dyslexic, normal, and retarded readers while sequentially fixating digits. *Am. J. Optom. Physiol. Opt.* **62**, 820–32.

87 Biscaldi, M., Fischer, B., Aiple, F. (1994) Saccadic eye movements of dyslexic and normal reading children. *Perception* **23**, 45–64.

88 Biscaldi, M., Fischer, B., Hartnegg, K. (2000) Voluntary saccadic control in dyslexia. *Perception* **29**, 509–21.

89 Griffin, D.C., Walton, H.N., and Ives, V. (1974) Saccades as related to reading disorders. *J. Learn. Disab.* **7**, 52–8.

90 Eskenazi, B. and Diamond, S.P. (1983) Visual exploration of non-verbal material by dyslexic children. *Cortex* **19**, 353–70.

91 Stanley, G., Smith, G.A., and Howell, E.A. (1983) Eye movements and sequential tracking in dyslexic and control children. *Brit. J. Psychol.* **74**, 181–7.

92 Brown, B., Haegerstrom-Portnoy, G., Adams, A.J., Yingling, C.D., Herron, J., and Marcus, M. (1983) Predictive eye movements do not discriminate between dyslexic and control children. *Neuropsych.* **21**, 121–8.

93 Garzia, R.P., Richman, J.E., Nicholson, S.B., and Gaines, C.S. (1990) A new visual-verbal saccadic test: the Developmental Eye Movement test (DEM). *J. Am. Optom. Assoc.* **61**, 124–135.

94 Fernandez-Velazquez, F.J., Fernandez-Fidalgo, M.J. (1995) Do DEM test scores change weth respect to the language? Norms for Spanish-speaking people. *Optom. Vis. Sci.* **72**, 902–6.

95 Taylor-Kulp, M., Schmidt, P.P. (1998) Relationship between visual skills and performance on saccadic eye movement testing. *Optom. Vis. Sci.* **75**, 284–7.

96 Rouse, M.W., Nestor, E.M., Parot, C.J. (1991) A re-evaluation of the reliability of the developmental eye movement (DEM) test. *Optom. And Vis. Sci. (supp.)* **68**, 90.

97 Taylor-Kulp, M., Schmidt, P.P. (1997) The relation of clinical saccadic eye movement testing to reading in kindergartners and first graders. *Optom. Vis. Sci.* **74**, 37–42.

98 Coulter, R.A., Shallo-Hoffmann, J. (2000) The presumed influence of attention on accuracy in the developmental eye movement (DEM) test. *Optom. Vis. Sci.* **77** (8), 428–32.

99 Hoffman, J.E., Subramaniam, B. (1995) The role of visual attention in saccadic eye movements. *Percept. Psychophys.* **57**, 787–95.

100 Prechtl, H.F.R. and Stemmer, C.J. (1962) The choreiform syndrome in children. *Dev. Med. Child Neurol.* **4**, 119–27.

101 Lefton, L.A., Lahey, B.B., and Stagg, D.I. (1978) Eye movements in reading disabled and normal children : a study of systems and strategies. *J. Learn. Disab.* **11**, 22–31.

102 Currie, J.N., Goldberg, M.E., Matsuo, V., FitzGibbon, E.J. (1986) Dyslexia with saccadic intrusions: a treatable reading disorder with a characteristic oculomotor sign (abstract).. *Neurology* **36** (**suppl.**), 134–5.

103 Bala, S.P., Cohen, B., Morris, A.G., et al. (1981) Saccades of hyperactive and normal boys during ocular pursuit. *Dev. Med. Child Neurol.* **23**, 323–36.

104 Shapira, Y.A., Jones, M.H., Sherman, S.P. (1980) Abnormal eye movements in hyperkinetic children with learning disability. *Neuropadiatrie* **11**, 36–44.

105 Bylsma, F.W,., Pivik, R.T. (1989) The effects of background illumination and stimulant medication on smooth pursuit eye movements of hyperactive children. J. Abnorm. Child Psychol. 17 (1), 73–90.

106 Dykman, R.A. and Ackerman, P.T. (1991) Attention deficit disorder and specific reading disability: separate but often overlapping disorders. *J. Learn. Disab.* **24**, 96–103.

107 Colby, C.L. (1991) The neuroanatomy and neurophysiology of attention. *J. Child Neurol. (suppl.)* **6**, S88–S116.

108 Adler-Grinberg, D. and Stark, L (1978) Eye movements, scan paths, and dyslexia. *Am. J. Optom. Phys. Opt.* **55**, 557–70.

109 Black, J.L., Collins, D.W. de Roach, J.N., Zubrick, S. (1984) Smooth pursuit eye movements in normal and dyslexic children. *Percept. Mot. Skills* **59**, 91–100.

110 Bogacz, J., Mendilaharsu, C., de Mendilaharsu, S.A. (1974) Electro-oculographic abnormalities during pursuit movements in developmental dyslexia. *Electroencephalogr. Clin. Neurophysiol.* **36**, 651–6.

111 Hodges, K. (1993) Structured interviews for assessing children. *J. Child Psychol. Psychiat.* **34**, 49–68.

112 Hartje, W. (1972) Reading disturbances in the presence of oculomotor disorders. *Europ. Neurol.* **7**, 249–64.

113 Voeller, K.K.S., Heilman, K. (1988) Motor impersistence in children with attention deficit hyperactivity disorder: evidence for right-hemisphere dysfunction. *Ann. Neurol.* **24**, 323.

114 Hardman, P.K., Clay, J.A., and Lieberman, A.D. (1989) The effects of diet and sublingual provocative testing on eye movements with dyslexics individuals. *J. Am. Optom. Assoc.* **60**, 10–13.

115 Pirozzolo, F.J. (1982) Eye movements and visual information processing in developmental reading disability.In. *Neuropsychology and Cognition: Volume 1* , Martinus Nijhoff, The Hague, pp. 147–67.

116 Stein, J., Talcott, J. (1999) Impaired neuronal timing in developmental dyslexia – the magnocellular hypothesis. *Dyslexia* **5**, 59–77.

117 Singleton, C.H. (1988) The early diagnosis of developmental dyslexia. *Support for Learning* **3**, 108–21.

118 Olson, R.K., Conners, F.A., Rack, J.P. (1991) Eye movements in dyslexic and normal readers. In *Vision and Visual Dysfunction* **Vol. 13**, (ed. J Cronly-Dillon), Macmillan Press, London, pp. 243–50.

119 Pirozzolo, F.J. and Hansch, E.C. (1982) The neurobiology of developmental reading disorders. In *Reading disorders* (eds. R.N. Malatesha and P.G. Aaron), Academic Press, New York, pp. 215–32.

120 Zangwill, O.L. and Blakemore, C. (1972) Note. Dyslexia : reversal of eye movements during reading. *Neuropsych.* **10**, 371–3.

121 Hendriks, A.W. (1996) Vergence eye movements during fixations in reading. *Acta Psychologica* **92**, 131–51.

122 Fischer, B., Hartnegg, K., Mokler, A. (2000) Dynamic visual perception of dyslexic children. *Perception* **29**, 523–30.

123 Fischer, B., Hartnegg, K. (2000) Effects of visual training on saccade control in dyslexia. *Perception* **29**, 531–42.

4 Ocular dominance

1 Evans, B.J.W. (1991) *Ophthalmic factors in dyslexia*. PhD Thesis, Aston University, Birmingham, UK.

2 Millodot, M. (1986) *Dictionary of Optometry*. Butterworth-Heinemann, Oxford.

3 Bennett, A.G. and Rabbetts, R.B. (1984) *Clinical Visual Optics*, Butterworths, London.

4 Griffin, J.R. (1982) *Binocular Anomalies: Procedures for Vision Therapy*, Professional Press, Chicago.

5 Walls, G.L. (1951) A theory of ocular dominance. *Arch. Ophthalmol.* **45**, 387–412.

6 Mallett, R. (1988) Techniques of investigation of binocular vision anomalies. In *Optometry*, (eds. K. Edwards and R. Llewellyn), Butterworths, London, pp. 238–69.

7 Dunlop, D.B., Dunlop, P., and Fenelon, B. (1973) Vision-laterality analysis in children with reading disability: the results of new techniques of examination. *Cortex* **9**, 227–36.

8 Coren, S., Kaplan, C.P. (1973) Patterns of ocular dominance. *Am. J. Optom.* **50**, 283–92.

9 Gilchrist, J.M. (1976) Dominance in the visual system. *Br. J. Physiol. Opt.* **30**, 32–44.

10 Collinge, A.J. (1979) A possible physiological basis for ocular dominance. *Brit. J. Physiol. Optics* **33**, 21–8.

11 Reading, R.W. (1983) *Binocular Vision: Foundations and Applications*, Butterworths, Boston.

12 Moseley, D. (1988) Dominance, reading and spelling. *Bull. Audiophonol. Ann. Sc. Univ. Franche-Comté* **4**, 443–64.

13 Humphriss, D. (1982) The psychological septum: an investigation into its function. *Am. J. Optom. Physiol. Opt.* **59**, 639–41.

14 Jasper, J.J. and Raney, E.T. (1937) The Phi test of lateral dominance. *Am. J. Psychol.* **49**, 450.

15 Ogle, K.N. (1962) Ocular dominance and binocular retinal rivalry. In *The Eye: Volume 4* (ed. H. Davson), Academic Press, London, pp. 409–17.

16 Simons, H.D. and Grisham, J.D. (1987) Binocular anomalies and reading problems. *J. Am. Optom. Assoc.* **58**, 578–87.

17 Joynt, R.J. (1985) Editorial: cerebral dominance. *Arch. Neurol.* **42**, 427.

18 Hermann, H.T., Zeevi, Y.Y. (1991) Interhemispheric interactions and dyslexia. In. *Vision and Visual Dysfunction* **Vol. 13**, (ed. J Cronly-Dillon), Macmillan Press, London, pp. 271–80.

19 Beaumont, J.G. and Rugg, M.D. (1978) Neuro-physhological laterality of function and dyslexia: a new hypothesis. *Dyslexia Review* **1**, 18–21.

20 Mallett, R.F.J. (1966) The investigation of oculo-motor balance. *The Ophthalmic Optician* **25 June**, 654–7.

21 Spache, G. (1947) A binocular reading test. *J. App. Psych.* **27**, 109–13.

22 Logothetis, N.K. and Schall, J.D. (1990) Binocular motion rivalry in Macaque monkeys: eye dominance and tracking eye movements. *Vision Research* **30**, 1409–19.

23 Leat, S.J., Woodhouse, J.M. (1984) Rivalry with continuous and flashed stimuli as a measure of ocular dominance across the visual field. *Perception* **13**, 351–7.

24 McFie, J. (1952) Cerebral dominance in cases of reading disability. *J. Neurol. Neurosurg. Psychiat.* **15**, 194–9.

25 Pickwell, L.D. (1972) Variation in ocular motor dominance. *Br. J. Physiol. Optics* **27**, 115–9.

26 Collinge, A.J. and Pickwell, L.D. (1976) Dominance in ocular movements. *B. J. Physiol. Opt.* **31**, 40–4.

27 Barbeito, R. (1981) Sighting dominance: An explanation based on the processing of visual direction in tests of sighting dominance. *Vision Research* **21**, 855–60.

28 Dengis, C.A., Steinbach, M.G., Goltz, H.C., Stager, C. (1993) Visual alignment from the midline: a declining developmental trend in normal, strabismic, and monocularly enucleated children. *J. Pediatr. Ophthalmol. Strabismus* **30**, 323–6.

29 Coren, S., Porac, C. (1976) Size accentuation in the dominant eye. *Nature* **260**, 527–8.

30 Porac, C., Coren, S. (1979) Monocular asymmetries in recognition after an eye movement: Sighting dominance and dextrality. *Perception and Psychophysics* **25**, 55–9.

31 Barbeito, R., Simpson, T.L. (1991) The relationship between eye position and egocentric visual direction. *Perception & Psychophysics* **50**, 373–82.

32 Mapp, A.P., Ono, H. (1999) Wondering about the wandering cyclopean eye. *Vision Research* **39**, 2381–86.

33 Hughes, H. (1953) An investigation into ocular dominancy. *B. J. Physiol. Opt.* **10**, 119–43.

34 Charnwood, Lord (1949) Observations on ocular dominance. *The Optician* **August 19**, 85–96.

35 Shearer, R. (1966) Eye findings in children with reading difficulties. *J. Ped. Ophthalmol. Strabismus* **3**, 47–53.

36 Benton, C.D. and McCann, J.W. (1969) Dyslexia and dominance. *J. Ped. Ophthalmol.* **6**, 220–2.

37 Orton, S.T. (1943) Visual functions in strephosymbolia. *AMA Archives of Ophthalmology* **30**, 707–17.

38 Vernon, M.D. (1971) *Reading and its Difficulties.* Cambridge University Press, London, pp.131–44.

39 Singleton, C.H. (1988) The early diagnosis of developmental dyslexia. *Support for Learning* **3**, 108–21.

40 Benton, C.D., McCann, J.W., and Larsen, M. (1965) Dyslexia and dominance. *Journal of Pediatric Ophthalmology* **2**, 3, 53–7.

41 Shepherd, E.M. (1956) Reading ability of 809 average school children (the effect of reversal on their performance). *Am. J. Ophthalmol.* **41**, 1029–39.

42 Michaels, D.D. (1972) Review: ocular dominance. *Survey Ophthalmology* **17**, 151–63.

43 McMonnies, C.W. (1993) Early intervention: Left/right body awareness and letter reversals. *Austral. J. Remed. Educ.* **25**, 8–13.

44 Vellutino, F.R. (1987) Dyslexia. *Scientific American* **256**, 20–7.

45 Bettman, J.W., Stern, E.L., Whitsell, W.J., and Gofman, H.F. (1967) Cerebral dominance in developmental dyslexia. *Arch. Ophthal.* **78**, 722–9.

46 Annett, M., Eglington, E., Smythe, P. (1996) Types of dyslexia and the shift to dextrality. *J. Child Psychol. Psychiat.* **37**, 167–80.

47 Bishop, D.V.M., Jancey, C., and Mc P. Steel, A. (1979) Orthoptic status and reading disability. *Cortex* **15**, 659–66.

48 Helveston, E.M., Billips, W.C., Weber, J.C. (1970) Controlling eye-dominant hemisphere relationship as a factor in reading ability. *Am. J. Ophthal.* **70**, 1.

49 Eden, G.F., Stein, J.F., Wood, M.H., Wood, F.B. (1995) Verbal and visual problems in reading disability. *J. Learning Disabilities* **28**, 272–90.

50 Chakrabarti, J. and Barker, K.G. (1966) Lateral dominance and reading ability. *Percept. Motor Skills* **22**, 881–2.

51 Miles, T.R., Haslum, M.N., Wheeler, T.J. (1996 or 1997) Handedness in dyslexia: should this be routinely recorded?. *Dyslexia Review* , 7–9.

52 MacMeeken, M. (1939) . *Ocular Dominance in Relation to Developmental Aphasia* , University of London Press, London.

53 Brod, N., Hamilton, D. (1971) Monocular-binocular coordination vs. Hand-eye dominance as a factor in reading performance. *Am. J. Optom. Arch. Am. Acad. Optom.* **48**, 123–9.

54 Spitzer, R.L., Rabkin, R., and Kramer, Y. (1959) The relationship between "mixed dominance" and reading disabilities. *J. Pediatrics* **54**, 76–80.

55 Rengstorff, R.H. (1967) The types and incidence of hand-eye preference and its relationship with certain reading abilities. *Am. J. Optom. Physiol. Opt.* **44**, 233–8.

56 Fendrick, P. (1935) *Visual characteristics of poor readers.* Bureau of publications, Teachers college, Columbia University, New York City, New York.

57 Riddell, P.M., Stein, J.F., and Fowler, M.S. (1987) A comparison of sighting dominance and the reference eye in reading disabled children. *Brit. Orth. J.* **44**, 64–9.

58 Annett, M. (1991) Right hemisphere costs of right handedness. In. *Vision and Visual Dysfunction* **Vol. 13**, (ed. J Cronly-Dillon), Macmillan Press, London, pp. 84–93.

59 McManus, I.C. (1991) The genetics of dyslexia. In. *Vision and Visual Dysfunction* **Vol. 13**, (ed. J Cronly-Dillon), Macmillan Press, London, pp. 94–112.

60 Dunlop, P. and Banks, E.M. (1974) New binocular factors in reading disability. *Austral. Orth. J.* **13**, 7–13.

61 Dunlop, P. (1976) The changing role of orthoptics in dyslexia. *Brit. Orth. J.* **33**, 22–8.

62 Dunlop, D.B. and Dunlop, P. (1974) New concepts of visual laterality in relation to dyslexia. *Australian Journal of Ophthalmology* **2**, 101–12.

63 Dunlop, P. (1975) The orthoptist's contribution to the multi-disciplinary group concerned with learning difficulties. *Austral. Orth. J.* **14**, 9–15.

64 Dunlop, P. (1979) Orthoptic management of learning disbility. *Brit. Orth. J.* **36**, 25–35.

65 Spooner, V. (1978) The assessment by an orthoptist of a group of children attending remedial reading classes. *Brit. Orth. J.* **35**, 40–5.

66 Stein, J. and Fowler, S. (1981) Visual dyslexia. *TINS*, **Apr**, 77–80.

67 Stein, J. and Fowler, S. (1985) The effect of monocular occlusion on visuomotor perception and reading in dyslexic children. *The Lancet.* 13th July, 69–73.

68 Stein, J. (1989) Visuospatial perception and reading problems. *Irish J. Psychol.* **10**, 521–33.

69 Stein, J., Riddell, P., and Fowler, S. (1989) Disordered right hemisphere function in developmental dyslexia. In *Brain and Reading* (eds. C. Von Euler, I. Lundberg, and G. Lennerstrand), Stockton, New York, pp. 139–57.

70 Fowler, M.S. (1991) Binocular control in dyslexia. In *Dyslexia* (ed. J. Stein), Vol. 13 of "Vision and Visual Dysfunction" (ed. J.R. Cronly Dillon), MacMillan, London.

71 Stein, J.F. (1991) Vision and Language. In *Dyslexia: Integrating Theory and Practice* (eds M. Snowling and M. Thomson), Whurr, London, pp. 31–43.

72 Stein, J.F., Richardson, A.J., Fowler, M.S. (2000) Monocular occlusion can improve binocular control and reading in dyslexics. *Brain* **123**, 164–70.

73 Polikoff, B.R., Evans, B.J.W., Legg, C.R. (1995) Is there a visual deficit in dyslexia resulting from a lesion of the right posterior parietal lobe?. *Ophthal. Physiol. Opt.* **15**, 513–7.

74 Fowler, M.S. and Stein, J.F. (1983) Consideration of ocular motor dominance as an aetiological factor in some orthoptic problems. *Brit. Orth. J.* **40**, 43–5.

75 Franklin, A.R. (1985) Retinal rivalry in dyslexia: a literary catastrophe? *Unpublished paper.*

76 Personal observation of the author.

77 Kertesz, A.E. (1981) Effect of stimulus size on fusion and vergence. *J. Opt. Soc. Am.* **71**, 699–704.

78 Bigelow, E.R. and McKenzie, B.E. (1985) Unstable ocular dominance and reading ability. *Perception* **14**, 329–55

79 Liu, J., Margolis, N., Mitchell, R. (1989) Binocular eye dominance in dyslexia. OD Thesis, University of California, Berkeley.

80 Evans, B.J.W., Drasdo, N., Richards I.L. (1994) Investigation of accommodative and binocular function in dyslexia. *Ophthal. Physiol. Opt.* **14**, 5–19.

81 Stein, J.F., Riddell, P.M., and Fowler, M.S. (1986) The Dunlop Test and reading in primary school children. *Br. J. Ophthal.* **70**, 317–20.

82 Buckley, C.Y. and Robertson, J.L. (1991) The Dunlop test – fact or fiction. *Br. Orthopt. J.* **48**, 39–40.

83 Bishop, D.V.M. (1989) Unfixed reference, monocular occlusion, and developmental dyslexia – a critique. *Br. J. Ophthalmol.* **73**, 209–15.

84 Goulandris, N., McIntyre, A., Snowling, M., Bethel, J., Lee, J.P. (1998) A comparison of dyslexic and normal readers using orthoptic assessment procedures. *Dyslexia* **4**, 30–48.

85 Riddell, P.M., Fowler, M.S., Stein, J.F. (1990) Spatial discrimination in children with poor vergence control. *Perceptual Motor Skills* **70**, 707–18.

86 Stein, J.F., Riddell, P.M., and Fowler, S. (1988) Disordered vergence control in dyslexic children. *Brit. J. Ophthal.* **72**, 162–6.

87 Fowler, M.S., Riddell, P.M., and Stein, J.F. (1988) The effect of varying vergence speed and target size on the amplitude of vergence eye movements. *British Orthoptic Journal* **45**, 49–55.

88 Riddell, P.M., Stein, J.F., and Fowler, M.S. (1988) Impaired vergence eye movement control in dyslexic children. *Invest. Ophthal. Vis. Sci.* **29** (suppl.), 346.

89 Stein, J.F. (1991) Visuospatial sense, hemispheric asymmetry and dyslexia. In. *Vision and Visual Dysfunction* **Vol. 13**, (ed. J Cronly-Dillon), Macmillan Press, London, pp. 181–188.

90 Mason, A., Cornelissen, P., Fowler, S. , Stein, J.F. (1993) Contrast sensitivity, ocular dominance and specific reading disability. *Clinical Vision Sciences* **8**, 345–53.

91 Evans, B.J.W. (1997) *Pickwell's Binocular Vision Anomalies: Investigation and Treatment.* Third edition, Butterworth-Heinemann, Oxford.

92 Evans, B.J.W., Drasdo, N., Richards, I.L. (1996) Dyslexia: the link with visual deficits. *Ophthal. Physiol. Opt.* **16**, 3–10.

93 Stein, J. and Fowler, S. (1982) Diagnosis of dyslexia by means of a new indicator of eye dominance. *Brit. J. Ophthalmol.* **66**, 332–6.

94 Newman, S.P., Wadsworth, J.F., Archer, R., Hockly, R. (1985) Ocular dominance, reading, and spelling ability in schoolchildren. *Br. J. Ophthal.* **69**, 228–32.

95 Ygge, J., Lennerstrand, G., Axelsson, I., Rydberg, A., Wijecoon, S., Pettersson, B.M. (1993) Visual functions and oculomotor functions in a Swedish population of 9-year-old dyslexics and normal readers. A preliminary report. *Acta Ophthalmol.* **71**, 10–21.

96 Aasved, H. (1987) Ophthalmological status of schoolchildren with dyslexia. *Eye* **1**, 61–8.

97 Watkins, E.J. (1991) Visual Dyslexia. In *Paediatric Ophthalmology – Surgical, Medical and Developmental Aspects, 16–25 May, 1991, Speakers notes 9120*, The British Council, London.

98 Stein, J.F. (1989) Correspondence: Unfixed reference, monocular occlusion, and developmental dyslexia – a critique. *B. J. Ophthal.* **73**, 319–20.

99 Evans, B.J.W. (2000) Decompensated exophoria at near, convergence insufficiency and binocular instability. *Optician* **219**, 20–8.

100 Evans, B.J.W. (2000) An open trial of the Institute Free-space Stereogram (IFS) exercises. *British Journal of Optometry & Dispensing* **8**, 5–14.

101 Cornelissen, P., Bradley, L., Fowler, S., Stein, J. (1991) What children see affects how they read. *Devel. Med. Child. Neurol.* **33**, 755–62.

102 Cornelissen, P., Bradley, L., Fowler, S., Stein, J. (1992) Covering one eye affects how some children read. *Dev. Med. Child. Neurol.* **34**, 296–304.

103 Cornelissen, P., Bradley, L., Fowler, S., Stein, J. (1994) What children see affects how they spell. *Developmental Medicine and Child Neurology* **36**, 716–27.

5 Behavioural optometry and other controversial visual approaches

1 Evans, B.J.W. (1991) *Ophthalmic factors in dyslexia.* PhD Thesis, Aston University, Birmingham, UK.

2 Gilman, G. (1990) The behavioral model of vision. In *Conference Notes: First International Congress of Behavioral Optometry*, Monte Carlo, 2–5th November.

3 Cohen, A.H., Lowe, S.E., Steele, G.T., Suchoff, I.B., Gottlieb, D.D., Trevorrow, T.L. (1988) The efficacy of optometric vision therapy. *J. Am. Optom. Assoc.* **59**, 95–105.

4 Keogh, B.K. (1974) Optometric vision training programs for children with learning disability: review of issues and research. *J. Learn. Disab.* **7**, 36–48.

5 Jennings, A. (2000) Behavioural optometry: a critical review. *Optometry in Practice* **1**, 67–78.

6 Adler, P.M. (1994) Behavioural optometry. *Optometry Today* **September 26**, 24–32.

7 Greenspan, S.B., Weisz, C.L. (1977) Psychological factors in pediatric optometry. *J. Am. Optom. Assoc.* **48** (1), 79–86.

8 Rounds, B.B., Manlley, C.W., Norris, R.H. (1991) The effect of oculomotor training on reading efficiency. *J. Am. Optom. Assoc.* **62**, 92–7.

9 Wesson, M.D. (1993) Diagnosis and management of reading dysfunction for the primary care optometrist. *Optom. Vis. Sci.* **70**, 357–68.

10 Adler, P. (1997) Understanding vision therapy. *Optometry Today* **May 2**, 38–9.

11 Forrest, E.B. (1981) Visual imagery as an information processing strategy. *J. Learn. Disab.* **14**, 584–6.

12 Hendrickson, H. (1990) Functional vision. In *Conference Notes: First International Congress of Behavioral Optometry*, Monte Carlo, 2–5th November.

13 Pierce, J.R. (1977) Vision therapy and academic achievement: part 1. *Review of Optometry* June 1977, 48–63.

14 Christenson, G.N., Griffin, J.R., DeLand, P.N. (1991) Validity of the dyslexia screener. *Optom. Vis. Sci.* **68**, 275–81.

15 Wood, J.M., Abernethy, B. (1997) An assessment of the efficacy of sports vision training programs. *Optom. Vis. Sci.* **74**, 646–59.

16 Cohen, A.H., Lowe, S.E., Steele, G.T., Suchoff, I.B., Gottlieb, D.D., Trevorrow, T.L. (1988) The efficacy of optometric vision training. *J. Am. Optom. Assoc.* **59**, 95–105.

17 Metzger, R.L. and Werner, D.B. (1984) The use of visual training for reading disabilities: a review. *Pediatrics* **73**, 824–9.

18 Levine, M.D. (1984) Commentary – Reading disability : do the eyes have it ? *Ped.* **73**, 869–70.

19 Keys, M.P., Silver, L.B. (1990) Learning disabilities and vision problems: are they related?. *Pediatrician* **17**, 194–201.

20 Silver, L.B. (1986) Review: Controversial approaches to treating learning disabilities and attention deficit disorder. *Am. J. Diseases Childhood* **140**, 1045–52.

21 Worrall, R.S., Nevyas, J. (1993) The eye exorcisors. In. *The Health Robbers: A Close Look at Quackery in America* , (Eds. S. Barrett and W.T. Jarvis, pp. 347–54.

22 Helveston, E.M. (1987) Management of dyslexia and related learning disabilities. *J. Learn. Disab.* **20**, 415–21.

23 Beauchamp, G.R. (1986) Optometric vision training. *Pediat.* **77**, 121–4.

24 Healy, A., Erengerg, G., Kaminer, R.K., La Camera, R., Nackashi, J.A., Poncher, J.R., Randall, V., Wachtel, R.C., Ziring, P.R. (1992) Learning disabilities, Dyslexia, and vision. *Pediatrics* **90**, 124–6.

25 Committee on Children with Disabilities et al. (1998) Learning disabilities, dyslexia, and vision: a subject review. *Pediatrics* **102**, 1217–19.

26 American Academy of Optometry & American Optometric Association (1997) Vision, learning, and dyslexia: a joint organizational policy statement. *Optom. Vis. Sci.* **74**, 868–70.

27 American Academy of Optometry, American Optometric Association (1999) Vision therapy: Information for health care and other allied professionals. *Optom. Vis. Sci.* **76**, 739–40.

28 Shaywitz, S.E. (1996) Dyslexia. *Scientific American* **November**, 78–84.

29 Zadnik, K. (1997) Myopia development in childhood. *Optom. Vis. Sci.* **74**, 603–8.

30 Grosvenor, T., Perrigin, D.M., Perrigin, J., Maslovitz, B. (1987) Houston myopia control study: a randomized clinical trial: Final report by the patient care team. *Am. J. Optom. Physiol. Opt.* **64**, 482–98.

31 Wildsoet, C.F. (1997) Active emmetropization: evidence for its existence and ramifications for clinical practice. *Ophthal. Physiol. Opt.* **17**, 279–90.

32 Gilmartin, B., Rosenfield, M. (2000) Myopia and nearwork: an overview. *Optician* **219**, 16–21.

33 Woods, A.C. (1945) Report from the Wilmer Institute on the results obtained in the treatment of myopia by visual training. *Trans. Am. Acad. Ophthalmol. Otol.* **Nov–Dec**, 3–31.

34 Angi, M., Caucci, S., Pilotto, E., Racano, E. (1996) Changes in myopia, visual acuity, and psychological distress after biofeedback training. *Optom. Vis. Sci.* **73**, 35–42.

35 Details of initial literature search: Medline and Silver Platter Ophthalmology databases searched September 2000 for *behavioral optometry*. BO articles are often published in publications which are not inter-disciplinary peer-reviewed journals, which may not be covered by usual search criteria. Therefore, the VISIONET (held by Southern College of Optometry) database (journal articles 1992–present) was searched, which was recommended to the author as holding many BO publications. Keywords that were used in this search included: *controlled trial, vision therapy* and *control, learning lenses, low plus, tracking, saccad* and *reading, pursuit* and *dyslexia, percept* and *reading, syntonic* [see Chapter 7].

36 Seiderman, A.S. (1980) Optometric vision therapy – results of a demonstration project with a learning disabled population. *J. Am. Optom. Assoc.* **51**, 489–93.

37 Fischer, B., Hartnegg, K. (2000) Effects of visual training on saccade control in dyslexia. *Perception* **29**, 531–42.

38 Kavale, K. (1982) Meta-analysis of the relationship between visual perceptual skills and reading achievement. *J. Learn. Disab.* **15**, 42–51.

39 Solan, H.A., Mozlin, R. (1986) Correlations of perceptual-motor maturation to readiness and reading in kindergarten and the primary glades. *J. Am. Optom. Assoc.* **57**, 28–35.

40 Richman, J.E. (1999) The influence of visual attention and automaticity on the diagnosis and treatment of clinical oculomotor, accommodative, and vergence dysfunctions. *J. Optom. Vision Development* **30**, 132–41.

41 Pirozzolo, F.J. (1979). *The Neuropsychology of developmental reading disorders*, Praeger, New York.

42 Details of initial literature search: Medline database and Silver Platter Ophthalmology databases searched August 2000 for *neuro-developmental retraining* or *neurodevelopmental retraining* or *neuro-developmental retraining* or *neurodevelopmental retraining*.

43 Frank, J. and Levinson, H. (1973) Dysmetric dyslexia and dyspraxia: hypothesis and study. *J. Am. Acad. Child Psychiat.* **12**, 690–701.

44 Frank, J. and Levinson, H.N. (1975) Dysmetric dyslexia and dyspraxia. *Academic Therapy* **11**, 133–43.

Frank, J. and Levinson, H.N. (1976) Compensatory mechanisms in cerebello-vestibular dysfunction, dysmetric dyslexia and dyspraxia. *Academic Therapy* **12**, 5–27.

45 Frank, J. and Levinson, H.N. (1976) Compensatory mechanisms in cerebello-vestibular dysfunction, dysmetric dyslexia and dyspraxia. *Academic Therapy* **12**, 5–27.

46 Levinson, H.N. (1988) The cereballar-vestibular basis of learning disabilities in children, adolescents and adults: hypothesis and study. *Percept. Mot. Skills* **67**, 983–1006.

47 Brown, B., Haegerstrom-Portnoy, G., Yingling, C.D., Herron, J., Galin, D., and Marcus, M. (1983) Dyslexic children have normal vestibular responses to rotation. *Arch. Neurol.* **f40**, 370–3.

48 Raymond, J.E., Ogden, N.A., Fagan, J.E., and Kaplan, B.J. (1988) Fixation instability and saccadic eye movements of dyslexia children with subtle cerebellar dysfunction. *Am. J. Optom. Vis. Sci.* **65**, 174–81.

49 Fawcett, A.J., Nicolson, R.I. (1994) Naming speed in children with dyslexia. *J. Learn. Disab.* **27**, 641–6.

50 Nicolson, R.I., Fawcett, A.J., Dean, P. (1995) Time estimation deficits in developmental dyslexia: evidence of cerebellar involvement. *Proc. R. Soc. Lond. B. Biol. Sci.* **259**, 43–7.

51 Rae, C., Lee, M.A., Dixon, R.M., Blamire, A.M., Thompson, C.H., Styles, P., Talcott, J., Richardson, A.J., Stein, J.F. (1998) Metabolic abnormalities in developmental dyslexia detected by 1H magnetic resonance spectroscopy. *Lancet* **351**, 1849–52.

52 Nicolson, R.I., Fawcett, A.J., Berry, E.L., Jenkins, I.H., Dean, P., Brooks, D.J. (1999) Association of abnormal cerebellar activation with motor learning difficulties in dyslexic adults. *Lancet* **353**, 1662–67.

53 Beauchamp, G.R. and Kosmorsky, G.S. (1989) The neurophysiology of reading. *Internat. Ophthalmol. Clin.* **29**, 16–19.

54 Details of initial literature search: Medline and Silver Platter Ophthalmology databases searched August 2000 for *dyslexia* and *ocular lock* or *chiropractic*.

6 Visual processing

1 Evans, B.J.W. (1991) *Ophthalmic factors in dyslexia*. PhD Thesis, Aston University, Birmingham, UK.

2 Seymour, P.H.K., Evans, H.M. (c. 1994) The visual (Orthographic) processor and developmental dyslexia. Chapter 16 in. , 347–76.

3 Slaghuis, W.L., Lovegrove, W.J., Davidson, J.A. (1993) Visual and language processing deficits are concurrent in dyslexia. *Cortex* **29**, 601–15.

4 Livingstone, M., Hubel, D. (1987) Psychophysical evidence for separate channels for the perception of form, color, movement, and depth. *J. Neurosci.* **7**, 3416.

5 Hubel, D. (1988) *Eye, Brain, and Vision*, Scientific American Library, New York.

6 Bassi, C.J. and Lehmkuhle, S. (1990) Clinical implications of parallel visual pathways. *J. Am. Optom. Assoc.* **61**, 98–109.

7 Ungerleider, L.G. and Mishkin, M. (1982) Two cortical visual systems. In *Analysis of Visual Behavior*, (eds. D.J. Ingle, M.A. Goodale, and R.J.W. Mansfield), MIT Press, Cambridge, MA, pp. 549–86.

8 Mishkin, M., Ungerleider, L.G., Macko, K.A. (1983) Object vision and spatial vision: two cortical pathways. *Trends Investig. Neurosci.*, October, 1983, 414–7.

9 Lennie, P., Trevarthen, C., Van Essen, D., Wassle, H. (1990) Parallel processing of visual information. In *Visual Perception: The Neurophysiological Foundations*, (eds. L. Spillmann and J.S. Werner), Academic Press, San Diego, pp. 163–203.

10 Kulikowski, J.J. and Tolhurst, D.J. (1973) Psychophysical evidence for sustained and transient detectors in human vision. *J. Physiol. (Lond.)* **232**, 149–62.

11 Green, M. (1981) Psychophysical relationships among mechanisms sensitive to pattern, motion and flicker. *Vision Research* **21**, 971–83.

12 Zeki, S. and Shipp, S. (1988) The functional logic of cortical connections. *Nature (Lond.)* **335**, 311–7.

13 Gilchrist, J. (1988) The psychology of vision. In *Optometry*, (eds. K. Edwards and R. Llewellyn), Butterworths, London, pp. 25–43.

14 Kaplan, E., Lee, B.B., Shapley, R.M. (1991) New views of primate retinal function. In *Progress in Retinal Research, Volume 9*, (eds. N. Osborne and J.Chader), Pergamon, Oxford, pp. 275–336.

15 Wilson, H.R., Levi, D., Maffei, L., Rovamo, J., and DeValois, R. (1990) The perception of form: retina to striate cortex. In *Visual Perception: The Neurophysiological Foundations*, (eds. L. Spillmann and J.S. Werner), Academic Press, San Diego, pp. 231–72.

16 Merigen, W.H., Maunsell, J.H. (1993) How parallel are the primate visual pathways?. *Ann. Rev. Neurosci.* **16**, 369–402.

17 Lovegrove, W., Martin, F., and Slaghuis, W. (1986) A theoretical and experimental case for a visual deficit in specific reading disability. *Cognitive Neuropsychol.*, **3**, 225–67.

18 Lovegrove, W. (1991) Spatial frequency processing in dyslexic and normal readers. In *Dyslexia* (ed. J. Stein), Vol. 13 of "Vision and Visual Dysfunction" (ed. J.R. Cronly Dillon), MacMillan, London.

19 Greatrex, J.C., Drasdo, N. (1995) The magnocellular deficit hypothesis in dyslexia: a review of reported evidence. *Ophthal. Physiol. Opt.* **15**, 501–6.

20 Greatrex, J.C., Drasdo, N. (1998) Methods of investigating a visual deficit in dyslexia. *Ophthal. Physiol. Opt.* **18**, 160–6.

21 Lovegrove, W., Martin, F., Bowling, A., Blackwood, M., Badcock, D., and Paxton, S. (1982) Contrast sensitivity functions and specific reading disability. *Neuropsych.* **20**, 309–15.

22 Müller, P. and Groner, R. (1991) Spatio-temporal characteristics of visual information processing in dyslexics and controls. Presented at: *Rodin Remediation 18th Scientific Conference – Reading and Reading Disorders: Interdisciplinary Perspectives*, Berne, Switzerland.

23 Georgeson, M.A. and Georgeson, J.M. (1985) Research note: on seeing temporal gaps between gratings: a criterion problem for measurement of visual persistence. *Vision Research* **25**, 1729–33.

24 Edwards, V.T., Hogben, J.H., Clark, C.D., Pratt, C. (1996) Effects of a red background on magnocellular functioning in average and specifically disabled readers. *Vision Research* **36**, 1037–46.

25 Spinelli, D., Angelelli, P., Deluca, M., Dipace, E., Judica, A., Zoccolotti, P. (1997) Developmental surface dyslexia is not associated with deficits in the transient visual system. *Neuroreport* **8**, 1807–12.

26 Evans, B.J.W., Drasdo, N., Richards, I.L. (1994) Refractive and sensory visual correlates of dyslexia. *Vision Research* **34**, 1913–26.

27 Talcott, J.B., Hansen, P.C., Willis-Owen, C., McKinnell, I.W., Richardson, A.J., Stein, J.F. (1998) Visual magnocellular impairment in adult developmental dyslexics. *Neuro-Ophthalmology* **20**, 187–201.

28 Martin, F. and Lovegrove, W. (1987) Flicker contrast sensitivity in normal and specifically disabled readers. *Perception* **16**, 215–21.

29 Hill, R., Lovegrove, W.J. (1993) One word at a time: a solution to the visual deficit in SRDs? *Facets of Dyslexia and its Remediation*, eds. S.F. Wright and R. Groner, pp. 65–76, North-Holland, Amsterdam.

30 Felmingham, K.L., Jakobson, L.S. (1995) Visual and visuomotor performance in dyslexic children. *Exp. Brain Research* **106**, 467–74.

31 Walther-Muller, P.U. (1995) Is there a visual deficit of early vision in dyslexia. *Perception* **24**, 919–36.

32 Lovegrove, W.J., Bowling, A., Badcock, D., and Blackwood, M. (1980) Specific reading disability: differences in contrast sensitivity as a function of spatial frequency. *Science* **210**, 439–40.

33 Martin, F. and Lovegrove, W.J. (1988) Uniform field flicker masking in control and specifically-disabled readers. *Perception* **17**, 203–14.

34 Slaghuis, W.L., Ryan, J.F. (1999) Spatio-temporal contrast sensitivity, coherent motion, and visible persistence in developmental dyslexia. *Vision Research* **39**, 651–68.

35 Cornelissen, P., Richardson, A., Mason, A., Fowler, S., Stein, J. (1995) Contrast sensitivity and coherent motion detection measured at photopic luminance levels in dyslexics and controls. *Vision Res.* **35**, 1483–94.

36 Badcock, D. and Lovegrove, W. (1981) The effects of contrast, stimulus duration, and spatial frequency on visible persistence in normal and specifically disabled readers. *J. Exper. Psychol.: Human Percept. & Perform.*, **7**, 495–505.

37 Høien, T. (1982) The relationship between iconic persistence and reading disabilities. In *Dyslexia. Proceedings of an International Symposium held at the Wenner-Gren Center, Stockholm, June3–4, 1980* (ed. Y. Zotterman), Pergamon Press, Oxford, pp. 93–107.

38 Lovegrove, W.J., Heddle, M., and Slaghuis, W. (1980) Reading disability : spatial frequency specific deficits in visual information store. *Neuropsych.* **18**, 111–5.

39 Di Lollo, V., Hanson, D., McIntyre, J.S. (1983) Initial stages of visual information processing in dyslexia. *J. Exp. Psychol.* **9**, 923–35.

40 Slaghuis, W.L., Lovegrove, W. (1984) Flicker masking of spatial-frequency-dependent visible persistence and specific reading disability. *Perception* **13**, 527–34.

41 Riding, R.J. and Pugh, J.C. (1977) Iconic memory and reading performance in nine-year-old children. *Br. J. educ. Psychol.* **47**, 132–7.

42 Hogben, J.H., Rodino, I.S., Clark, C.D., Pratt, C. (1995) A comparison of temporal integration in children with a specific reading disability and normal readers. *Vision Res.* **35**, 2067–74.

43 Slaghuis, W.L., Lovegrove, W.J., Freestun, J. (1992) Letter recognition in peripheral vision and metacontrast masking in dyslexic and normal readers. *Clin. Vision Sci.* **7**, 53–65.

44 Slaghuis, W.L., Pinkus, S.Z. (1993) Visual backward masking in central and peripheral vision in late-adolescent dyslexics. *Clin. Vis. Sci.* **8**, 187–99.

45 Casco, C. (1993) Visual processing of static and dynamic information in disabled readers. *Clin. Vision Sci.* **8**, 461–71.

46 Eden, G.F., VanMeter, J.W., Rumsey, J.M., Maisog, J.M., Woods, R.P., Zeffiro, T.A. (1996) Abnormal processing of visual motion in dyslexia revealed by functional brain imaging. *Nature* **382**, 66–9.

47 Demb, J.B., Boynton, G.M., Best, M., Heeger, D.J. (1998) Psychophysical evidence for a magnocellular pathway deficit in dyslexia. *Vision Research* **38**, 1555–9.

48 Witton, C., Talcott, J.B., Hansen, P.C., Richardson, A.J., Griffiths, T.D., Rees, A. (1998) Sensitivity to dynamic auditory and visual stimuli predicts nonword reading ability in both dyslexic and normal readers. *Current Biology* **8**, 791–7.

49 Bear, D.M. (1987) Letter to the editor. *New Eng. J. Med.* **317**, 1738–9.

50 Vellutino, F.R. (1977) Alternative conceptualizations of dyslexia: evidence in support of a verbal-deficit hypothesis. *Harvard Educational Review* **47**, 334–54.

51 Vellutino, F.R., Steger, B.M., Moyer, S.C., et al. (1977) Has the perceptual deficit hypothesis led us astray? *J. Learn. Disab.*, **10**, 375–85.

52 Lovegrove, W.J., Garzia, R.P., and Nicholson, S.B. (1990) Experimental evidence for a transient system deficit in specific reading disability. *J. Am. Optom. Assoc.* **61**, 37–146.

53 May, J.G., Lovegrove, W.J., Martin, F., and Nelson, P. (1991) Pattern-elicited visual evoked potentials in good and poor readers. *Clin. Vision Sci.* **62**, 131–6.

54 Livingstone, M.S., Rosen, G.D., Drislane, F.W., Galaburda, A.M. (1991) Physiological and anatomical evidence for a magnocellular defect in developmental dyslexia. *Proc. Nat. Acad. Sci.* **88**, 7943–7.

55 Galaburda, A., Livingstone, M. (1993) Evidence for a magnocellular defect in developmental dyslexia. *Ann. New York Acad. Sci.* , 70–82.

56 Lehmkuhle, S., Garzia, R.P., Turner, L., Hash, T., Baro, J.A. (1993) A defective visual pathway in children with reading disability. *New England J. Medicine* **328**, 989–96

57 May, J.G., Dunlap, W.P., Lovegrove, W.J. (1992) Factor scores derived from visual evoked potential latencies differentiate good and poor readers (letter). *Clin. Vision Sci.* **1**, 67–70.

58 Kubova, Z., Kuba, M., Peregrin, J., Novakova, V. (1995) Short communication: Visual evoked potential evidence for magnocellular system deficit in dyslexia. *Physiol. Res.* **44**, 87–9.

59 Demb, J.B., Boynton, G.M., Heeger, D.J. (1997) Brain activity in visual cortex predicts individual differences in reading performance. *Proc. Nat. Acad. Sci. USA* **94**, 13363–6.

60 Brannan, J.R., Solan, H.A., Ficarra, A.P., Ong, E. (1998) Effect of luminance on visual evoked potential amplitudes in normal and disabled readers. *Optom. Vis. Sci.* **75**, 279–83.

61 Victor, J.D., Conte, M.M., Burton, L., Nass, R.D. (1993) Visual evoked potentials in dyslexics and normals: failure to find a difference in transient or steady-state responses. *Visual Neuroscience* **10**, 939–46.

62 Johannes, S., Kussmaul, C.L., Munte, T.F., Mangun, G.R. (1996) Developmental dyslexia – passive visual stimulation provides no evidence for a magnocellular processing defect. *Neuropsychologia* **34**, 1123–7.

63 Snowling, M., Davidoff, J. (1992) Visual deficits in dyslexia?. *Current Biology* **2**, 196–7.

64 Garzia, R.P., Nicholson, S.B. (1990) Visual function and reading disability: an optometric viewpoint. *J. Am. Optom. Assoc.* **61**, 88–97.

65 Solan, H.A. (1994) Transient and sustained processing: A dual subsystem theory of reading disability. *J. Behavioral Optometry* **5**, 149–54.

66 Croyle, L. (1998) Rate of reading, visual processing, colour and contrast. *Australian Journal of Learning Disabilities* **3**, 13–21.

67 Visyasagar, T., R., Pammer, K. (1999) Impaired visual serch in dyslexia relates to the role of the magnocellular pathway in attention. *NeuroReport* **10**, 1283–7.

68 Hulme, C. (1988) The implausibility of low-level visual deficits as a cause of children's reading difficulties. *Cognitive Neuropsychology* **5**, 369–74.

69 Casco, C., Tressoldi, P.E., Dellantonio, A. (1998) Visual selective attention and reading efficiency are related in children. *Cortex* **34**, 531–46.

70 Cornelissen, P.L., Hansen, P.C., Hutton, J.L., Evangelinou, V., Stein, J.F. (1998) Magnocellular visual function and children's single word reading. *Vision Research* **38**, 471–82.

71 Cornelissen, P.L., Hansen, P.C., Gilchrist, I., Cormack, F., Essex, E., Frankish, C. (1998) Coherent motion detection and letter position encoding. *Vision Research* **38**, 2181–91.

72 May, J.G., Williams, M.C., Dunlap, W.P. (1988) Temporal order judgement in good and poor readers. *Neuropsychologia* **26**, 917–24.

73 Lovegrove, W., Slaghuis, W., Bowling, A., Nelson, P., and Geeves, E. (1986) Spatial frequency processing and the prediction of reading ability: a preliminary investigation. *Percept. & Psychophys.*, **40**, 440–44.

74 Kruk, R. and Willows, D. (1991) Toward an ecologically valid analysis of visual processes in dyslexic readers. *Facets of Dyslexia and its Remediation*, eds. S.F. Wright and R. Groner, pp. 193–206, North-Holland, Amsterdam.

75 Lovegrove, W.J. (1993) Do dyslexics have a visual deficit? *Facets of Dyslexia and its Remediation*, eds. S.F. Wright and R. Groner, pp. 33–49, North-Holland, Amsterdam.

76 Williams, M.C., and LeCluyse K. (1990) Perceptual consequences of a temporal processing deficit in reading disabled children. *J. Am. Optom. Assoc.* **61**, 111–21.

77 Williams, M.C. and Bologna, N.B. (1985) Perceptual grouping in good and poor readers. *Perception and Psychophysics* **38**, 367–374.

78 Solman, R.T., Cho, H., and Dain, S.J. (1991) Colour-mediated grouping effects in good and disabled readers. *Ophthal. Physiol. Opt.* **11**, 320–7.

79 Williams, M.C., Molinet, K., LeCluyse, K. (1989) Visual masking as a measure of temporal processing in normal and disabled readers. *Clin. Vision Sci.*, **4**, 137–44.

80 Williams, M.C., LeCluyse, K., and Bologna, N. (1990) Masking of light as a measure of visual integration in normal and disabled readers. *Clin. Vision Sci.*, **5**, 335–43.

81 Solman, R.T., May, J.G. (1990) Spatial localization discrepencies: a visual deficiency in poor readers. *Am. J. Psychol.* **103**, 243–263.

82 Williams, M.C., Brannan, J.R., and Lartigue, E.K. (1987) Visual search in good and poor readers. *Clin. Vision Sci.* **1**, 367–71.

83 Williams, M.C., May, J.G., Solman, R., Zhou, H. (1995) The effects of spatial filtering and contrast reduction on visual search times in good and poor readers. *Vision Res.* **35**, 285–91.

84 Rock-Faucheux, A., LeCluyse, K., Williams, M. (1993) The effects of wavelength on visual processing and reading performance in normal and disabled readers. *Facets of Dyslexia and its Remediation*, eds. S.F. Wright and R. Groner, pp. 77–94, North-Holland, Amsterdam.

85 Solan, H.A., Ficarra, A., Brannan, J.R., Rucker, F. (1998) Eye movement efficiency in normal and reading disabled elementary school children: effects of varying luminance and wavelength. *J. Am. Optom. Assoc.* **69**, 455–64.

86 Breitmeyer, B.G. (1980) Unmasking visual masking: a look at the "why" behind the veil of "how". *Psychological Review* **87**, 52–69.

87 Breitmeyer, B.G. (1983) Sensory masking, persistence, and enhancement in visual exploration and reading. In *Eye Movements in Reading: Perceptual and Language Processes* (ed. K. Rayner), Academic Press, New York, pp. 3–30.

88 Robinson, G.L., Conway, R.N. (1994) Irlen filters and reading strategies: effect of coloured filters on reading achievement, Specific reading strategies, and perception of ability. *Perceptual and Motor Skills* **79**, 467–83.

89 Breitmeyer, B.G. and Ganz, L. (1976) Implications of sustained and transient channels for visual pattern masking, saccadic suppresion, and information processing. *Psychol. Rev.* **83**, 1–35.

90 Macknik, S.L., Bridgeman, B., and Switkes, E. (1991) Saccadic suppression of displacement at isoluminance. *Invest. Ophthal. Vis. Sci.* **32**, 899.

91 Burr, D.C., Morrone, M.C., Ross, J. (1994) Selective suppression of the magnocellular visual pathway during saccadic eye movements. *Nature* **371**, 511–3.

92 Skottun, B.C., Parke, L.A. (1999) The possible relationship between visual deficits and dyslexia: examination of a critical assumption. *J. Learning Disab.* **32**, 2–5.

93 Stein, J., Talcott, J. (1999) Impaired neuronal timing in developmental dyslexia – the magnocellular hypothesis. *Dyslexia* **5**, 59–77.

94 Stein, J.F. (1989) Review article: Representation of egocentric space in the posterior parietal cortex. *Quart. J. Exp. Physiol.* **74**, 583–606.

95 Stein, J.F. (1991) Vision and Language. In *Dyslexia: Integrating Theory and Practice* (eds M. Snowling and M. Thomson), Whurr, London, pp. 31–43.

96 Evans, B.J.W., Drasdo, N., Richards, I.L. (1996) Dyslexia: the link with visual deficits. *Ophthal. Physiol. Opt.* **16**, 3–10.

97 Barnard, N., Gillard Crewther, S., Crewther, D.P. (1998) Development of a magnocellular function in good and poor primary school-age readers. *Optom. Vis. Sci.* **75**, 62–8.

98 Mason, A., Cornelissen, P., Fowler, S. , Stein, J.F. (1993) Contrast sensitivity, ocular dominance and specific reading disability. *Clinical Vision Sciences* **8**, 345–53.

99 Lovegrove, W.J. (1991) Visual deficits in dyslexia. Presented at *Meeting the Challenge: The Second International Conference of the British Dyslexia Association*, Oxford.

100 Talcott, J.B., Witton, C., McClean, M., Hansen, P.C., Rees, A., Green, G.G., Stein, J.F. (1999) Can sensitivity to auditory frequency modulation predict children's phonological and reading skills?. *Neuroreport* **10**, 1045–2050.

101 Talcott, J.B., Witton, C., McLean, M.F., Hansen, P.C., Rees, A., Green, G.G., Stein, J.F. (2000) Dynamic sensory sensitivity and children's word decoding skills. *Proc. Natl. Acad. Sci. USA* **97**, 2952–57.

102 Hulme, C. (1981) *Reading Retardation and Multi-Sensory Teaching*, Routledge, London.

103 Eden, G.F., Vanmeter, J.W., Rumsey, J.M., Zeffiro, T.A. (1996) The visual deficit theory of developmental dyslexia. *Neuroimage* **4**, S108–S17.

104 Borsting, E., Ridder, W.H., Dudeck, K., Kelley, C., Matsui, L., Motoyama, J. (1996) Visual processing in adult dyseidectic dyslexics. *Vision Research* **36**, 1047–54.

105 Ridder, W.H., Borsting, E., Cooper, M., McNeel, B., Huang, E. (1997) Not all dyslexics are created equal. *Optom. Vis. Sci.* **74**, 99–104.

106 Grosser, G.S. and Spafford, C.S. (1990) Light sensitivity in peripheral retinal fields of dyslexic and proficient readers. *Perceptual Motor Skills* **71**, 467–77.

107 Spafford, C., Grosser, G.S. (1991) Retinal differences in light sensitivity between dyslexic and proficient reading children: new prospects for optometric input in diagnosing dyslexia. *J. Am. Optom. Assoc.* **62**, 610–5.

108 Grosser, G.S., Spafford, C.S. (1989) Perceptual evidence for an anomalous distribution of rods and cones in the retinas of dyslexics: a new hypothesis. *Percept. Mot. Skills* **68**, 683–98.

109 Spafford, C.S., Grosser, G.S., Donatelle, J.R., Squillance, S.R., Dana, J.P. (1995) Contrast sensitivity differences between proficient and disabled readers using colored lenses. *J. Learning Disabilities* **28**, 240–52.

110 Geiger, G. and Lettvin, J.Y. (1987) Peripheral vision in persons with dyslexia. *New Eng. J. Med.* **316**, 1238–43.

111 Dunn, P.M. (1987) Letter to the editor. *New Eng. J. Med.* **317**, 1737.

112 Helveston, E.M. (1987) Management of dyslexia and related learning disabilities. *J. Learn. Disab.* **20**, 415–21.

113 Geiger, G., Lettvin, J. (1993) Manifesto on dyslexia. In. *Facets of Dyslexia and its Remediation (Eds. S.F. Wright and R. Groner), Elsevier*, 51–63.

114 Geiger, G., Lettvin, J.Y., Zegarra-Moran, O. (1992) Task-determined strategies of visual process. *Cognitive Brain Research* **1**, 39–52.

115 Geiger, G., Lettvin, J.Y., Fahle, M. (1994) Dyslexic children learn a new visual strategy for reading: a controlled experiment. *Vision Res.* **34**, 1223–33.

116 Fahle, M., Luberichs, J. (1995) Extension of a recent therapy for dyslexia. *German J. Ophthalmol.* **4**, 350–4.

117 Dautrich, B.R. (1993) Visual perceptual differences in the dyslexic reader: evidence of greater visual peripheral sensitivity to color and letter stimuli. *Percept. Mot. Skills* **76**, 755–64.

118 Bjaalid, I. et al. (1993) Letter identification and lateral masking in dyslexics and normal readers. *Scandinavian J. Educ. Res.* **37** (2), 151–61.

119 Pirozzolo, F.J. (1982) Eye movements and visual information processing in developmental reading disability.In. *Neuropsychology and Cognition: Volume 1*, Martinus Nijhoff, The Hague, pp. 147–67.

120 Critchley, M. (1964) *Developmental dyslexia*, Whitefriars, London.

121 Stordy, B.J. (1995) Benefit of cocosahexaenoic acid supplements to dark adaptation in dyslexics. *Lancet (letter)* **346**, 385.

122 Stordy, J. (1997) Dyslexia, attention deficit disorder, dyspraxia: do fatty acid supplements help? *Dyslexia Review* **9**, 5–7.

123 Carroll, T.A., Mullaney, P., Eustace, P. (1994) Dark adaptation in disabled readers screened for Scotopic Sensitivity Syndrome. *Percept. Mot. Skills* **78**, 131–41.

124 Greatrex, J.C., Drasdo, N., Dresser, K. (2000) Scotopic sensitivity in dyslexia and requirements for DHA supplementation. *Lancet* **355**, 1429–30.

7 Coloured filters

1 Evans, B.J.W. (1991) *Ophthalmic factors in dyslexia*. PhD Thesis, Aston University, Birmingham, UK.

2 Evans, B.J.W. and Drasdo, N. (1991) Tinted lenses and related therapies for learning disabilities: a review. *Ophthalmic Physiol. Opt.* **11**, 206–17.

3 Rosner, J. and Rosner, J. (1987) The Irlen treatment – a review of the literature. *The Optician* **25 Sep**.

4 Fitzgerald, A. (1989) Tinted lenses and dyslexia: a review of the literature. *Austral. Orthoptic J.* **25**, 1–6.

5 Anon (1987) Foreign Influence. *Life Magazine* **Fall**, 29–35.

6 Joint Committee on Industrial Ophthalmology Report (1953), cited by Borish, I.M. (1975) *Clinical Refraction*, The Professional Press Inc., Chicago, pp. 1126–7.

7 Sasieni, L.S. (1975) *The principles and practice of optical dispensing and fitting*, Butterworths, London, pp.402–9.

8 British Standard 2724 (1987)

9 Trevor-Roper, P.D. (1974) *The eye and its disorders*. 2nd edition, Blackwell, Oxford, p. 261.

10 Howard, R.J.W.M. and Valori, R.M. (1989) Hospital patiets who wear tinted spectacles – physical sign of psychoneurosis: a controlled study. *J. Royal Soc. Med.* **82**, 606–8.

11 Critchley, M. (1964) *Developmental dyslexia*, Whitefriars, London.

12 Meares, O. (1980) Figure/ground, brightness contrast, and reading disabilities. *Visible Language*, **14**, 13–29.

13 Irlen, H. (1983) Successful treatment of learning difficulties. Presented at: *The Annual Convention of the Americal Psychological Association*, Anaheim, California.

14 Irlen, H. and Lass, M.J. (1989) Improving reading problems due to symptoms of scotopic sensitivity syndrome using Irlen lenses and overlays. *Education*. **109**, 413–7.

15 Irlen, H. (1991) . *Reading by the Colours: Overcoming Dyslexia and Other Reading Disabilities by the Irlen Method* , Avery, New York.

16 Irlen, H.L. (1985) *Method and Apparatus of Treatment of Symptoms of The Irlen Syndrom* (sic). US Patent No 4961640. The United States Patent Office.

17 Evans, B.J.W. (1997) Coloured filters and dyslexia: what's in a name?. *Dyslexia Review* **9**, 18–19.

18 Whiting, P.R. (1985) How difficult can reading be ? New insight into reading problems. *J. Eng. Teach. Assoc.* **49**, 49–55.

19 Millodot, M. (1993) *Dictionary of Optometry* , Third Edition, Butterworth-Heinemann, Oxford.

20 Sharp, D.M., Arden, G.B., Kemp, C.M., Hogg, C.R., and Bird, A.C. (1990) Mechanisms and sites of loss of scotopic sensitivity: a clinical analysis of congenital stationary night blindness. *Clin. Vis. Sci.* **5**, 217–30.

21 Robinson, G.L. and Miles, J. (1987) The use of coloured overlays to improve visual processing – a preliminary survey. *The Except. Child.* **34**, 65–70.

22 Irlen, H.L. (1994) Scotopic Sensitivity/Irlen Syndrome: Hypothesis and explanation of the syndrome. *J. Behavioral Optometry* **5**, 62, 65–6.

23 Wilkins, A. (1993) Overlays for classroom and optometric use. *Ophthal. Physiol. Opt.* **14**, 97–9.

24 Conlon, E.G., Lovegrove, W.J., Chekaluk, E., Pattison, P.E. (2000) Measuring visual discomfort. *Visual Cognition* **6** (6), 637–63.

25 Warnock, T.H., Freeman, R., Moran, D.J., and Halford, J. (1988) Tinted lenses: a study in children with learning disabilities. (Abstract). *Austral. Paed. J.* **24**, 392.

26 Wright, A. (2000) Specific learning difficulties: the development of Irlen technology. *Optometry Today* **Sept 8**, 39–42.

27 Robinson, G.L., Foreman, P.J., Dear, K.B.G. (1996) The familial incidence of symptoms of scotopic sensitivity/irlen syndrome. *Perceptual and Motor Skills* **83**, 1043–55.

28 Lea, A.R. and Hailey, D.M. (1990) *Tinted Lenses in Treatment of the Reading Disabled*, Australian Institute of Health: Health Care Technology Series No. 2, Australia Government Publishing Service, Canberra.

29 Helveston, E.M. (1990) Scotopic Sensitivity Syndrome. *Arch. Ophthalmol.* **108**, 1232–3.

30 Stanley, G. (1987) Coloured filters and dyslexia. *Austral. J. Remed. Educat;* **19**, 8–9.

31 Wilsher, C.R. and Taylor, J.A. (1988) Commentary – tinted glasses and dyslexia. *J. Res. Rdg.* **11**, 50–2.

32 Rosner, J. and Rosner, J. (1988) Another cure for dyslexia: guest editorial. *J. Am. Optom. Assoc.* **59**, 832–4.

33 Cotton, M.M., Evans, K.M. (1990) A review of the use of Irlen (tinted) lenses. *Aust. New Zeal. J. Ophthalmol.* **18**, 307–12.

34 Sadun, A.A. (1992) Dyslexia at the New York Times – (Mis)understanding of parallel visual processing. *Arch. Ophthal.* **110**, 933–4.

35 Healy, A., Erengerg, G., Kaminer, R.K., La Camera, R., Nackashi, J.A., Poncher, J.R., Randall, V., Wachtel, R.C., Ziring, P.R. (1992) Learning disabilities, Dyslexia, and vision. *Pediatrics* **90**, 124–6.

36 Hunt, R.W.G. (1998) *Measuring Colour.* Third edition. Fountain Press, Kingston-upon-Thames.

37 Fletcher, R., Voke, J. (1985) *Defective Colour Vision: Fundamentals, Diagnosis and Management.* Hilger, Bristol.

38 Wald, G. (1945) Human vision and the spectrum. *Science* **101**, 653–8.

39 Dwyer, J.I. (1991) Colour vision defects in children with learning difficulties. *Clin. Exp. Optom.* **74**, 30–8.

40 Wilkins, A.J., Nimmo-Smith, I., Jansons, J.E. (1992) Colorimeter for the intuitive manipulation of hue and saturation and its role in the study of perceptual distortion. *Ophthal. Physiol. Opt.* **12**, 381–5.

41 Wilkins, A., Milroy, R., Nimmo-Smith, I., Wright, A., Tyrell, R., Holland, K., et al. (1992) Preliminary observations concerning treatment of visual discomfort and associated perceptual distortion. *Ophthal. Physiol. Opt.* **12**, 257–63.

42 Wilkins, A.J., Jeanes, R.J., Pumfrey, P.D., Laskier, M. (1996) Rate of Reading Test: its reliability, and its validity in the assessment of the effects of coloured overlays. *Ophthal. Physiol. Opt.* **16**, 491–7.

43 Lightstone, A. (1995) The Intuitive Colorimeter. *Optical Practitioner* **August**, 17–22.

44 Evans, B.J.W., Patel, R., Wilkins, A.J., Lightstone, A., Eperjesi, F., Speedwell, L., Duffy, J. (1999) A review of the management of 323 consecutive patients seen in a specific learning difficulties clinic. *Ophthal. Physiol. Opt.* **19**, 454–66.

45 McNamara, R. (1999) Detecting children who will benefit from treatment in an orthoptic clinic for specific learning difficulties. *Br. Orthopt. J.* **56**, 22–30.

46 Jeanes, R., Busby, A., Martin, J., Lewis, E., Stevenson, N., Pointon, D., Wilkins, A. (1997) Prolonged use of coloured overlays for classroom reading. *Br. J. Psychol.* **88**, 531–48.

47 Wilkins, A. and Neary, C. (1991) Some visual, optometric and perceptual effects of coloured glasses. *Ophthal. Physiol. Opt.* **11**, 163–71.

48 Gole, G.A., Dibden, S.N., Pearson, C.C., Pidgeon, K.J., Mann, J.W., Rice, D., Rooney, K.F., Hannell, G., Fitzgerald, B.A., Kortman, J.Y., McGlinchey, N.D'A. (1989) Tinted lenses and dyslexics – a controlled study. *Australian and New Zealand J. Ophthal.* **17**, 137–41.

49 Lightstone, A., Lightstone, T., Wilkins, A. (1999) Both coloured overlays and coloured lenses can improve reading fluency, but their optimal chromaticities differ. *Ophthal. Physiol. Opt.* **19**, 279–85.

50 Whiting, P.R., Robinson, G.L.W., Parrott, C.F. (?1995) Irlen coloured filters for reading: a six year follow-up. *Austral. J. Remed. Educat.* **26**, 13–19.

51 Hovis, J.K. (1997) Long wavelength pass filters designed for the management of color vision dificiencies. *Optom. Vis. Sci.* **74**, 222–30.

52 Harris, D.A. (1998) Interim report on the use of the ChromaGen contact lenses in patients with specific learning difficulties. *Optometry Today* **July 31**, 24–5.

53 Wilkins, A.J. (1998) Comparative study concerns (Letter to the editor). *Optometry Today* **August 21**, 8.

54 Young, G. (1996) Insufficient clinical evidence (Letter to the editor). *Optometry Today* **August 21**, 8.

55 Harris, D., MacRow-Hill, S.J. (1999) Application of ChromaGen haploscopic lenses to patients with dyslexia: a double-masked, placebo-controlled trial. *J. Am. Optom. Assoc.* **70** (10), 629–40.

56 Jordan, I. (1993) Pair of lenses, one clear, one coloured, for treating dyslexia. *UK Patent Application* **GB 2 266 786.**

57 Kaplan, R. (1983) Changes in form visual fields in reading disabled children produced by syntonic (coloured light) stimulation. *Internat. J. Biosocial Res.* **5**, 20–33.

58 Wurtman, R.J. (1975) The effects of light on the human body. *Sci. Am.* **233**, 68–80.

59 Liberman, J. (1986) The effect of Syntonic (coloured light) stimulation on certian visual and cognitive functions. *J. Optom. Vis. Devel.* **17**, 4–15.

60 Shayler, G. (2000) Functional visual fields: their importance in the assessment of children with educational difficulties. *Optician* **220**, 26–32.

61 Details of literature search: Medline and Silver Platter Ophthalmology databases searched August 2000 for *syntonic*.

62 Details of literature search: Medline and Silver Platter Ophthalmology databases searched August 2000 for *Downing technique* and *dyslexia* or *reading*.

63 Wilkins, A.J., Evans, B.J.W., Brown, J., Busby, A., Wingfield, A.E., Jeanes, R., Bald, J. (1994) Double-masked placebo-controlled trial of precision spectral filters in children who use coloured overlays.. *Ophthal. Physiol. Opt.* **14**, 365–70.

64 Tyrrell, R., Holland, K., Dennis, D., Wilkins, A. (1995) Coloured overlays, visual discomfort, visual search and classroom reading. *Journal of Research in Reading* **18**, 10–23.

65 Robinson, G.L., Conway, R.N. (1994) Irlen filters and reading strategies: effect of coloured filters on reading achievement, Specific reading strategies, and perception of ability. *Perceptual and Motor Skills* **79**, 467–83.

66 Winter, S. (1987) Irlen lenses: an appraisal. *The Austral. Educ. and Develop. Psychol.* 1–5.

67 Saint-John, L.M. and White, M.A. (1988) The effect of coloured transparencies on the reading performance of reading disabled children. *Austral. J. Psychol.* **40**, 403–11.

68 Giddings, E.H., Carmean, S.L. (1989) Reduced brightness contrast as a reading aid. *Perceptual Motor Skills* **69**, 383–6.

69 Chan, L.K.S. and Robinson, G.L.W. (1989) Effects of comprehension monitoring instruction for reading disabled students with and without tinted glasses. *Austral. J. Special Educ.* **13**, 4–13.

70 O'Connor, P.D., Sofo, F., Kendall, L., and Olsen, G. (1990) Reading disabilities and the effects of colored filters. *J. Learn. Disab.* **23**, 597–603.

71 Blaskey, P., Scheiman, M., Parisi, M., Ciner, E.B., Gallaway, M., and Selznick, R. (1990) The effectiveness of Irlen filters for improving reading performance: a pilot study. *J. Learn. Disab.* **23**, 604–12.

72 Robinson, G.L.W. and Conway, R.N.F. (1990) The effects of Irlen colored lenses on student's specific reading skills and their perception of ability: a 12-month validity study. *J. Learn. Disab.* **23**, 589–96.

73 Cotton, M.M., Evans, K.M. (1990) An evaluation of the Irlen lenses as a treatment for specific reading disorders. *Austral. J. Psychol.* **42**, 1–12.

74 Solman, R.T., Dain, S.J., Keech, S.L. (1991) Color-mediated contrast sensitivity in disabled readers. *Optom. Vis. Sci.* **68**, 331–7.

75 Williams, M.C., Lecluyse, K., Rock-Faucheux, A. (1992) Effective interventions for reading disability. *J. Am. Optom. Assoc.* **63**, 411–7. Also published as: Rock-Faucheux, A., LeCluyse, K., Williams, M. (1993) The effects of wavelength on visual processing and reading performance in normal and disabled readers. *Facets of Dyslexia and its Remediation*, eds. S.F. Wright and R. Groner, pp. 77–94, North-Holland, Amsterdam.

76 Menacker, S., Breton, M.E., Breton, M.L., Radcliffe, J., Gole, G.A. (1993) Do tinted lenses improve the reading performance of dyslexic children?. *Arch. Ophthalmol.* **111**, 213–8.

77 Maclachlan, A., Yale, S., Wilkins, A. (1993) Research note: open trial of subjective precision tinting. *Ophthal. Physiol. Opt.* **13**, 175–8.

78 Williams, M.C., Littell, R.R., Reinoso, C., Greve, K. (1994) Effect of wavelength on performance of attention disorded and normal children on the Wisconsin Card Sorting Test. *Neuropsychology* **8**, 187–93.

79 Sawyer, C., Taylor, S., Willcocks, S. (1994) Transparent coloured overlays and specific learning difficulties. *Educational Psychology in Practice* **9**, 217–20.

80 Solman, R.T., Dain, S.J., Lim, H., May, J.G. (1995) Reading-related wavelength and spatial frequency effects in visual spatial location. *Ophthal. Physiol. Opt.* **15**, 125–32.

81 Solan, H.A., Ficarra, A., Brannan, J.R., Rucker, F. (1998) Eye movement efficiency in normal and reading disabled elementary school children: effects of varying luminance and wavelength. *J. Am. Optom. Assoc.* **69**, 455–64.

82 Croyle, L. (1998) Rate of reading, visual processing, colour and contrast. *Australian Journal of Learning Disabilities* **3**, 13–21.

83 Robinson, G.L., Foreman, P.J. (1999) The effects of Irlen coloured filters on eye movement: a long-term placebo controlled and masked study. *Behavioral Optometry* **7**, 5–18.

84 Robinson, G.L., Foreman, P.J. (1999) Scotopic sensitivity/Irlen Syndrome and the use of coloured filters: a long-term placebo-controlled and masked study of reading achievement and perception of ability. *Perceptual & Motor Skills* **88**, 35–52.

85 Robinson, G.L., Foreman, P.J. (1999) Scotopic sensitivity/Irlen Syndrome and the use of coloured filters: a long-term placebo-controlled study of reading strategies using analysis of miscue. *Perceptual & Motor Skills* **88**, 35–52.

86 Robinson, G.L., Conway, R.N.F. (2000) Irlen lenses and adults: a small-scale study of reading speed, accuracy, comprehension and self-image`. *Australian Journal of Learning Disabilities* **5**, 4–12.

87 Ball, G.V. (1982) *Symptoms in Eye Examination*, Butterworth Scientific, London.

88 Eustace, P., Weston, E., Druby, D.J. (1973) The effect of illumination on intermittent divergent squint of the divergence excess type. *Transactions of the Ophthalmological Society of Great Britain* **93**, 559–90.

89 Francis, M., Taylor, S., Sawyer, C. (1992) Coloured lenses and the Dex frame: New issues. *Support for Learning* **7**, 25–7.

90 Howell, E. and Stanley, G. (1988) Colour and learning disability. *Clin. & Exper. Optom.* **71**, 66–71.

91 Solan, H.A. and Richman, J. (1990) Irlen lenses: a critical appraisal. *J. Am. Optom. Assoc.*, **61**, 789–96.

92 Scheiman, M., Blaskey, P., Ciner, E.B., Gallaway, M., Parisi, M., Pollack, K., Selznick, R. (1990) Vision charecteristics of individuals identified as Irlen filter candidates. *J. Am. Optom. Assoc.* **61**, 600–5.

93 Evans, B.J.W., Wilkins, A.J., Brown, J., Busby, A., Wingfield, A.E., Jeanes, R., Bald, J. (1996) A preliminary investigation into the aetiology of Meares-Irlen Syndrome. *Ophthal. Physiol. Opt.* **16**, 286–96.

94 Evans, B.J.W., Busby, A. , Jeanes, R, Wilkins, A.J. (1995) Optometric correlates of Meares-Irlen Syndrome: a matched group study.. *Ophthal. Physiol. Opt.* **15**, 481–7.

95 British College of Optometrists (1995) *Notes for the prescribing of tinted lenses for dyslexia, migraine, and visual discomfort.*

96 Wilkins, A.J. (1995) . *Visual Stress* , Oxford University Press, Oxford.

97 Evans, B.J.W. (1997) Guest editorial: Coloured filters and reading difficulties: a continuing controversy. *Optom. Vis. Sci.* **74**, 239–40.

98 Bradley, A. (1992) Perceptual manifestations of imperfect optics in the human eye: attempts to correct for ocular chromatic aberration. *Optom. Vis. Sci.* **69**, 515–21.

99 Wilkins, A.J., Nimmo-Smith, I., Slater, A.I., Bedocs, L. (1989) Fluorescent lighting, headaches and eyestrain. *Lighting Res. Technol.* **21**, 11–18.

100 Wilkins, A.J. and Wilkinson, P. (1991) Research note: a tint to reduce eye-strain from fluorescent lighting? Preliminary observations. *Ophthal. Physiol. Opt.* **11**, 172–5.

101 Neary, C. (1989) The effect of high frequency flicker on accommodation. *Ophthalmic & Physiol. Opt.* **9**, 440–6.

102 Wilkins, A.J. (1986) Intermittent illumination from visual display units and fluorescent lighting affects movement of the eyes across text. *Human Factors.* **28**, 75–81.

103 Baccino, T. (1999) Research Note: Exploring the flicker effect: the influence of in-flight pulsations on saccadic control. *Ophthal. Physiol. Opt.* **19**, 266–73.

104 Pammer, K., Lovegrove, W. (1998) A psychophysical study on the effect of colour on transient activity. *Austral. J. Psychol.* **50 (supp.)**, 60.

105 Greatrex, J.C., Drasdo, N., Dresser, K. (2000) Scotopic sensitivity in dyslexia and requirements for DHA supplementation. *Lancet* **355**, 1429–30.

106 Wilkins, A. (1991) Visual discomfort and reading. In *Dyslexia* (ed. J. Stein), Vol. 13 of 'Vision and Visual Dysfunction' (ed. J.R. Cronly Dillon), MacMillan, London.

107 Solman, R.T., Dain, S.J., and Keech, S.L. (1991) Color-mediated contrast sensitivity in disabled readers. *Optom. Vis. Sci.* **68**, 331–7.

108 Lopez, R., Yolton, R.L., Kohl, P., Smith, D.L., Saxerud, M.H. (1994) Comparison of Irlen Scotopic Sensitivity Syndrome test results to academic and visual performance data. *J. Am. Optom. Assoc.* **65**, 705–14.

109 Ciuffreda, K.J., Scheiman, M., Ong, E., Rosenfield, M., Solan, H.A. (1997) Irlen lenses do not improve accommodative accuracy at near. *Optom. Vis. Sci.* **74**, 298–302.

110 Grisham, D., Winston Alwes, W., Frisby, S., and Lasher, D. (1990) The efficacy of using coloured lenses to improve reading ease and performance (Abstract). *Supplement to Optom. & Vis. Sci.,* **67**, 93.

111 Robinson, G.L. (1994) Coloured lenses and reading: a review of research into reading achievement, reading strategies and causal mechanisms. *Australasian Journal of Special Education* **18**, 3–14.

112 Wilkins, A.J., Nimmo-Smith, I., Tait, A., Mc Manus, C., Della Sala, S., Tilley, A., Arnold, K., Barrie, M., and Scott, S. (1984) A neurobiological basis for visual discomfort. *Brain* **107**, 989–1017

113 Conlon, E. (1993) A model of visual discomfort and its implications for efficient reading performance. *PhD Thesis* , University of Wollongong, Australia.

114 Conlon, E., Lovegrove, W., Hine, T., Chekaluk, E., Piatek, K., Hayes-Williams, K. (1998) The effects of visual discomfort and pattern structure on visual search. *Perception* **27**, 21–33.

115 Wilkins, A.J. and Nimmo-Smith, I. (1984) On the reduction of eye-strain when reading. *Ophthal. Physiol. Opt.* **4**, 53–9.

116 Wilkins, A.J. and Nimmo-Smith, M.I. (1987) The clarity and comfort of printed text. *Ergonomics*, **30**, 1705–20.

117 Wilkins, A.J., Andermann, F., and Ives, J. (1975) Stripes, complex cells and seizures. *Brain.* **98**, 365–80.

118 Weston, H.C. (1962) Sight, light and work. , Lewis, London, p. 52.

119 Evans, B.J.W. (1999) Do visual problems cause dyslexia? (Guest Editorial). *Ophthal. Physiol. Opt.*, **19** (4), 277–8.

120 Johnson, D.J., Zecker, S.G. (1991) Visual processing and dyslexia. In. *Vision and Visual Dysfunction* **13**, (ed. J Cronly-Dillon), Macmillan Press, London, pp. 132–140.

121 Casco, C., Tressoldi, P.E., Dellantonio, A. (1998) Visual selective attention and reading efficiency are related in children. *Cortex* **34**, 531–46.

122 Marcus, D.A. and Soso, M.J. (1989) Migraine and stripe-induced visual discomfort. *Arch. Neurol.* **46**, 1129–32.

123 Chronicle, E.P. (1993) Visual discomfort and visual dysfunction in migraine. *D. Phil. Thesis*, University of Cambridge, UK, pp. iii–iv, 24–53, 196–227.

124 Bickford, R.G., Daly, D., and Keith, H.M. (1953) Convulsive effects of light stimulation in children. *Am. J. Diseases of Children* **86**, 170–83.

125 Jeavons, P.M., Harding, G.F.A., Panayiotopoulos, C.P., and Drasdo, N. (1972) Clinical note: the effect of geometric patterns combined with intermittent photic stimulation in photosensitive epilepsy. *Electroenceph. clin. Neurophysiol.* **33**, 221–4 .

126 Wilkins, A.J., Darby, C.E., and Binnie, C.D. (1979) Neurophysiological aspects of pattern-sensitive epilepsy. *Brain.* **102**, 1–25.

127 Darby, C.E., Wilkins, A.J., Binnie, C.D., and de Korte, R. (1980) Technical Note: Routine testing for pattern sensitivity. *J. Electrophysiol. Technol.* **6**, 202–10.

128 Meldrum, B.S. and Wilkins, A.J. (1984) Photosensitive epilepsy: integration of pharmacological and psychophysical evidence. In: *Electrophysiology of Epilepsy*, (eds. P. Schwartzdroin and H.W. Wheal), Academic Press, London, pp. 51–77.

129 Chronicle, E. (1993) The influence of colour on visual discomfort in migraineurs and controls. In. *Headache and Migraine* , T.J. Steiner and L.A.H. Hogenhuis (eds.), Utrecht, Bunge, pp. 10–15.

130 Griffin, J. (1996) Specific tinting and migraine: a retrospective questionnaire. *Optometry Today* **November 18**, 35–8.

131 Wilkins, A.J., Patel, R., Adjamian, P., Evans, B.J.W. Tinted spectacles and visually-precipitated migraine. *In press. Cephalgia.*

132 Abu-Arefeh, I., Russell, G. (1994) Prevalence of headache and migraine in schoolchildren. *Br. Med. J.* **309**, 765–9.

133 Hess, R.F., Harding, G.F.A., and Drasdo, N. (1974) Seizures induced by flickering light. *Am. J. Optom. Physiol. Optics* **51**, 517–29.

134 Jeavons, P.M. and Harding, G.F.A. (1975) *Photosensitive Epilepsy*, William Heinemann Medical Books Ltd., Philadelphia, pp. 15–16 and 83–4.

135 Wilkins, A.J., Baker, A., Smith, S., Bradford, J., Zaiwalla, Z., Besag, F.M., Binnie, C.D., Fish, D. (1999) Treatment of photosensitive epilepsy using coloured glasses. *Seizure* **8**, 444–9.

136 Koutroumanidis, M., Koepp, M.J., Richardson, M.P., Camfield, C., Agathonikou, A., Ried, S., Papadimitriou, A., Plant, G., Duncan, J.S., Panayiotopoulos, P. (1998) The variants of reading epilepsy. A clinical and video-EEG study of 17 patients with reading-induced seizures. *Brain* **121**, 1409–27.

137 Wilkins, A. and Lindsay, J. (1985) Common forms of reflex epilepsy: physiological mechanisms and techniques for treatment. In *Recent Advances in Epilepsy: Number 2* (eds. T.A. Pedley and B.S. Meldrum), pp. 239–71, Churchill Livingstone, Edinburgh.

138 Taylor, S., Francis, M., Sawyer, C. (1992) Clinical note: Preliminary assessment of the Dex Frame for assisting children with specific learning difficulties. *Ophthal. Physiol. Opt.* **12**, 386–9.

139 Kirk, R. (1999) Management of visual dyslexia. *Dispensing Optics* **November**, 6–7.

140 Bowers, A.R. (2000) Eye movements and reading with plus-lens magnifiers. *Optom. Vis. Sci.* **77**, 25–33.

141 Williams, M.C., Brannan, J.R., and Lartigue, E.K. (1987) Visual search in good and poor readers. *Clin. Vision Sci.* **1**, 367–71.

142 Williams, M.C., May, J.G., Solman, R., Zhou, H. (1995) The effects of spatial filtering and contrast reduction on visual search times in good and poor readers. *Vision Res.* **35**, 285–91.

143 Sheedy, J.E., McCarthy, M. (1994) Reading performance and visual comfort with scale to gray compared with black and white scanned print. *Displays* **15**, 27–30.

144 O'Brien, B.A., Mansfield, J.S., Legge, G.E. (2000) The effect of contrast on reading speed in dyslexia. *Vision Research* **40** (14), 1921–35.

8 Conclusions

1 Solan, H.A. (1993) Dyslexia and learning disabilities: Epilogue. *Optom. Vis. Sci.* **70**, 392–3.

2 Evans, B.J.W., Drasdo, N., Richards, I.L. (1996) Dyslexia: the link with visual deficits. *Ophthal. Physiol. Opt.* **16**, 3–10.

3 Suchoff, I.B. (1981) Research on the relationship between reading and vision – what does it mean?. *J. Learn. Disab.* **14**, 573–6.

4 Eden, G.F., Stein, J.F., Wood, H.M., Wood, F.B. (1994) Differences in eye movements and reading problems in dyslexic and normal children. *Vision Res.* **34**, 1345–58.

5 Eden, G.F., Stein, J.F., Wood, M.H., Wood, F.B. (1995) Verbal and visual problems in reading disability. *J. Learning Disabilities* **28**, 272–90.

6 Stein, J.F., Richardson, A.J., Fowler, M.S. (2000) Monocular occlusion can improve binocular control and reading in dyslexics. *Brain* **123**, 164–70.

7 Hung, G.K., Wang, K.J., Ciuffreda, K.J., Semmlow, J.L. (1989) Suppression of sensitivity to surround displacement during vergence eye movements. *Experimental Neurology* **105**, 300–5.

8 Witton, C., Talcott, J.B., Hansen, P.C., Richardson, A.J., Griffiths, T.D., Rees, A. (1998) Sensitivity to dynamic auditory and visual stimuli predicts nonword reading ability in both dyslexic and normal readers. *Current Biology* **8**, 791–7.

9 Stein, J., Talcott, J. (1999) Impaired neuronal timing in developmental dyslexia – the magnocellular hypothesis. *Dyslexia* **5**, 59–77.

10 Schneider, W., Dumais, S.T., Shiffrin, R.M. (1984) Automatic and control processing and attention. *In Varieties of Attention (eds. R. Parasuraman and D.R. Davies)*, **Academic Press**, 1–27.

11 Kahneman, D. And Treisman, A. (1984) Changing views of attention and automaticity. *In Varieties of Attention (eds. R. Parasuraman and D.R. Davies)*, **Academic Press**, 27–61.

12 Taylor, E.A. (1994) Development and psychopathology of attention. Chapter 8 in. *Development Through Life* (Eds. M.L. Rutter, D.F. Hay), Blackwells, pp. 185–211.

13 Nicolson, R.I. and Fawcett, A.J. (1990) Automaticity: a new framework for dyslexia research? *Cognition* **35**, 159–82.

14 Davies, D.R., Jones, D.M., and Taylor, A. (1984) Selective- and sustained-attention tasks: individual and group differences. *In Varieties of Attention (eds. R. Parasuraman and D.R. Davies)*, **Academic Press**, 395–447.

15 Colby, C.L. (1991) The neuroanatomy and neurophysiology of attention. *J. Child Neurol. (suppl.)* **6**, S88–S116.

16 Parasuraman, R. (1984) Sustained attention in detection and discrimination. In. *Varieties of Attention* , (eds. R. Parasuraman and D.R. Davies), Academic Press, London, 243–71.

17 Lahey, B.B., Carlson, C.L. (1991) Validity of the diagnostic category of attention deficit disorder without hyperactivity: a review of the literature. *J. Learn. Disab.* **24**, 110–20.

18 Hynd, G.W., Lorys, A.R., Semrud-Clikeman, M., Nieves, N., Huettner, M.I.S., Lahey, B.B. (1991) Attention deficit disorder without hyperactivity: a distinct behavioral and neurocognitive syndrome. *J. Child Neurol. (supp.)* **6**, S37–43.

19 Swanson, J.M., Posner, M., Potkin, S., Bonforte, S., Youpa, D., Fiore, C., Cantwell, D., Crinella, F. (1991) Activating tasks for the study of visual-spatial attention in ADHD children: a cognitive anatomic approach. *J. Child Neurol. (suppl.)* **6**, S117–S25.

20 Details of literature search: Medline database searched October 2000 for *ADD* and *visual attention.*

21 Richards, I. (1994) ADHD, ADD and dyslexia. *Therapeutic Care and Education* **3**, 145–58.

22 Steinman, S.B., Steinman, B.A. (1998) Vision and attention. 1: Current models of visual attention. *Optom. Vis. Sci.* **75**, 146–55.

23 Steinman, S.B., Steinman, B.A., Trick, G.L., Lehmkuhle (1994) A sensory explanation for visual attention deficits in the elderly. *Optom. Vis. Sci.* **71**, 743–9.

24 Harter, M.R. and Aine, C.J. (1984) Brain mechanisms of visual selective attention. *In Varieties of Attention (eds. R. Parasuraman and D.R. Davies)*, **Academic Press**, 293–321.

25 Steinman, S.B., Steinman, B.A., Garzia, R.P. (1998) Vision and Attention. II: Is visual attention a mechanism through which a deficient magnocellular pathway might cause reading disability?. *Optom. Vis. Sci.* **75**, 674–81.

26 Facoetti, A., Paganoni, P., Turatto, M., Marzola, V., Mascetti, G.G. (2000) Visual-spatial attention in developmental dyslexia. *Cortex* **36**, 109–23.

27 Casco, C., Tressoldi, P.E., Dellantonio, A. (1998) Visual selective attention and reading efficiency are related in children. *Cortex* **34**, 531–46.

28 Visyasagar, T., R., Pammer, K. (1999) Impaired visual serch in dyslexia relates to the role of the magnocellular pathway in attention. *NeuroReport* **10**, 1283–87.

29 Hoffman, J.E., Subramaniam, B. (1995) The role of visual attention in saccadic eye movements. *Percept. Psychophys.* **57**, 787–95.

30 Shelhamer, M., Merfeld, D.M., Mendoza, J.C. (1994) Vergence can be controlled by audio feedback, and induces downward ocular deviation. *Exp. Brain Research* **101**, 169–72.

31 Stein, J.F. (1989) Review article: Representation of egocentric space in the posterior parietal cortex. *Quart. J. Exp. Physiol.* **74**, 583–606.

32 Voeller, K.K.S., Heilman, K. (1988) Motor impersistence in children with attention deficit hyperactivity disorder: evidence for right-hemisphere dysfunction. *Ann. Neurol.* **24**, 323.

33 Evans, B.J.W. (1999) Do visual problems cause dyslexia? (Guest Editorial). *Ophthal. Physiol. Opt.,* **19** (4), 277–278.

34 Conlon, E., Lovegrove, W., Hine, T., Chekaluk, E., Piatek, K., Hayes-Williams, K. (1998) The effects of visual discomfort and pattern structure on visual search. *Perception* **27**, 21–33.

35 Richman, J.E. (1999) The influence of visual attention and automaticity on the diagnosis and treatment of clinical oculomotor, accommodative, and vergence dysfunctions. *J. Optom. Vision Development* **30**, 132–41.

36 Eden, G.F., VanMeter, J.W., Rumsey, J.M., Maisog, J.M., Woods, R.P., Zeffiro, T.A. (1996) Abnormal processing of visual motion in dyslexia revealed by functional brain imaging. *Nature* **382**, 66–9.

37 Frith, C., Frith, U. (1996) A biological marker for dyslexia. *Nature* **382**, 19–20.

38 Cornelissen, P.L., Hansen, P.C., Hutton, J.L., Evangelinou, V., Stein, J.F. (1998) Magnocellular visual function and children's single word reading. *Vision Research* **38**, 471–82.

39 Seymour, P.H.K., Evans, H.M. (c. 1994) The visual (Orthographic) processor and developmental dyslexia. Chapter 16 in. , 347–76.

40 Williams, M.C., Lovegrove, W. (1992) Sensory and perceptual processing in reading disability. In. *Applications of Parallel Processing in Vision* , (Ed. J. Brannan), Elsevier Science, Amsterdam, pp. 263–302.

41 Bishop, A.M. (1991) Vision screening of children: a review of methods and personnel involved within the UK. *Ophthal. Physiol. Opt.* **11**, 3–9.

42 Francis, M., Taylor, S., Sawyer, C. (1992) Coloured lenses and the Dex frame: New issues. *Support for Learning* **7**, 25–7.

43 Thomson, W.D., Evans, B. (1999) A new approach to vision screening in schools. *Ophthal. Physiol. Opt.* **19**, 196–209.

44 Department for Education (1994) Special educational needs: a guide for parents.

45 Lightstone, A., Evans, B.J.W. (1995) A new protocol for the optometric management of patients with reading difficulties. *Ophthal. Physiol. Opt.* **15**, 507–12.

46 Evans, B.J.W., Patel, R., Wilkins, A.J., Lightstone, A., Eperjesi, F., Speedwell, L., Duffy, J. (1999) A review of the management of 323 consecutive patients seen in a specific learning difficulties clinic. *Ophthal. Physiol. Opt.* **19**, 454–66.

47 Perez-Carpinell, J., de Fez, M.D., Climent, V. (1994) Vision evaluation in people with Down's syndrome. *Ophthal. Physiol. Opt.* **14**, 115–21.

48 Woodhouse, J.M., Pakeman, V.H., Cregg, M., Saunders, K.J., Parker, M., Fraser, W.I., Sastry, P., Lobo, S. (1997) Refractive errors in young children with Down syndrome. *Optom. Vis. Sci.* **74**, 844–51.

49 Woodhouse, J.M. (1998) Investigating and managing the child with special needs. *Ophthal. Physiol. Opt.* **18**, 147–52.

Index

Printed in the United Kingdom
by Lightning Source UK Ltd.
131859UK00001B/37-42/P